To my dearest D

with love from Ross xxx

Christmas 1990

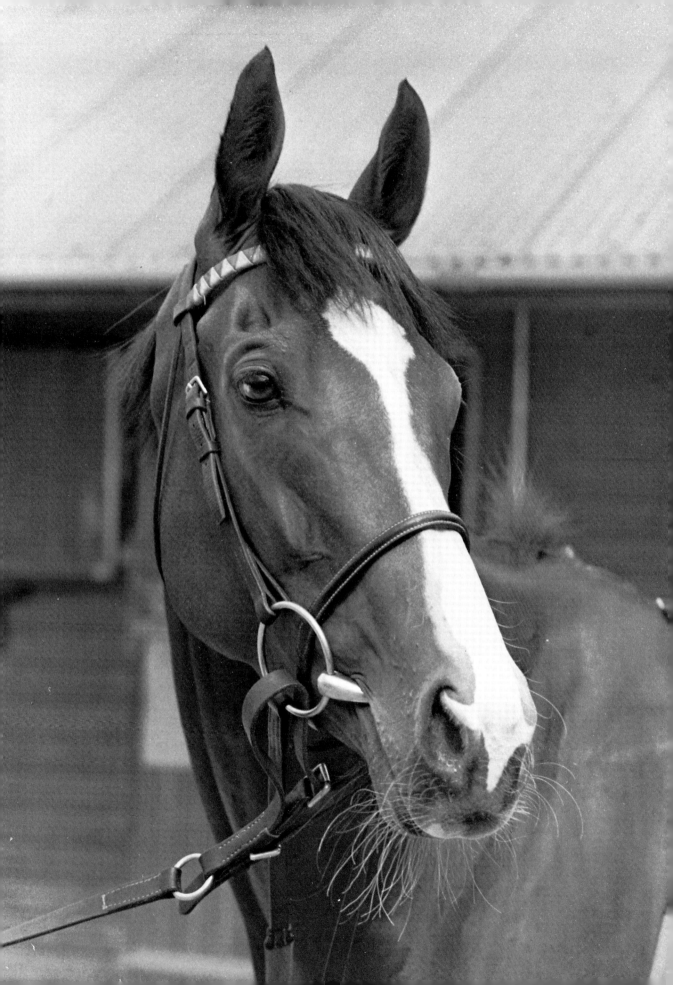

The Channel Four Book of
THE RACING YEAR

Sean Magee

With contributions from
JOHN FRANCOME
GRAHAM GOODE
JOHN McCRIRICK
JIM McGRATH
JOHN OAKSEY
BROUGH SCOTT
DEREK THOMPSON
JOHN TYRREL

Sidgwick and Jackson
LONDON
in association with
Channel Four Television Company

CONTENTS

First published in Great Britain 1990
by Sidgwick & Jackson Limited

Copyright © Sean Magee 1990

ISBN 0 283 06059 X

Phototypeset by Opus, Oxford
Printed in Great Britain by Butler and
Tanner Ltd, Frome and London
for Sidgwick & Jackson Limited,
1 Tavistock Chambers,
Bloomsbury Way,
London WC1A 2SG

Half-title
Salsabil.

Title spread
Tirol winning the 1990 Two
Thousand Guineas at Newmarket
from Machiavellian.

INTRODUCTION

ILLUSTRATIONS

The photographs in the colour section (between pages 64 and 65) were all entries to the Bonusprint/Channel Four Racing photography awards, and are reproduced by permission of the individual photographers listed with each picture. All the other photographs in the book are from the Gerry Cranham Library, with the following exceptions: page 46, Hulton Picture Co.; pages 49, 50, Popperfoto; page 75, Laurie Morton; pages 71, 105, 126, Alec Russell. The photographs of the Channel Four presenters were all taken by Mel Fordham on Derby Day 1990.

The course plans in this book have been drawn by Jackie Hunt. Where a meeting is described a full plan of the course is given, with the area over which a particular race within that meeting is run shown by shading in the relevant piece of the course plan at the start of the entry. Where a race described is not within such a meeting a brief description of the course is offered or the reader is referred to the full description elsewhere. Course plans have not been supplied for the American tracks (pages 184–9): Breeders' Cup Day moves from course to course, and in any case the general uniformity of US tracks (flat left-hand ovals about seven furlongs round) makes the inclusion of individual plans unnecessary.

In the plans of steeplechase circuits 'OD' signifies open ditch and 'W' water jump; all other jumps marked are plain fences.

One of the abiding attractions of horse racing is the variety of occasions it has on offer. No one week in the year's sport is like the one before, and each of the major events of the racing year – meetings and individual races – has a character of its own.

This book seeks to express that character by looking at what makes each of the big races important, a moment greeted with special anticipation by those visiting the course or watching on television, and is intended for use throughout the year as a companion for racing fans wanting to know more about the history and background of the great contests which provide the waypoints of each season. Every running of the Classics, the King George VI and Queen Elizabeth Diamond Stakes, the Arc, the Grand National, the Champion Hurdle and the Cheltenham Gold Cup alters the face of the sport, while many of the races in this book are trials or build-up races for those pivotal events and must be judged on the subsequent record of the runners, but each of the different races has a different feel. This special character is a mixture of elements – the quality of previous winners, the nature and conditions of the race itself, the course on which it is run, the time of year, and so on – but all such elements come together under the umbrella of history, and no apology is made for teasing out the special character of each big race by concentrating on the historical aspect. Much of this, of course, is ancient history in Turf terms, and the fact that Sceptre ran twice in the Lincoln Handicap has little to do with the cavalry charge up the Doncaster straight mile on the first Saturday of the new Flat season. Or does it? Sceptre may have been from a different age, but the essence of the race itself – a highly competitive handicap often used as the medium for a hefty gamble – was the same in her day as it is now. Nor need history be ancient. The great ten-furlong event on the opening day of the York August Meeting started life in sensational style by producing Brigadier Gerard's only defeat, and that historic moment less than twenty years ago has remained a potent part of the appeal of the International Stakes.

Each individual's racing year is constructed from personal taste, circumstance and experience – my own best day's racing in the first half of 1990 was a wonderfully enjoyable cold, wet and windy Tuesday at Towcester – but restrictions of space have meant that the book has to focus on the big races, and these have been grouped into three sections: Flat, National Hunt, and International. (A chart showing how these different events relate to each other chronologically can be found on pages 8–9.)

If *The Racing Year* enhances your enjoyment of the great races which provide the framework for the annual round of Turf events, it will have served its purpose.

A few words of explanation. Pattern races are the cream of Flat races; divided into Groups One, Two and Three and Listed Races by the European Pattern Committee, they are subject to constant scrutiny and frequent revision of the gradings. The book describes all the Flat races in Britain designated Group One in the European Pattern for

1990 (and gives winners of these races since 1970, or their inauguration if later), in addition to many of the Group Two and Three races and the major handicaps (with winners since 1980). From the start of the 1990–1 season National Hunt racing has been subjected to a new system of grading its major races, with the top events divided into Grades One (conditions races only), Two (conditions races plus a few handicaps with a restricted weight range) and Three (to include the major handicaps such as the Grand National and the Whitbread). The book describes those races – of whatever Grade – which continue to provide the focal points of the jumping season.

And a few words of apology, to sponsors of some of the races described in the pages that follow. It is quite impossible to take account of every change in a race's name when describing so many different runnings, and unless the sponsor's name is an integral part of the race's title – that is, if the contest would be unrecognizable without it – names are given in their basic form. Where feasible, details of the history of any particularly significant sponsorship have been included.

And a few words of acknowledgement. Andrew Franklin, producer of the Channel Four coverage, has for the second successive year lugged a set of proofs of a Channel Four Racing book with him when snatching his summer holiday after the July Meeting: while he's been in foreign parts we've indulged in mammoth discussions over the telephone, during which he has imparted a huge amount of useful suggestion and comment. British Telecom is grateful to him and so am I, as I am to Teresa Wadeson and the rest of the Channel Four Racing team, especially the presenters for their contributions to this book and in particular to John Tyrrel for much advice and discussion. JT alone, it seems, knows the true date of the first running of the Lincoln Handicap. The lists of winners in the book cannot go back that far, mercifully for Chris Jones of Turf Statistics who compiled them: his efforts are much appreciated. The ratings from the International Classification are reproduced by kind permission of the Jockey Club, and I am delighted that Major David Swannell has agreed to provide ratings for the period before the International Classification and to supply the explanation of the ratings which can be found on page 13. Roger Stokes of the Sturt Farm Stud – where one of the resident stallions is Roman Warrior, whose greatest hour is described on page 105 – gave me much guidance on the year in breeding, while the National Horseracing Museum and the Newmarket Public Library have again proved mines of information. Michael and Louise Wigley provided support in the form in which it was most needed. On the publishing and production front I have a special word for Hilary Davies at Sidgwick and Jackson (though I cannot say what it is) and am very grateful to her sidekick Ingrid Connell; to Charlie Webster and Nick Withers at Opus; to Susanna Yager; and to Gillian Bromley.

And finally, a word of warning. The book does not presume to suggest how to pick winners. Such impertinence would be highly inappropriate from one whose car sticker 'I slow down for horses' should be accompanied by one reading 'Horses slow down for me'.

S.M.

FURTHER READING

Several of the great races described in this book have been the subjects of recent individual histories:

Cheltenham Gold Cup
John Welcome's *The Cheltenham Gold Cup* (third edition, 1984) brings the story up to the Michael Dickinson first five in 1983.

Champion Hurdle
Michael Tanner's *The Champion Hurdle* (1989) is similar in format – and in quality – to Welcome's *Gold Cup*.

The Grand National
Like the Derby, the National has spawned a host of books. Reg Green's *A Race Apart* (1988) is an accurate year-by-year account, though for the flavour of the race conveyed by a massive gallery of pictures and two of the best racing writers of recent times, take a look at *The Grand National* by Clive Graham and Bill Curling (1972).

The Derby
The standard racing history is Roger Mortimer's wonderfully authoritative and entertaining year-by-year account *The History of the Derby Stakes*, the new edition of which was published in 1973; *The Epsom Derby*, published in 1984, brings the story up to Secreto and El Gran Senor.

King George VI and Queen Elizabeth Diamond Stakes
Stephen Michael Brie's *Diamond Days* (1990) is a year-by-year description to 1989.

Prix de l'Arc de Triomphe
The definitive history is Arthur Fitzgerald's three-decker *Prix de l'Arc de Triomphe*, the final volume of which (1983) covers the years 1965 to 1982.

King George VI Chase
Michael Tanner's highly readable *The King George VI Steeplechase* (1984) tells the story to 1983.

THE RACING YEAR MONTH BY MONTH

The chart shows how the events described in this book (with the opening page number of that entry), plus the key moments for the bloodstock industry, fall through the year.

	FLAT	NATIONAL HUNT	INTERNATIONAL	BREEDING
JANUARY		Mildmay, Cazalet Chase (p. 139)		1: All Thoroughbred horses' official birthday
FEBRUARY		Tote Gold Trophy (p. 140)		15: Covering season begins
		Racing Post Chase (p. 141)		
MARCH		Cheltenham National Hunt Festival (p. 142)		
	Flat season (turf) begins Lincoln Handicap (p. 16)			
APRIL		Grand National (p. 152)	Irish Grand National (p. 168)	
	Newmarket Craven Meeting (p. 18)	Scottish National (p. 159)		
	Sandown Park April Meeting (p. 22)	Whitbread Gold Cup (p. 161)		
MAY	Newmarket Spring Meeting (Guineas) (p. 26)		Kentucky Derby (p. 184) Poule. . .des Poulains (p. 173) Poule. . .des Pouliches (p. 173)	
	Chester May Meeting (p. 34) York May Meeting (p. 38)		Preakness (p. 185) Irish 2000 Guineas (p. 169) Irish 1000 Guineas (p. 169)	
JUNE	Epsom Summer Meeting (Derby/Oaks) (p. 42) Royal Ascot (p. 62)	*National Hunt season ends*	Belmont Stakes (p. 185) Prix du Jockey-Club (p. 174) Prix de Diane (p. 175) Irish Derby (p. 170)	
	Northumberland Plate (p. 70)			

	FLAT	NATIONAL HUNT	INTERNATIONAL	BREEDING
JULY	Eclipse Stakes (p. 72) Newmarket July Meeting (p. 76) King George VI and Queen Elizabeth Diamond Stakes (p. 80) Goodwood July Meeting (p. 84)		Irish Oaks (p. 172)	15: Covering season ends. Keeneland yearling sales
AUGUST	York August Meeting (p. 88)	*National Hunt season begins*		Deauville Sales
SEPTEMBER	Ladbroke Sprint Cup (p. 96) Doncaster September Meeting (St Leger) (p. 98) Ascot September Meeting (p. 106)		Arlington Million (p. 186)	Doncaster Sales
OCTOBER	Newmarket October Meeting (p. 112) Newmarket Houghton Meeting (p. 118)		Prix de l'Arc de Triomphe/Prix de l'Abbaye (p. 176) Irish St Leger (p. 172) Prix Royal-Oak (p. 175) Breeders' Cup (p. 187)	Highflyer Sales Goffs Sales Tattersalls October Sales
NOVEMBER	November Handicap (p. 127) *Flat season (turf) ends*	Mackeson Gold Cup (p. 130) Hennessy Gold Cup (p. 131)	Melbourne Cup (p. 182) Japan Cup (p. 183)	
DECEMBER		Welsh National (p. 133) King George VI Chase (p. 134) Christmas Hurdle (p. 138)		

THE YEAR IN BREEDING AND TRAINING

On 1 January, the day when all Thoroughbreds in the Northern Hemisphere become one year older, birthday celebrations are muted, for the turn of the year is a comparatively quiet time in the breeding cycle. But the start of the real action is not far away, and the stallion will be being brought to peak fitness for the rigorous duties to come by undertaking an increasing amount of exercise – being led out for long walks or turned out in his paddock – and by having his diet enhanced after comparatively short rations through the idle weeks of the winter. From early January his next batch of mates will be arriving.

Then on 15 February the covering season begins, and for the next five months the stallion will serve his mares (often several a day) until the season ends on 15 July; he may be asked to cover a few jumping mares after the end of the formal season. If a visiting mare is pregnant with a foal conceived the previous year, she gives birth to that foal soon after she has arrived at the stud, before the next covering. After being mated with the stallion she will remain at the stud for subsequent coverings by the same stallion as necessary to ensure conception (in so far as this is possible), and will then return home with her recently born foal 'at foot'. (Of course, many studs breed from their own as well as taking in visiting mares.) That foal will be weaned at about five months and may be sold before it has reached the age of one, though the more common practice for commercial breeders is to sell when the foal has become a yearling.

To prepare a young horse for the sales requires a great deal of skill and care and by the end of July the breeder has started to get the yearlings ready for their date in the sale ring by teaching them to trot round on a lungeing rein – they will need to trot at the sales to show would-be purchasers the condition of their wind – and to walk on a leading rein. (They will have been led with a halter since the morning after being born.) They will also be got fit and well muscled so that they are in prime condition when they come under the hammer. Sales of different categories of horse take place throughout the year, but most attention in Britain focuses on the three big yearling sales: the Doncaster St Leger Sales in September, the Highflyer Sales at Newmarket in early October (the highlight of the year for auctioneers Tattersalls) and the Newmarket October Sales, which coincide with the Cesarewitch meeting on the Rowley Mile and where more than twice as many horses are sold as at any other auction: 911 lots were sold there in 1989 as against 446 at the St Leger and 352 at the very select Highflyer. But compare the average price of the lots – 90,693 guineas at the Highflyer, 14,201 guineas at the October, 9,794 guineas at the St Leger. So the Highflyer is clearly the place to go to buy (or to sell) the best stock – an occasion on a par with the world's other great yearling sales at Keeneland, Kentucky (in late July), Deauville in France (August) or Goffs in Ireland (October).

As autumn arrives, far from the great international bonanza of sales the stallion is being 'let down' after the exertions of the covering season and has returned to the less hectic regime of lounging around in his paddock (or box when the weather is extreme) during the day

Reprimand at the National Stud in 1990.

and being shut away at night. His diet is reduced in order to aid the process of calming him down, but he will still need regular exercise in order to keep in trim. The mares with whom he had such a fleeting acquaintance are turned out in the paddocks. The foals are growing rapidly and gathering strength, and some will be put up for sale in November and December. And the yearlings are off to Lambourn or Newmarket or Malton to learn the business of racing.

If the yearling sales in the autumn mark something of an ending in the annual cycle of the breeder's year, they mark a beginning in the year of the trainer – at least on the Flat – for the influx of a new batch of yearlings is the start of the whole training process.

Imagine you are a trainer with a hundred-horse Newmarket yard. With the benefit of your advice an unconscionably rich Arab owner has picked up at the Highflyer Sales a yearling colt by Sadler's Wells out of a middle-distance Classic-winning mare; the colt arrives in your yard, where he will remain for probably the next two years, and already the whisper is of the Derby. How will his time be spent?

The priority that first autumn is to break him in, to teach him how to be ridden. This may take several weeks but cannot be rushed. He must also be made accustomed to starting stalls, and shown how to exert himself at the gallop and to remain balanced going round turns. (In the USA horses are even taught to change their legs once they have come off the bend into the stretch.) By the spring of his two-year-old year the colt will have grown appreciably and will be getting used to the routine of training. Unless he is a highly precocious fellow (and if your thoughts are of the Derby you will be hoping he is not) it will be too soon to start thinking about his first race, but throughout the late winter and early spring he will, like the the rest of your string, slowly build up his fitness: for several weeks he will spend every day walking and then trotting for mile upon mile along the roads in order to lay the foundation for the strength which will be the bedrock of his racing ability. Eventually he canters gently with some of his fellow two-year-olds – probably given a lead by an older and wiser horse – and then the time comes when he is to be put through his paces in a home gallop, his first taste of 'work'. However easy he finds it to catch pigeons on the gallops, the racecourse is the true test, and if a prolonged three-year-old career is planned he will not be brought to his peak too soon by being tested in the very top two-year-old races. A gentle introduction in a maiden race at Newbury in August, perhaps, then a graduation race to consolidate the experience, and perhaps a stab at one of the Pattern races in the autumn. If in doubt, patience is the watchword; no matter if he is put away for the winter with only limited experience, so long as he has plenty to think about as the shadows lengthen.

He has an easy time through the winter, and in February is beginning to walk and trot the winter idleness out of his limbs as you snatch a brief holiday in Barbados, where you will lie on the beach composing letters to the *Sporting Life* about how tough life is as a trainer. When the colt's three-year-old career will begin in earnest depends on how forward in condition he is, and that – to some extent – depends on the weather. A hot and dry spring and early summer can

Henry Cecil on his hack supervising his string.

11

prove disastrous for Classic hopes, not just because of the risk of running them on very firm ground, but because despite the widespread use of all-weather training surfaces it is very difficult to get a horse fully fit when the gallops are firm, as he will not stretch out and exert himself properly. But assume that all is well, that the colt is in good shape and raring to go. Where will he run? Put him in the Craven Stakes in April: he won't be completely fit, but the timing of the race leaves enough of a gap before the Two Thousand Guineas to bring him to his peak for the first Classic. He wins the Guineas, and then goes straight to Epsom: once a horse is fit he is likely to remain so for a while with only a token amount of work, and it is vital that he should stay fresh through his summer campaign. With the Derby safely in the bag, all sorts of possibilities unfold for the rest of the year. Pick up the Irish Derby while the colt is still in good form; or take the Eclipse over a shorter distance and against older horses – that will impress breeders. Then to Ascot for the King George to impose your colt's presence indelibly on the complexion of international racing. Then what? Let him down a bit: he's had several big races in the space of three months and can't go on showing his best form for ever. Give him a rest, then bring him back in September for his preparation race for the Arc the following month (you could even make this the St Leger if you think him tough enough), then go and win at Longchamp early in October. The colt is now a multi-million-pound stallion prospect, so you may as well leave it at that; you resist the lure of the Breeders' Cup Turf and let him wind down, reducing his exercise and cutting down on his feed until the supercharged racing machine is more amenable to the quieter life at stud. In November, little more than two years after he arrived in the yard, he's gone. Meanwhile the latest class of new boys have arrived . . .

For a jumping trainer, of course, the year has a completely different shape. January finds him (or her) in the middle of a season which has begun way back at the beginning of August and which stretches ahead to early June, and from the turn of the year all eyes are on the Cheltenham National Hunt Festival, followed soon after by the big Liverpool meeting which culminates in the Grand National. Thereafter most trainers will start to slow down their operations, turning the horses out to unwind, sending some away for a change of scene and a summer holiday. Although the new season begins even as Glorious Goodwood is in full swing, the ground will still be very firm and a long term beckons, so it is unusual for the best chasers and hurdlers to be brought back into training until much later in the year, with the Mackeson meeting at Cheltenham the unofficial marker of the moment when the new season begins in earnest. Next attention focuses on the big Rank Holiday Festival at Kempton Park, the mid-season peak. And then, in the words of the song – 'Bloody January again!'

A NOTE ON THE RATINGS *by David Swannell*

Since 1977 the racing authorities of Great Britain, France and Ireland (joined in 1985 by those of Germany and Italy) have produced annually the International Classification of the best horses to have raced in that season, the *official* rating of the cream. With the descriptions in this book of the five English Classics and the King George VI and Queen Elizabeth Diamond Stakes contemporary ratings are given to allow the reader to see – and, as appropriate, take issue with – how the best horses have been ranked in the past. I have supplied my own unofficial ratings for the seasons 1973 to 1976 and translated those of my predecessor from 1970 to 1972 to complete the picture of the last two decades.

The rating expresses the merit of a horse in terms of pounds carried (so a horse rated 140 – ten stone – would be expected to concede three pounds in a hypothetical handicap to a horse rated 137). The ratings listed in this book are taken from the year of the race in question and not necessarily the highest rating a particular horse ever achieved: for instance, Pebbles was rated 122 in 1984 and ten pounds higher in 1985. The ratings in the International Classification are now divided into distance categories, but the defining criteria of these categories have not been constant throughout the life of the system and can produce anomalies: in 1986 Dancing Brave was rated 141 in the long-distance category (over eleven furlongs), 134 in the intermediate (nine and a half to eleven furlongs) and 130 in the mile (seven to nine and a half furlongs), but he did not race over a mile after the Two Thousand Guineas, so who is to say that he was really eleven pounds inferior at one mile in the spring than at a mile and a half five vital months later? (For another anomaly consider Reference Point in 1987.) The ratings in the book represent each horse's highest rating as assessed at the end of the year (*in the relevant distance category*) when the full form picture is available. For obvious reasons such ratings for 1990 are not yet to hand.

It is important to understand how these ratings are arrived at. The system of classifying each generation against a 'norm' was introduced in order to move beyond the stage where subjective judgements were accepted as the best evidence of the level of a horse's ability. This recognized standard, necessarily arbitrary to some extent, links successive Thoroughbred crops and thus provides a means of comparing horses many generations apart. When official ratings were introduced in 1973 with the founding of a centralized system of handicapping, the 'norm' was equated to the figure 100. This figure was recently (for technical reasons) changed to 140. In order to avoid confusion in the comparisons I have, for the purposes of the ratings reproduced in this book, amended all figures to their present-day equivalent: for example, Grundy (141) was actually rated 101 in 1975. Overwhelming dominance or dominance in an above-average year leads to a rating of well over 140. Overwhelming dominance of a good crop has been achieved, in my time, only by Sea Bird II in 1965, which was reflected in a pre-International Classification rating of 150.

THE FLAT

Lincoln Handicap

Doncaster: 1 mile

Handicap: four-year-olds and upwards

It is some indication of how important a race the Lincoln used to be that its running was not interrupted by the Second World War. Between 1942 and 1945 it was staged at Pontefract rather than Lincoln itself, where the Lincolnshire Handicap was first run in 1849. The historic course on the Carholme at Lincoln closed down in 1964, at which point the race was transferred to its current home at Doncaster.

In times gone by the Lincoln was for Flat fans the light at the end of the tunnel through the dark days of winter, and once the weights were published vast quantities of midnight oil would be burnt in an effort to find a blot on the handicap. The race attracted a huge amount of ante-post betting interest and was the object of many a coup, not all of them successful. The professional punter Alex Bird has described how in the 1951 race he backed his own horse Newton Heath to win £40,000 (think of that in today's money!). Ridden by the young apprentice Herbert Jones, Newton Heath had taken the lead when in the final furlong his saddle started slipping back: his jockey could do nothing but twist his fingers into the horse's mane and cling on, but he was unable to ride a finish and was caught close home by 33–1 outsider Barnes Park. Alex Bird was stoical: 'These things happen in racing. I lit a cigar and strolled to the unsaddling enclosure, to congratulate my great friend Harry Lane, who owned Barnes Park. I bought the Pathe Gazette newsreel of the race, and whenever I wanted to torture myself, I played it over and over again.' What Bird did not know as he puffed on his cigar was that Newton Heath's saddle had slipped in a previous race, and his jockey on that occasion had suggested to trainer Jack Pearce that he should always run the horse in a breast-girth to prevent the saddle slipping: but the advice was not acted upon. Of such omissions are hard-luck stories made.

Without doubt the finest horse to take part in the Lincoln was Sceptre, one of the greatest fillies ever to run in England. Foaled in 1899, Sceptre was bred by the Duke of Westminster along the best classic lines, by the outstanding Derby winner Persimmon out of Ornament, a full sister to Ormonde. On the Duke's death she was sold at auction for 10,000 guineas, at the time considerably more than had ever been paid for a yearling, to Bob Sievier, born (he would insist) in a hansom cab and one of the great characters of Turf history: 'I was dubbed by some "an ass", by the majority as "mad", while a few kindly referred to the proverb of "a fool and his money"', wrote Sievier, but the critics were confounded in 1902 when Sceptre

Course description on page 98.

Previous pages: The 1984 Eclipse Stakes at Sandown Park: Sadler's Wells beats Time Charter and Morcon.

became the only horse in history to win four Classics outright. Given her breeding and her ability, how on earth could Sceptre have run twice in a tough one-mile handicap at the very beginning of the season? At that time the race was open to three-year-olds, and Sievier hatched a plan whereby a coup on Sceptre in the Lincolnshire Handicap could help alleviate his chronic cash-flow difficulties. The filly had been trained as a two-year-old by Charles Morton and won two of her three races, but when Morton became private trainer to J. B. Joel for the 1902 season Sievier decided to train her himself. Shortly before the Lincoln he had to make a trip to Paris, leaving the filly in the care of his American assistant trainer. On his return he was horrified to find that the assistant had been working Sceptre too hard, galloping her severely four days running, and had, so early in the season, pushed her over the top: she was morose and off her feed. The assistant was soon on his way, but Sievier had little time to restore Sceptre's *joie de vivre*; she was still not right by the day of the race, when she put up a heroic performance to finish just a head behind the winner, St Maclou. She then won every Classic except the Derby (in which she was fourth). How the owner of such a horse could find himself in financial trouble at the end of her Classic year begs questions, but Sievier was indeed strapped for cash again and sent Sceptre to the December Sales. When she failed to reach her reserve of 24,000 guineas he chose to keep her for another crack at the Lincoln in 1903: she carried nine stone one pound but could only finish fifth behind Over Norton, ridden by Otto Madden, who later that year would partner Ard Patrick to a famous victory over Sceptre – by then trained at Manton by Alec Taylor for her new owner William Bass – in the Eclipse Stakes (see page 73). Admittedly this was a different age, but just imagine Salsabil starting her seasonal campaign with a run in the Lincoln!

If Sceptre's participation adds an element of the bizarre to the history of the race, it is no less weird that the Lincoln should attract such a degree of betting interest. For one thing, practically every horse in the race will be having its first run of the season and interpretation of the previous year's form must be tempered by informed knowledge of the fitness of the runners. For another, the safety limit of twenty-five runners means that many horses at the bottom of the handicap may be balloted out. And really to query the mental state of anyone who has a serious ante-post bet on the Lincoln, there is the draw, made the day before the race. So marked is the effect of the starting position at the beginning of Doncaster's straight mile that those not favoured might as well not bother to turn up, but a further complication is that the favoured side changes. High numbers used to have a considerable advantage, but in recent years low numbers have been favoured, though the 1990 winner Evichstar was drawn 14 and raced on the stands side. (In 1978 the race was run on the round course in an attempt to remove the effect of the draw, but the experiment was not deemed a success.)

From wherever it starts, the horse that wins the Lincoln will need to last home every inch of the mile up the Doncaster straight, and though you won't see a Sceptre in the race these days, the sight of that huge field belting out of the distance announces that the Flat is back.

WINNERS SINCE 1980

1980 King's Ride
  G. Baxter 10–1 (18 ran)

1981 Saher
  R. Cochrane 14–1 (19 ran)

1982 King's Glory
  B. Crossley 11–1 (26 ran)

1983 Mighty Fly
  S. Cauthen 14–1 (26 ran)

1984 Saving Mercy
  W. R. Swinburn 14–1 (26 ran)

1985 Cataldi
  G. Starkey 10–1 (26 ran)

1986 K-Battery
  J. Lowe 25–1 (25 ran)

1987 Star Of A Gunner
  J. Reid 9–1 (25 ran)

1988 Cuvee Charlie
  M. Rimmer 33–1 (25 ran)

1989 Fact Finder
  T. Williams 20–1 (25 ran)

1990 Evichstar
  A. Munro 33–1 (24 ran)

Fifty-eight horses lined up at the start of the 1948 Lincolnshire Handicap, the largest field ever to run in a Flat race in Britain.

Babur in 1957 and 1958 is the only horse to have won the Lincoln twice. On both occasions he started at 25–1.

NEWMARKET CRAVEN MEETING

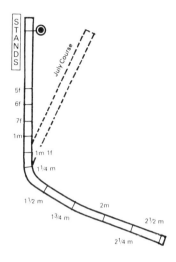

All races up to and including ten furlongs are perfectly straight; at longer distances the runners have an easy turn towards home some eleven furlongs out. The course is flat until about a quarter of a mile from home, at the Bushes, it runs downhill for about a furlong into the Dip, then climbs to the winning post.

The new Flat season has awakened elsewhere – usually at Doncaster – but with the Craven Meeting it gets out of bed, stretches, and looks forward to the day ahead. The Craven is the meeting which breathes life into the new term, combining important Classic trials with seasonal debut races for some of the best of the older horses and with competitive handicaps. It has something for everyone.

The characteristic mood of the meeting is anticipation, for as the first gathering of the season when many of the races see top-class horses in action it looks forward expectantly to bigger things in the future. This is especially so of the two main races of the Craven Meeting, the NELL GWYN STAKES (opposite) and the CRAVEN STAKES (page 21), trials respectively for the One Thousand and the Two Thousand Guineas – now barely two weeks away – which have have the great advantage over the trials run at other courses of taking place on the Guineas track itself: the full mile for the Craven, a furlong shorter for the Nell Gwyn. If a horse can handle the course in the trial, so much better does it augur for its chances in the real thing – as Tirol (winner of the Craven and Two Thousand) and Heart of Joy (winner of the Nell Gwyn and second in the One Thousand) emphatically announced in 1990.

But the meeting has other delights beyond the Classic trials and the FREE HANDICAP (page 20). There is the six-furlong ABERNANT STAKES, named after one of the greatest sprinters of all time; the EARL OF SEFTON STAKES over nine furlongs, a fascinating early-season event which has been won in recent years by Ela-Mana-Mou (1980) and Kalaglow (1982), both of whom went on to win the King George VI and Queen Elizabeth Diamond Stakes, while in 1990 Terimon, second in the 1989 Derby, won a thrilling race by a short head; the sometimes enthralling WOOD DITTON STAKES, over one mile, for three-year-olds which have never run before; and the FEILDEN STAKES, a Listed nine-furlong race for three-year-olds.

All these races offer pointers to the important events soon upon us. No wonder you can smell the expectation in the air at the Craven Meeting.

Nell Gwyn Stakes

Newmarket (Rowley Mile): 7 furlongs

Group Three: three-year-old fillies

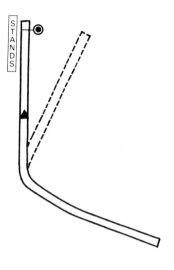

Nell Gwyn was born in 1650 and brought up in a brothel. She found employment as an orange girl at a London theatre and was soon one of the most popular actresses of the age. Then in 1669 it was arranged for her to take up the role which would secure her place in English history – becoming mistress to Charles II, in which position, according to the writer Gilbert Burnet, she was 'the indiscreetest and wildest creature that ever was in a court, yet continued to the end of the king's life in great favour'. When Charles was at Newmarket she lived in a house across the street from his palace (near where the Rutland Arms stands today), and an underground passage was constructed to facilitate the royal progress. She bore the king two sons, but died in poverty at the age of thirty-seven.

There is no better or more reliable trial for the first Classic of the season, the One Thousand Guineas, than the race which commemorates Nell Gwyn's association with Newmarket, for experience on the ups and downs of the Rowley Mile can prove invaluable two weeks later in the Classic. First run in 1962, the race has long been a natural three-year-old debut for fillies with Classic pretensions, and over the last two decades has produced several horses which have gone on to win the One Thousand: Flying Water (1976), One In A Million (1979), Fairy Footsteps (1981), Pebbles (1984) and Oh So Sharp (1985). But defeat in the Nell Gwyn does not rule out Guineas success: in 1971 Altesse Royale was second to Super Honey but won the One Thousand Guineas and Oaks, while in 1982 On The House was only fifth in the trial race but won the first Classic at 33–1. Sonic Lady (1986) and Ensconse (1989) went on from winning the Nell Gwyn to take the Irish One Thousand Guineas: both had been beaten in the One Thousand at Newmarket. Diminuendo, winner of the Oaks in 1988, had been runner-up to Ghariba in the Nell Gwyn.

For a typically exciting Nell Gwyn we need look no further than the 1990 running. Hasbah, Hamdan Al-Maktoum's daughter of Al Bahathri, leads out of the Dip, with Michael Stoute's Heart Of Joy challenging and Steve Cauthen on In The Groove pushing along. It looks as if Hasbah will hold on, but now In The Groove is stretching up the hill and Walter Swinburn has Heart Of Joy at full tilt. The three flash past the post together, and it takes the judge the best part of half an hour to decide: Heart Of Joy, In The Groove, Hasbah – two short heads. All three were back for the Guineas, Heart Of Joy being narrowly beaten by Salsabil, with In The Groove eighth (though she went on to win the Irish One Thousand) and Hasbah last.

WINNERS SINCE 1980

1980 Evita
    J. Mercer 7–2 (11 ran)

1981 Fairy Footsteps
    L. Piggott 4–6 (9 ran)

1982 Chalon
    L. Piggott 8–1 (12 ran)

1983 Favoridge
    Pat Eddery 13–8 (9 ran)

1984 Pebbles
    P. Robinson 7–1 (9 ran)

1985 Oh So Sharp
    S. Cauthen 8–13 (8 ran)

1986 Sonic Lady
    W. R. Swinburn 13–8 (9 ran)

1987 Martha Stevens
    S. Cauthen 4–1 (6 ran)

1988 Ghariba
    M. Roberts 11–2 (10 ran)

1989 Ensconse
    R. Cochrane 2–1 (8 ran)

1990 Heart Of Joy
    W. R. Swinburn 5–6 (6 ran)

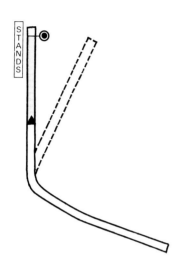

Free Handicap

Newmarket (Rowley Mile): 7 furlongs

Handicap: three-year-olds

The Free Handicap was first run in its current form in 1929, though an autumn race named the Free Handicap had been run at Newmarket long before that. The weights for the race, published in January, provide a complete order of merit of the leading two-year-olds from the previous season, though these days the very best two-year-olds will be aimed at the more traditional Classic trials, and it is unusual for top horses to be in the line-up.

Despite this it is not unknown for the Free Handicap winner to go on to Classic victory. The last horse to win an English Classic after taking the Free Handicap was Mrs McArdy, who won at 8–1 in 1977 and then started at 16–1 when lifting the One Thousand Guineas. Nearly two decades earlier the great Petite Etoile had given weight all round and shown electrifying acceleration to win the race at 9–1 at the start of a three-year-old campaign which brought triumphs in the One Thousand Guineas, the Oaks, the Sussex Stakes, the Yorkshire Oaks and the Champion Stakes. Privy Councillor in 1961 won the Free Handicap before taking the Two Thousand Guineas, and back in 1937 the winner Mid-day Sun had gone on from Newmarket to win the Derby. Remainder Man was second in the Two Thousand Guineas and third in the Derby in 1978 after winning the Free Handicap, while other top-class winners in recent times have been the great sprinter Moorestyle (1980) and Green Desert (1986), who went on to run second to Dancing Brave in the Two Thousand Guineas.

WINNERS SINCE 1980

1980 Moorestyle
L. Piggott 6–1 (13 ran)

1981 Motavato
S. Cauthen 13–2 (13 ran)

1982 Match Winner
L. Piggott 9–4 (13 ran)

1983 Boom Town Charlie
T. Ives 13–2 (8 ran)

1984 Cutting Wind
W. R. Swinburn 20–1 (17 ran)

1985 Over The Ocean
A. Lequeux 85–40 (11 ran)

1986 Green Desert
W. R. Swinburn 11–2 (8 ran)

1987 Noble Minstrel
A. Badel 7–1 (11 ran)

1988 Lapierre
M. Roberts 10–1 (9 ran)

1989 Danehill
Pat Eddery 6–1 (9 ran)

1990 Anshan
Pat Eddery 9–2 (10 ran)

Craven Stakes

Newmarket (Rowley Mile): 1 mile

Group Three: three-year-old colts and geldings

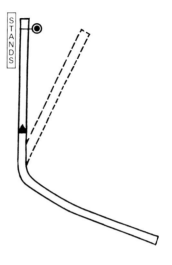

When Tirol powered up the hill to win the General Accident Two Thousand Guineas in May 1990 his victory was yet another advertisement for the worth of the Craven Stakes as a Two Thousand trial. For he was the fourth horse in the last six years to go on from a triumph in the Craven to Classic glory, following in the hoofprints of Shadeed (1985), Dancing Brave (1986) and Doyoun (1988). Before this fine group you have to go back to My Babu in 1948 for a horse which achieved the double.

First run in 1878 and the oldest of the established Guineas trials, the Craven Stakes is the ideal preparation race for the Two Thousand, run as it is over the full mile of the Classic distance and demanding the same qualities as the Classic itself: the speed to lay up close in the early stages of what is usually a fast-run race and then go for the winning post, with enough balance to run downhill from the Bushes and the grit to keep up the gallop as the ground rises towards the finish.

Since the war the race has been won by several horses who went on to great things apart from the Two Thousand, and it should not be seen purely in terms of a trial for the second Classic. Migoli (1947) was second in the Derby and third in the St Leger, but he beat Tudor Minstrel in the Eclipse Stakes and the following year won the Prix de l'Arc de Triomphe. Bald Eagle was trained by Cecil Boyd-Rochfort to win the Craven in 1958; he failed in the Guineas but was sent to be trained in the USA and won the Washington International in 1959 and 1960. Aurelius, the 1961 victor, won the St Leger later that year under Lester Piggott: he is best remembered now for his unusual subsequent career, for after failing to perform in the approved manner at stud he was gelded and put over jumps, winning over both hurdles and fences. Guineas or no Guineas, not many Craven Stakes winners in the future will be able to claim as much.

Green Desert wins the Ladbroke
European Free Handicap from Sperry
in 1986.

WINNERS SINCE 1980

1980 Tyrnavos
E. Hide 5–1 (9 ran)

1981 Kind Of Hush
S. Cauthen 25–1 (9 ran)

1982 Silver Hawk
A. Murray 11–2 (9 ran)

1983 Muscatite
B. Taylor 7–2 (5 ran)

1984 Lear Fan
G. Starkey 51–6 (5 ran)

1985 Shadeed
W. R. Swinburn 9–4 (6 ran)

1986 Dancing Brave
G. Starkey 11–8 (11 ran)

1987 Ajdal
W. R. Swinburn 6–5 (6 ran)

1988 Doyoun
W. R. Swinburn 100–30 (5 ran)

1989 Shaadi
W. R. Swinburn 5–2 (5 ran)

1990 Tirol
Pat Eddery 9–2 (6 ran)

SANDOWN PARK APRIL MEETING

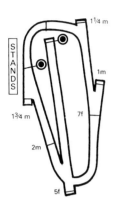

Oval in shape and galloping in nature, Sandown Park is an eminently fair test. The far straight is flat and the home straight climbs from the turn (about half a mile out) to the winning post, then continues to climb to the highest point of the course at the turn beyond the post. The sprint course cuts through the main course and has its own winning post.

In an old music-hall song a woman intent on a little extra-mural activity gleefully anticipates 'a lark in the light or the dark – my silly old man's at Sandown Park'. But if her old man has gone to the Esher track at the end of April for what is popularly known as the Whitbread meeting, she's the silly one if she doesn't go with him: for this is in many ways the most enjoyable fixture of the whole calendar.

The Saturday of the Sandown Park April Meeting is unique in the racing year in combining very high-class Flat racing with a top steeplechase, but the Friday has its own attraction in the TRUSTHOUSE FORTE MILE (Group Two), a comparatively recent addition to the programme but already established as the first big mile race of the season: its inaugural running in 1985 went to the unforgettable Pebbles, and in 1988 André Fabre sent over the brilliant Soviet Star to win for France. But the true joy of the Friday is that it's the day before the Saturday . . .

It is hardly cause for surprise that Whitbread Gold Cup Day is the most popular event in Sandown Park's year. There are few sights in racing to compare with the field for the WHITBREAD GOLD CUP itself (pages 161–5) setting off towards the stands on a sunny spring afternoon, then building up pace towards the downhill fence, sweeping along the back straight and over the Railway Fences, then making back towards the Pond Fence and the straight, then round once again before the climb up the hill to the winning post. That in itself would be enough to fill Sandown's excellent stands, but Whitbread Day has so much more. The CLASSIC TRIAL (page 23) has a wonderful record of pinpointing Derby winners, and the GORDON RICHARDS STAKES (page 25) always brings out many of the top ten-furlong horses who have remained in training. And that's not all. The ESHER CUP is a one-mile handicap for three-year-olds which often attracts a high-class field: Shareef Dancer, winner of the Irish Sweeps Derby, was beaten in this race in 1983.

Whitbread Gold Cup Day is like a favourite meal. You look forward to each course eagerly and, having consumed it, know that there is something different and hardly less appetising still to come.

Classic Trial

Sandown Park: 1¼ miles

Group Three: three-year-old colts and geldings

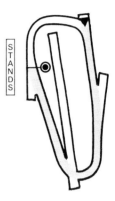

The early part of the Flat season is not short of trials for the Derby, but few races can boast the record of Sandown Park's Classic Trial for pointing out the identity of the horse which will go on to glory at Epsom on the first Wednesday of June. Formerly known as the Royal Stakes, the race was run as the Ladbroke Classic Trial from 1971 to 1973, and the 1972 winner Pentland Firth was third at Epsom, a respectful three lengths behind the desperate finish between Roberto and Rheingold. Two years later Bustino beat Snow Knight half a length at Sandown before finishing fourth behind the same horse – a 50–1 outsider at Epsom – in the Classic itself. Shirley Heights in 1978 ran an eye-catching second – though beaten ten lengths – to Whitstead in the Trial before getting home from Hawaiian Sound in the Derby (for which immediately after the Classic Trial he was quoted at 33–1), but the purple period for the Trial came with the next three runnings.

Troy in 1979, Henbit in 1980 and Shergar in 1981 really established the Sandown race as a harbinger of Epsom glory, and of the three it was Shergar's ten-length victory which most caught the eye: he took the lead three furlongs out and strode home with nonchalant ease. Shergar and Henbit won the Chester Vase and Troy the Predominate Stakes at Goodwood to complete their Derby preparations, but for all three the Sandown race had seen their seasonal reappearance and announced their arrival in the top bracket of three-year-olds.

The 1985 winner Damister was third to Slip Anchor at Epsom, but five years after Shergar another horse owned by the Aga Khan scooted home in the Classic Trial in his first race of the season and went on to win the Derby. Shahrastani strolled in four lengths clear of the 7–4 favourite Bonhomie at Sandown before taking the Dante Stakes *en route* to his controversial defeat of Dancing Brave at Epsom.

Why has the Classic Trial achieved such significance? For one thing, it is a very fair and uncomplicated test of an inexperienced three-year-old. The four horses who went on to take the Derby after winning the race had all had fairly light campaigns as two-year-olds: Troy had run four times and won twice, beaten on his last outing by Ela-Mana-Mou in the Royal Lodge Stakes at Ascot; Henbit had run three times, winning once; Shergar had run twice, winning his first race and coming second to Beldale Flutter in the William Hill Futurity at Doncaster; and Shahrastani had run just once, second at Newbury. So in all four cases the Sandown Park race was an ideal

---

WINNERS SINCE 1980

1980 Henbit
  W. Carson 9–4 (6 ran)

1981 Shergar
  W. R. Swinburn evens (9 ran)

1982 Peacetime
  Pat Eddery 9–2 (11 ran)

1983 Gordian
  G. Starkey 10–1 (7 ran)

1984 Alpabatim
  B. Rouse 4–1 (8 ran)

1985 Damister
  S. Cauthen 10–11 (4 ran)

1986 Shahrastani
  W. R. Swinburn 2–1 (4 ran)

1987 Gulf King
  P. Cook 25–1 (8 ran)

1988 Galitzin
  R. Cochrane 11–2 (5 ran)

1989 Old Vic
  S. Cauthen 4–9 (3 ran)

1990 Defensive Play
  Pat Eddery 7–4 (6 ran)

debut for the Classic season, and the timing of the race – the end of April – was perfect, for it both allowed time for the horses to mature before that crucial first appearance of the new term and still left enough to be gained from another preparatory race before Epsom.

The record of the Classic Trial, which was sponsored by *The Guardian* between 1981 and 1990, adds an exciting dimension to each new running. For it is very possible that the field will contain the Derby winner. Ah, but which one is it? . . .

Shahrastani (Walter Swinburn) wins the Guardian Classic Trial in 1986.

Indian Skimmer (Steve Cauthen), near side, goes past Carroll House to win the 1989 Gordon Richards Stakes.

Gordon Richards Stakes

Sandown Park: 1¼ miles

Group Three: four-year-olds and upwards

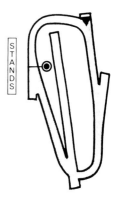

Gordon Richards, the most successful jockey in the history of British racing, rode the winners of 4,870 races in a career which began in 1920 and ended through injury in 1954. He was champion jockey twenty-six times and rode the winners of fourteen Classics. It was at Sandown Park that Richards suffered the accident that ended his riding career on 10 July 1954. In the race after the Eclipse (in which he finished third on the Queen's Landau) he was riding Her Majesty's two-year-old filly named Abergeldie, as he recounted in *My Story*:

> I was using a very little saddle which did not weigh more than two pounds. I think she felt it a bit cold on her back. The travelling head lad led her out of the paddock, and we were just going down the gravel track to the course when she half-reared. I said 'Let her go, Jim.' I ought to have kicked her on, but I did not, and so by this omission I let her do it again. All fillies are very unsafe when they rear. She came straight up, and went straight over with me underneath. I felt something crack. She tried to get up, and then came back on me again.

He had broken his pelvis. Gordon Richards died in November 1986, and the following year the ten-furlong race formerly known as the Westbury Stakes was renamed in his honour.

The Gordon Richards Stakes is a natural early-season target for the best of the older generation of middle-distance horses, and along with the Brigadier Gerard Stakes, run over the same course and distance a month later, provides the perfect preparation for the Eclipse Stakes at Sandown Park in early July (see pages 72–5). Brigadier Gerard himself won the Westbury in 1972, at which period it was run at the Sandown meeting at the end of May.

Although of Group Three status, the race usually attracts several Group One horses, and like so many top-class contests at Sandown Park often provides a wonderfully exciting finish, such as that in 1989 when the great grey mare Indian Skimmer got up in the final strides to beat Per Quod and Carroll House (destined to win the Arc at the end of the season) by two heads. The previous year another grey, the filly Infamy, had caused similar excitement when beating 1987 Derby runner-up Most Welcome by a head, and the 1990 race maintained the standard of pulsating finishes when Dolpour held off the renewed challenge of Ile De Chypre. The style of jockeyship which brought these races to their frenetic climaxes was a long way removed from that of Gordon Richards himself, who rode with a long rein and sat much more upright than the likes of Cauthen, Cochrane and Swinburn.

WINNERS SINCE 1980

1980 Gregorian
    L. Piggott 11–4 (9 ran)

1981 Hard Fought
    W. R. Swinburn 9–4 (7 ran)

1982 Prince's Gate
    G. Starkey 10–1 (9 ran)

1983 Ivano
    L. Piggott 4–6 (7 ran)

1984 Morcon
    W. Carson 6–1 (8 ran)

1985 Elegant Air
    J. Matthias 8–1 (12 ran)

1986 Supreme Leader
    P. Robinson 1–2 (9 ran)

1987 Allez Milord
    G. Starkey 15–8 (9 ran)

1988 Infamy
    R. Cochrane 5–1 (5 ran)

1989 Indian Skimmer
    S. Cauthen 8–15 (9 ran)

1990 Dolpour
    W. R. Swinburn 5–2 (8 ran)

NEWMARKET SPRING MEETING

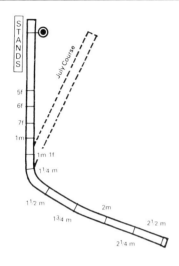

Course description on page 18.

Now it starts to get serious, for the trials have been run, and speculation must be put to the test. It's Classic time.

The Newmarket Spring Meeting is of course dominated by the ONE THOUSAND GUINEAS (pages 27–9) and the TWO THOUSAND GUINEAS (pages 31–3), but the meeting has much to offer beyond the first two Classics. The PRETTY POLLY STAKES commemorates the great racehorse who won twenty-two of her twenty-four races from 1903 to 1906: a ten-furlong Listed race for three-year-old fillies, it was won in 1987 by Indian Skimmer. Also in the Listed category is the NEWMARKET STAKES, for three-year-old colts over the same distance. And one of Newmarket's oddities is the NEWMARKET CHALLENGE WHIP over one mile, for three-year-old maidens, 'the property of Members of the Jockey Club or Jockey Club Rooms': no prize money is added to the stakes for this venerable old race, the conditions for which stipulate that 'in no case shall the whip leave Great Britain'.

On the Saturday of the meeting the Two Thousand Guineas is supported by the Group Three PALACE HOUSE STAKES, a five-furlong race which usually sees the seasonal debut of many of the best sprinters in training and often produces a wonderful finish – not least in 1990, when Statoblest just pipped Boozy to win by the shortest of short heads. In the last few years the Palace House Stakes has been won by such notable sprinters as Double Schwartz (1986) and Silver Fling (1989), both of whom went on to win the Prix de l'Abbaye at Longchamp at the other end of the season.

One Thousand Guineas

Newmarket (Rowley Mile): 1 mile

Group One: three-year-old fillies

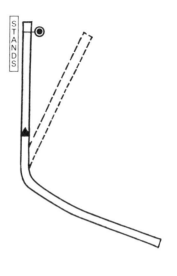

The One Thousand Guineas is the youngest of the five Classics, its first running in 1814 coming five years after the inaugural Two Thousand. It was run over the Ditch Mile, a flatter and easier terrain than the Rowley Mile, until joining the Two Thousand on the Rowley course in the early 1870s. The course really puts three-year-old fillies on their mettle, asking for an unusual combination of speed, toughness and balance, and it is no coincidence that a large proportion of One Thousand winners have already won or run well on the course in a top two-year-old contest such as the Cheveley Park Stakes (page 113) or the traditional Guineas trial, the Nell Gwyn Stakes (page 19).

The initial running of the race, when the bay filly Charlotte beat four opponents, saw the completion of a remarkable double for owner Christopher Wilson and jockey Billy Clift, for five years earlier they had won the first Two Thousand Guineas with Wizard. (Wilson had also owned Champion, who in 1800 had become the first horse to win the Derby and the St Leger.) The second running was won by a horse with no name – Lord Foley's brown filly by Selim, also ridden by Clift. Like its sibling Newmarket Classic, the One Thousand in its early years saw very small fields. The 1825 'race' was a walkover, unique in Classic history, taken by the appropriately named Tontine on the defection of her seven opponents. Tontine was owned by the Duke of Grafton, who won the race eight times in nine years between 1819 and 1827; during the same period he also won the Two Thousand Guineas five times, and he won the Derby in 1815 and had six winners of the Oaks between 1813 and 1831.

Among other famous nineteenth-century winners of the One Thousand Guineas was Crucifix, 10–1 on when taking the 1840 race – she also won the Two Thousand and the Oaks and became the dam of Surplice (see page 48); and special mention should be made of Virago, who took the Classic after beginning her three-year-old career by winning the Grand Metropolitan Handicap and the City and Suburban Handicap at Epsom on the same day!

The early years of the twentieth century formed a golden period for English fillies, with Sceptre winning four Classics in 1902 and Pretty Polly three in 1904. Both won the One Thousand with ease, Sceptre taking the race at 2–1 on after her unorthodox preparation in the Lincolnshire Handicap (see pages 16–17) and two days after winning the Two Thousand, which at that period was run before the fillies' Classic: she twisted a plate at the start and as no farrier was in attendance her owner Bob Sievier wrenched it off himself, leaving her

> Ten fillies were entered for the inaugural running, at a subscription of 100 guineas each – thus One Thousand Guineas.

> Tagalie, who won the One Thousand Guineas at 20–1 in 1911, is the only filly ever to go on and win the Derby.

WINNERS SINCE 1970
with ratings (see page 13)

1970 Humble Duty *137*
L. Piggott 3–1 (12 ran)

1971 Altesse Royale *134*
Y. Saint-Martin 25–1 (10 ran)

1972 Waterloo *124*
E. Hide 8–1 (18 ran)

1973 Mysterious *124*
G. Lewis 11–1 (14 ran)

1974 Highclere *133*
J. Mercer 12–1 (15 ran)

1975 Nocturnal Spree *124*
J. Roe 14–1 (16 ran)

1976 Flying Water *125*
Y. Saint-Martin 2–1 (25 ran)

1977 Mrs McArdy *125*
E. Hide 16–1 (18 ran)

1978 Enstone Spark *117*
E. Johnson 35–1 (16 ran)

1979 One In A Million *123*
J. Mercer evens (17 ran)

1980 Quick As Lightning *120*
B. Rouse 12–1 (23 ran)

1981 Fairy Footsteps *121*
L. Piggott 6–4 (14 ran)

1982 On The House *121*
J. Reid 33–1 (15 ran)

1983 Ma Biche *122*
F. Head 5–2 (18 ran)

1984 Pebbles *122*
P. Robinson 8–1 (15 ran)

1985 Oh So Sharp *122*
S. Cauthen 2–1 (17 ran)

1986 Midway Lady *124*
R. Cochrane 10–1 (15 ran)

1987 Miesque *132*
F. Head 15–8 (14 ran)

1988 Ravinella *121*
G. Moore 4–5 (12 ran)

1989 Musical Bliss *115*
W. R. Swinburn 7–2 (7 ran)

1990 Salsabil –
W. Carson 6–4 (10 ran)

MULTIPLE CLASSIC WINNERS

Only Sceptre has won four Classics outright. In 1902 she took the Two Thousand Guineas, One Thousand Guineas, Oaks and St Leger. Formosa in 1868 dead-heated for the Two Thousand and won the One Thousand, Oaks and St Leger.

Fifteen colts have won the Triple Crown of Two Thousand Guineas, Derby and St Leger: West Australian (1853), Gladiateur (1865), Lord Lyon (1866), Ormonde (1886), Common (1891), Isinglass (1893), Galtee More (1897), Flying Fox (1899), Diamond Jubilee (1900), Rock Sand (1903), Pommern (1915), Gay Crusader (1917), Gainsborough (1918), Bahram (1935) and Nijinsky (1970).

Seven fillies (in addition to Formosa and Sceptre) have won the One Thousand Guineas, Oaks and St Leger: Hannah (1871), Apology (1874), La Fleche (1892), Pretty Polly (1904), Sun Chariot (1942), Meld (1955) and Oh So Sharp (1985).

to race in three, but the loss of a shoe made no difference to her performance as she came home one and a half lengths clear of St Windeline. Just two years later Pretty Polly, unbeaten in nine races as a two-year-old and making her three-year-old debut in the Guineas, won in a canter by three lengths at 4–1 on in race record time.

The race was run on the July Course during the Second World War, and celebrated its return to the Rowley Mile in 1946 with a royal victory, King George VI's Hypericum winning at 100–6. The King's daughter Queen Elizabeth II owned another royal heroine when the blinkered Highclere, having her first run of the season, gamely held off Polygamy by a short head in 1974. Highclere's daughter Height Of Fashion is the dam of Nashwan. Possibly the greatest winner of the post-war period was Petite Etoile, who came home in 1959 at what with hindsight appear the extraordinarily generous odds of 8–1: ridden by Doug Smith, as Noel Murless's stable jockey Lester Piggott for once chose wrong and opted to partner Collyria, she burst into the lead after the Bushes and clocked a time more than two seconds faster than Taboun in that year's Two Thousand.

Petite Etoile went on to win the Oaks and many other big races, but it is curious how many One Thousand Guineas heroines never win again. Examples from the last few years include Nocturnal Spree in 1975; 35–1 winner Enstone Spark in 1978; Quick As Lightning in 1980; Fairy Footsteps the following year; and the 1989 winner Musical Bliss: trainer Michael Stoute's first One Thousand winner after five seconds and two thirds (and he had the second in the 1989 running), Musical Bliss beat just six opponents, the smallest field since Pretty Polly also beat six in 1904.

The One Thousand Guineas first attracted commercial sponsorship from the insurance company General Accident in 1984, the year of the enchanting and brilliant Pebbles.

┌─ **HOW THEY RATE** ─────────┐

Humble Duty *137*
Altesse Royale *134*
Highclere *133*
Miesque *132*
Flying Water *125*
Mrs McArdy *125*
Midway Lady *124*
Mysterious *124*
Nocturnal Spree *124*
Waterloo *124*
One In A Million *123*
Ma Biche *122*
Oh So Sharp *122*
Pebbles *122*
Fairy Footsteps *121*
On The House *121*
Ravinella *121*
Quick As Lightning *120*
Enstone Spark *117*
Musical Bliss *115*

└─────────────────────────┘

Above: the 1985 General Accident One Thousand Guineas: Oh So Sharp beats Al Bahathri by a short head, with Bella Colora (spots) the same distance away in third. Vilikaia is fourth. *Below:* the 1990 General Accident One Thousand Guineas: Salsabil goes clear of Heart Of Joy.

Jockey Club Stakes

STANDS

Newmarket (Rowley Mile): 1½ miles

Group Two: four-year-olds and upwards

The Jockey Club Stakes today is an ideal seasonal debut for top-class older horses who have been kept in training, and provides the highlight of the middle day of the Guineas meeting. But for much of its history it was open to three-year-olds and run during the autumn, and its distance was not reduced from its original one mile six furlongs until it was moved forward to the spring in 1963.

But whatever the timing, and whatever the distance, the list of horses who have won this race contains many of the most familiar names in Turf history. Its tenth running, in 1903, saw what was perhaps the finest hour of the immortal Sceptre, who carried ten stone to a four-length victory over that year's Triple Crown winner Rock Sand. The following year it was Rock Sand's own turn. The 1904 Derby winner St Amant took the 1905 renewal, and the 1910 race went to another Derby hero, Lemberg. In the period immediately following the Second World War the best winner was the great stayer Alycidon in 1948.

The last Derby winner to take the race was the four-year-old St Paddy in 1961: ridden by Lester Piggott, he eased past Sir Winston Churchill's High Hat (Scobie Breasley) to win by a length. But in its current guise the Jockey Club Stakes has seen deep disappointment for two Derby winners who, against the modern trend, were kept in training. Henbit in 1981 was last of six behind Master Willie, and another run confirmed that he had not recovered from the injury sustained in his heroic Derby victory the year before. And in 1986 Slip Anchor used the race as a springboard to a four-year-old campaign: he started at 11−4 on to beat two opponents, but went down by a neck to Phardante, who was given a brilliant tactical ride by Greville Starkey. Phardante would win the race for a second time in 1987, but Slip Anchor never ran again.

There was another major upset in 1990 when Brush Aside, the 5−2 on favourite, finished a dismal fifth behind Roseate Tern, who had been sold for 1,100,000 guineas the previous December to Peter Brant: her Newmarket victory repaid £42,912 of his investment.

WINNERS SINCE 1980

1980　More Light
　　W. Carson 4−1 (8 ran)

1981　Master Willie
　　P. Waldron 2−1 (6 ran)

1982　Ardross
　　L. Piggott evens (6 ran)

1983　Electric
　　W. R. Swinburn 12−1 (11 ran)

1984　Gay Lemur
　　G. Baxter 8−1 (6 ran)

1985　Kirmann
　　S. Cauthen 11−1 (8 ran)

1986　Phardante
　　G. Starkey 11−2 (3 ran)

1987　Phardante
　　G. Starkey 7−1 (7 ran)

1988　Almaraad
　　W. Carson 13−2 (4 ran)

1989　Unfuwain
　　W. Carson 5−6 (6 ran)

1990　Roseate Tern
　　L. Dettori 17−2 (7 ran)

Two Thousand Guineas

Newmarket (Rowley Mile): 1 mile

Group One: three-year-old colts and fillies

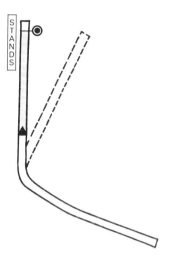

The Two Thousand Guineas was first run in 1809, nearly three decades after the inaugural Derby and five years before its sister Classic the One Thousand. The first running was won by Wizard, who beat seven opponents, and the following year the race went to Hephestion. His jockey, Frank Buckle, rode twenty-seven Classic winners, from John Bull in the 1792 Derby to Arab in the 1827 One Thousand Guineas: his record remained unbroken until Lester Piggott pushed Commanche Run home in the 1984 St Leger to land his twenty-eighth Classic.

In its early years the Two Thousand Guineas tended to attract small fields: only ten of the first fifty runnings saw the number of contestants into double figures, and in both 1829 and 1830 just two went to post. But as the Classic framework to the season gradually evolved during the nineteenth century the race became second only to the Derby as a test of a three-year-old. The first horse to go on from Newmarket success to win the Derby was Smolensko in 1813, and the first to win the Triple Crown of Two Thousand Guineas, Derby and St Leger was West Australian in 1853. In all, fifteen horses have won the Triple Crown, but to Pastille, in 1822 the first filly to win the Two Thousand, goes the unique distinction of a dual Classic haul of the Two Thousand Guineas and the Oaks, and Pilgrimage in 1878 won the Two Thousand and One Thousand. (Several other horses have included the Two Thousand Guineas in triple or even quadruple Classic success: see page 28.)

The Two Thousand Guineas is now the biggest race of the early part of the Flat calendar, and if the first month or so of the season can be an intriguing time as the Classic hopefuls make their reappearances, the Saturday of the Guineas is the moment of truth. Rarely is the race a disappointment either in prospect or in the running, and since the Second World War it has produced many famous moments. In 1947 the then unbeaten Tudor Minstrel, ridden by Gordon Richards, won with extraordinary ease by eight lengths: 'On that day', wrote Richards, 'Tudor Minstrel was the best miler I have ever ridden in all my career.' He was sensationally beaten in the Derby at 7–4 on, but at a mile was one of the most brilliant horses of the post-war period.

Nearly a quarter of a century later a horse came along who would take over Tudor Minstrel's position as the best post-war Guineas winner, and would do so in one of the most eagerly awaited races of modern times, for the 1971 running brought together three horses

> The inaugural running attracted twenty-three entries at a subscription of 100 guineas each – thus (roughly!) Two Thousand Guineas.

> There were 1001 horses entered for the 1974 running of the Two Thousand Guineas, the largest ever entry for a single race. In the event only twelve started, for Apalachee, who had been a brilliant two-year-old, scared away most of the opposition. He started at 9–4 on but could finish only third behind Nonoalco and Giacometti. Apalachee never ran again.

who the previous season had each shown himself an exceptional two-year-old. Top of the Free Handicap in 1970 was My Swallow, one pound above Mill Reef (whom he had beaten a short head in the Prix Robert Papin at Maisons-Laffitte – the only time Mill Reef had been beaten) and two pounds above the unbeaten Brigadier Gerard, winner of the Middle Park Stakes but thought to be slightly below his two rivals in the overall quality of his juvenile form. In addition, Brigadier Gerard came to Newmarket without a previous run that season (as another Dick Hern winner, Nashwan, was to do in 1989), and for the 1971 Two Thousand Guineas he started at 11–2, less well supported than the 6–4 favourite Mill Reef and 2–1 chance My Swallow. Brigadier Gerard never started again at odds against, for the Two Thousand announced his stature as a truly great horse. In a field of six, he lay in behind his two main rivals in the early part of the race and swept contemptuously past them in the Dip to win by three lengths, with Mill Reef depriving My Swallow of second place by a short head.

A performance almost as impressive was that of El Gran Senor in 1984. Ridden with supreme confidence by Pat Eddery, the Vincent O'Brien-trained colt powered away from a top-class field to beat Chief Singer and Lear Fan by two and a half lengths and four. El Gran Senor completely dominated his field and showed tremendous strength to pull away up the hill – as did Dancing Brave in 1986 and Nashwan in 1989 – but sometimes the Two Thousand produces a race of heart-stopping excitement, for that hill can change the complexion of a race dramatically in the final stages and only a horse with no chink in his armour will get home. In 1982 Zino beat Wind And Wuthering by a head in a thrilling finish, and the same distance brought Lester Piggott his twenty-ninth and final Classic success when Shadeed just got the verdict from Bairn in 1985. The 1980 race saw similar excitement and then sensation and controversy when Nureyev beat Known Fact by a neck only to be disqualified – the first horse in the history of the Two Thousand Guineas to lose the race in the Stewards' Room – for barging into Posse just over two furlongs out.

If the Two Thousand Guineas often produces a horse of exceptional calibre, how can you spot that calibre in advance? Above all, the race requires a horse that will not flinch from one of the toughest tasks that an immature three-year-old can face, for the Rowley Mile is no place for faint hearts. Its wide and dead straight expanse demands that the horse stay every yard of the trip: he will need the speed to remain handy in the early stages of a race which is always run at a fast pace, and then have enough in reserve to get up the final hill. Only very occasionally will a horse of doubtful stamina prevail in the Two Thousand Guineas: Charlie Smirke may have stolen the 1950 running on Palestine by using his mount's speed going into the Dip to set up a lead which Prince Simon failed to claw back by only a short head, but such enterprise is rarely rewarded, and in the final furlong the non-stayer will have his weakness ruthlessly exposed – which explains why so many races on the Rowley Mile end in frantically close finishes.

The war years of the 1940s apart – when it was transferred to the July Course at Newmarket while the Rowley Mile course was taken over by the RAF – the Two Thousand Guineas has always been run on the Rowley Mile, and the race was first supported by General Accident in 1984.

HOW THEY RATE

Brigadier Gerard *146*
Nijinsky *144*
El Gran Senor *138*
Bolkonski *135*
Nonoalco *135*
High Top *133*
Nashwan *131*
Shadeed *131*
Wollow *131*
Dancing Brave *130*
Known Fact *129*
To-Agori-Mou *128*
Tap On Wood *127*
Nebbiolo *126*
Mon Fils *125*
Don't Forget Me *123*
Lomond *123*
Zino *123*
Doyoun *122*
Roland Gardens *121*

Pat Eddery and El Gran Senor stride home in the 1984 General Accident Two Thousand Guineas.

CHESTER MAY MEETING

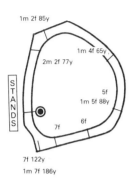

1m 2f 85y

1m 4f 65y

2m 2f 77y

STANDS

5f
1m 5f 88y

6f

7f

7f 122y
1m 7f 186y

Chester's exceptionally tight left-handed track is just over one mile in circumference, with a home straight of little more than one furlong. The track is completely flat, and favours the speedy but nimble sort of horse.

After the serious business of the Guineas races at Newmarket, the Chester May Meeting comes as a sort of light relief. The racing is of a high order but the overall atmosphere at the meeting is one of fun, engendered by the unique configuration of the course.

Chester is the tightest Flat racecourse in the country. Its peculiar size derives from its position between a sweeping bend in the River Dee and the old Roman walls of the city, from which spectators can enjoy a fine view of the racing. Chester is such fun because it is so different: its runners scurry like rabbits round the bends, its punters swarm between the stands and the parade ring, situated on the inside of the circuit (there's nowhere else to put it): everywhere is bustle. And the Roman wall which rises above the entrance to the straight provides physical expression of the great sense of history which forms the backdrop to modern racing at the course: racing has been taking place on the Roodee (or Roodeye) since the early sixteenth century.

The three-day May meeting is the high point of Chester's year and one of the most engaging fixtures of the season. The CHESTER VASE (opposite) is a well-established trial for the Derby, and the CHESHIRE OAKS, a Listed race over one mile three furlongs and about seventy yards, usually attracts a few fillies with Oaks pretensions. The CHESTER CUP (page 36) remains one of the most historic races of the calendar, and the ORMONDE STAKES (page 37) an important early-season target for middle-distance older horses. The May Meeting also has the DEE STAKES, a Listed Race over one and a quarter miles which has offered significant Classic pointers: Parthia in 1959 was the last horse to win the Derby after taking the Dee Stakes, but more recently the Irish Derby winner Sir Harry Lewis won in 1987; Blue Stag, who beat Saumarez in 1990, went on to finish second at Epsom and fourth at The Curragh.

On television or in the flesh, Chester has a magic all of its own.

Chester Vase

Chester: 1 mile, 4 furlongs, 65 yards

Group Three: three-year-olds only

Although the main interest of the Chester Vase in modern racing centres around its significance as a trial for the Derby, from its foundation in 1907 until 1958 it was open to four-year-olds as well as three-year-olds. But it is on the Classic contenders that attention now focuses, and although Chester is in many ways a completely different sort of course from Epsom, many trainers look to the tight turns of the Roodee for some indication of whether their Derby hopefuls will be nimble and adaptable enough to take a chance in the premier Classic.

The first horse to go on to win the Derby after landing the Chester Vase was Papyrus in 1923, to be emulated ten years later by the great Hyperion and in 1934 by Windsor Lad. Although it was not until Henbit in 1980 that the feat was repeated – and then Shergar pulled it off again in 1981 – the race could hardly be said to have fallen into decline in the meantime, either as a Derby trial or as a pointer to other big things to come. The 1949 winner Swallow Tail was beaten two heads into third at Epsom. In 1951 Supreme Court won the Vase on his way to victory in the first running of the King George VI and Queen Elizabeth Stakes at Ascot. Alcide, winner of the King George in 1959, had won the Vase as a three-year-old. Fidalgo (1959) was second to Parthia (who had won Chester's other significant Derby trial, the Dee Stakes) in the Derby. Indiana in 1964 was second to Santa Claus at Epsom and then won the St Leger. Remand in 1968 beat Connaught, who was to run second to Sir Ivor at Epsom, with Remand himself fourth. Linden Tree won the Vase and was second to Mill Reef in the Derby in 1971, and Hot Grove (1977) likewise took the runner-up berth at Epsom, second to The Minstrel after a desperate finish. Law Society (1985) won the Irish Derby, Unfuwain (1988) was second to Mtoto in the King George, and Old Vic (1989) went on to win the Prix du Jockey-Club and the Irish Derby.

In 1990 Quest For Fame finished second to Belmez, in whose absence at Epsom he scored an impressive Derby victory; but Belmez – whose retirement through injury was prematurely announced soon after the Vase – was restored to fitness and finished ahead of Quest For Fame when third to Salsabil in the Irish Derby and then just beat Old Vic in the King George. The form of the 1990 Chester Vase worked out pretty well!

WINNERS SINCE 1980

1980 Henbit
W. Carson evens (5 ran)

1981 Shergar
W. R. Swinburn 4–11 (10 ran)

1982 Super Sunrise
P. Cook 10–1 (8 ran)

1983 abandoned – waterlogged

1984 Kaytu
W. Carson 11–2 (7 ran)

1985 Law Society
Pat Eddery 5–2 (5 ran)

1986 Nomrood
T. Quinn 11–2 (7 ran)

1987 Dry Dock
W. Carson 11–2 (8 ran)

1988 Unfuwain
W. Carson 1–3 (4 ran)

1989 Old Vic
S. Cauthen 6–4 (5 ran)

1990 Belmez
S. Cauthen 8–13 (3 ran)

Chester Cup

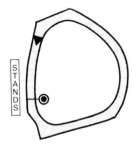

Chester: 2 miles, 2 furlongs, 77 yards

Handicap: four-year-olds and upwards

There is no race in the racing year quite like the Chester Cup. In which other big race on the Flat does the field pass the winning post three times?

The Cup was first run in 1824, when it was known as the Tradesmen's Cup, and before long was one of the biggest betting races of the calendar (for a time second only to the Derby). Alice Hawthorn, a famous mare who won fifty-two races in her career, landed a big gamble when taking the 1842 running under a mere six stone, but when in 1844 she attempted to concede seventy-eight pounds to the three-year-old Red Deer she was unable to obstruct one of the most massive gambles of the age. The three-year-old carried four stone, of which three stone four pounds consisted of his diminutive jockey named Kitchener, and Red Deer went straight to the front and won by a huge margin – 'about fifty lengths': so easily was he going at the finish that Kitchener could not pull him up until he had reached the opposite side of the course. Fifty years later the prize for the race included for the first time a Cheshire cheese.

The status of the Chester Cup has declined during recent decades but it still attracts many of the best staying handicappers around, and plenty of horses whose exploits will be remembered long after those of briefly famous Classic winners figure in the list of winners. Trelawny, the most loved stayer since Brown Jack (winner in 1931), won in 1960; Peter O'Sullevan's Attivo took the 1974 race not long after showing his versatility when winning the Triumph Hurdle at Cheltenham; John Cherry lifted the 1976 running under nine stone four pounds, and the next two Chester Cups went to the indomitable Sea Pigeon. In 1978 he carried nine stone seven to victory a couple of months after the first of his tremendous Champion Hurdle finishes with Monksfield, and the following year won the Ebor Handicap, a double also achieved by Western Dancer, who took the York race in 1985 and the Chester Cup in 1986. Donegal Prince (1981) followed Sea Pigeon in combining the flat with hurdling: he won the Schweppes Gold Trophy at Newbury in 1982, and Grey Salute, the 1989 winner of that race (then the Tote Gold Trophy) swapped Richard Dunwoody for Pat Eddery and won the Cup three months later.

WINNERS SINCE 1980

1980 Arapahos
S. Cauthen 7–2 (10 ran)

1981 Donegal Prince
P. Young 12–1 (15 ran)

1982 Dawn Johnny
W. R. Swinburn 14–1 (16 ran)

1983 abandoned – waterlogged

1984 Contester
G. Baxter 22–1 (19 ran)

1985 Morgans Choice
W. Carson 13–2 (16 ran)

1986 Western Dancer
P. Cook 14–1 (22 ran)

1987 Just David
M. Roberts 10–1 (13 ran)

1988 Old Hubert
M. L. Thomas 33–1 (17 ran)

1989 Grey Salute
Pat Eddery 7–1 (14 ran)

1990 Travelling Light
A. Munro 5–2 (16 ran)

Ormonde Stakes

Chester: 1 mile, 5 furlongs, 88 yards

Group Three: four-year-olds and upwards

Ormonde was one of the greatest horses of the nineteenth century, the unbeaten winner of sixteen races over three seasons from 1885 to 1887, including the Triple Crown in 1886. By Bend Or out of Lily Agnes (winner twenty-one times and like her son commemorated in a race at Chester), Ormonde beat the hot favourite Minting in the Two Thousand Guineas before taking the Derby at 9–4 on from The Bard; he then won twice at Royal Ascot, and after winning the St Leger in a canter he notched up another four victories at Newmarket. Despite a wind affliction (it was said that he could be heard half a mile away) he was kept in training as a four-year-old, and his final race advertised his versatility: he won the six-furlong Imperial Gold Cup at Newmarket (the precursor of the July Cup).

There have been many distinguished winners of the Ormonde Stakes (which before 1936 was a five-furlong contest for two-year-olds). The first running of the race in its current form went to Quashed, the 1935 Oaks winner, who beat the five-year-old Cecil by a head after a ding-dong tussle: six weeks later she just got the better of Omaha in the Ascot Gold Cup, generally regarded as the greatest race of the inter-war period. Alycidon won the Ormonde Stakes as a four-year-old in 1949, and three years later the three-year-old Tulyar beat three opponents before going on to win the Lingfield Derby Trial and then the Derby itself. Since Tulyar two Derby winners have won the race – Blakeney (1970) and Teenoso (1984) – while Indiana (1965) and Crow (1978) had won the St Leger the previous autumn. Those four are typical Ormonde Stakes winners – high-class four-year-olds warming up for bigger dates elsewhere – but sometimes things don't quite work out as expected: in 1990 the St Leger winner Michelozzo was odds-on to open his four-year-old account in the Ormonde, but could finish only second to Braashee.

WINNERS SINCE 1980

1980 Niniski
    W. Carson 4–7 (5 ran)

1981 Pelerin
    B. Taylor 11–8 (5 ran)

1982 Six Mile Bottom
    S. Cauthen 12–1 (6 ran)

1983 abandoned – waterlogged

1984 Teenoso
    Pat Eddery 11–8 (5 ran)

1985 Seismic Wave
    B. Thomson 7–1 (8 ran)

1986 Brunico
    B. Thomson 33–1 (8 ran)

1987 Rakaposhi King
    S. Cauthen 1–3 (5 ran)

1988 Mr Pintips
    W. Carson 20–1 (6 ran)

1989 Mountain Kingdom
    S. Cauthen 4–6 (3 ran)

1990 Braashee
    M. Roberts 6–1 (6 ran)

YORK MAY MEETING

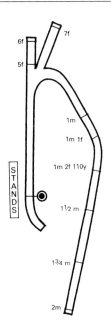

York is as fair and as testing a racecourse as any in the country. Wide and flat with easy bends, it is perfect for the long-striding horse.

The circus of early-season Flat racing moves on from Chester to York, and there could hardly be a greater contrast between the two courses in terms of the shape of the circuit. While Chester is 'the soup-plate', York is magnificently spacious, heaven for the relentless galloper. But as at Chester, racing at York is designed to give maximum enjoyment, not only in the facilities on offer to those on the course but also in the overall quality of racing. If the August Meeting (pages 88–95) is as fine a fixture as the Flat can boast all year, the May Meeting is a fascinating taste of what is to come.

As with so many of the early-season occasions on the major courses, the meeting is dominated by Classic trials: the MUSIDORA STAKES (opposite) and the DANTE STAKES (page 40) regularly provide important pieces for the jigsaw of form building up for the Oaks and the Derby respectively. Three-year-olds also have two significant graduation races at the meeting: the MIDDLETON STAKES for fillies over one mile two and a half furlongs and the GLASGOW STAKES for colts and geldings over the same distance. Other delights of the meeting are a race for top-class older horses – the YORKSHIRE CUP (page 41) – and the Group Three DUKE OF YORK STAKES, run over six furlongs and won in recent years by the likes of Indian Ridge (1989), Handsome Sailor (1987 and 1988), Gabitat (1984) and Vorvados (1983). York is a wonderful course for competitive handicaps, and the NORWEST HOLST TROPHY is a valuable seven-furlong affair which always provides a stirring finish.

There's no need any longer to refer to York as 'the Ascot of the North': it's one of the world's great racecourses in its own right, and the May Meeting is its second most important fixture.

Musidora Stakes

York: 1 mile 2½ furlongs

Group Three: three-year-old fillies only

Like the Dante Stakes, the Musidora Stakes perpetuates the memory of a famous northern racehorse. Bred in Ireland, Musidora was trained at Malton by Charles Elsey. After one victory from six starts as a two-year-old she won on her three-year-old debut and then took the 1949 One Thousand Guineas at 100–8. Edgar Britt described in his autobiography *Post Haste* how he was riding 'that strange filly' alongside Gordon Richards a quarter of a mile out: 'Gordon looked across the line of horses and said, "I do believe you're going best of all Edgar," and when I replied, "I think so, too," he added, "Well away you go lad, while you have the advantage." I said, "No" and sat there until we got well in the dip and Gordon cried, "Go on, go on."' Britt took the advice, and although Musidora idled in front she won easily. In the Oaks she started 4–1 favourite and scrambled home by a neck from Marcel Boussac's Coronation V, with Britt careful not to use the whip on her. She did not win again, failing to reach the first three in the Yorkshire Oaks, the St Leger and the Doonside Plate at Ayr. Like so many good racing fillies she proved a disappointment at stud, her three winning progeny being of little consequence.

It is as a trial for the Oaks that the Musidora Stakes, first run in 1961, keeps its significant place in the racing year. Noblesse, trained by Paddy Prendergast, won the 1963 race by six lengths on her seasonal debut and started at 11–4 on in the Oaks: even those odds were made to look generous as she bolted in by ten lengths. It was not until 1980 that another filly – Bireme – won both races. The 1987 winner Indian Skimmer was not entered in the Oaks but proved herself one of the very best of her sex of the post-war period: she came to York via a small graduation race at Wolverhampton and the Pretty Polly Stakes at Newmarket, and slammed Bourbon Girl (later second in the Oaks) before going on to win the Prix Saint-Alary and the Prix de Diane (French Oaks), in which she beat Miesque. In 1988 Diminuendo won the Musidora emphatically and then scampered to a four-length victory at Epsom, and in 1989 the race went to Snow Bride, who finished second behind Aliysa in the Classic.

WINNERS SINCE 1980

1980 Bireme
  W. Carson 5–1 (9 ran)

1981 Condessa
  D. Gillespie 16–1 (5 ran)

1982 Last Feather
  S. Cauthen 7–4 (5 ran)

1983 Give Thanks
  D. Gillespie 13–8 (8 ran)

1984 Optimistic Lass
  W. R. Swinburn 9–1 (9 ran)

1985 Fatah Flare
  S. Cauthen 10–1 (9 ran)

1986 Rejuvenate
  B. Thomson 9–2 (7 ran)

1987 Indian Skimmer
  S. Cauthen 1–2 (3 ran)

1988 Diminuendo
  S. Cauthen 8–13 (6 ran)

1989 Snow Bride
  S. Cauthen 4–1 (6 ran)

1990 In The Groove
  R. Cochrane 15–2 (5 ran)

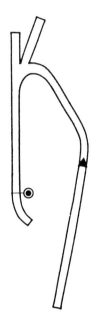

Dante Stakes

York: 1 mile 2½ furlongs

Group Two: three-year-olds only

No wonder Dante was the idol of northern racing. His victory in the 1945 Derby, displaced by the war to the July Course at Newmarket, was the first Derby triumph for a northern-trained horse since that of Pretender in 1869, and no northern horse has won since. Dante was a brilliant two-year-old, winning all his six races, and after a facile victory at Stockton in April 1945 went to Newmarket for the Two Thousand Guineas. An inflammation two days before the race lost him the sight of one eye, and Court Martial sneaked up on his blind side to beat him by a neck. But ridden by Billy Nevett and starting 100–30 favourite, Dante took his revenge in the Derby, winning by two lengths from Midas, with Court Martial third: the victory was received with rapturous enthusiasm in Yorkshire, and the Bell at Middleham – where he was trained by Matthew Peacock – was rung; later a Dante Ball was held. It proved impossible to get him ready for the St Leger and he was retired to stud, where he became completely blind, and by the time he died in 1956 he had sired the winners of 256 races.

It is fitting that the North's top Derby trial should commemorate its last winner of the premier Classic. The Dante Stakes was first run in 1958, when it was won by Bald Eagle, destined to become a dual winner of the Washington International. Only two years later it produced its first Derby winner in St Paddy, but there was then a gap of nearly two decades before the next – Shirley Heights in 1978 – though in the interim the race maintained its reputation as a reliable indicator of Epsom chances, going to Merchant Venturer in 1963 (second to Relko at Epsom) and Rheingold in 1972 (second to Roberto). Shahrastani in 1986 and Reference Point in 1987 both added to the reputation of the race by going on to take the Derby after winning the Dante, and its record justifies its position as the most valuable of the Derby trials: the 1990 running was worth £75,600 to Khalid Abdullah, owner of the winner, Sanglamore, who then went over to Chantilly for a battling victory in the Prix du Jockey-Club.

The main factor that has made the Dante Stakes and the Musidora Stakes such good trials of would-be Classic horses is the York track itself, which with its long, easy bends and wide straight is a fair but searching test of the three-year-old Thoroughbred.

Yorkshire Cup

York: 1¾ miles

Group Two: four-year-olds and upwards

The Yorkshire Cup is the first of the four big weight-for-age staying races of the season, though coming as it does early in the season it tends to be used as a trial for the later Cup races at Ascot, Goodwood and Doncaster. Significantly shorter than those races, it often attracts some very high-class performers.

It was first run in 1927 over two miles, and was not reduced to its present distance until 1966. Among the early winners was the charmingly named The Bastard (1930), who after winning four races in Britain was exported to Australia – where more delicate sensibilities caused him to be renamed The Buzzard – and was the great-grandsire of Carbine, possibly the greatest Australian-bred horse ever. Trimdon (1932) took the Ascot Gold Cup twice, as did Ardross, who prefaced both his 1981 and 1982 Ascot victories with success in the Yorkshire Cup. Felicitation won the Cup in 1935, the year *after* he had won the Ascot Gold Cup, while Pandofell in 1961 used the York race as a stepping-stone to winning the centrepiece of Royal Ascot. Ardross was a typical Yorkshire Cup winner of the period since the distance was shortened – high-class over middle distances but even better over a longer trip. It has become increasingly difficult for trainers to know how to race such horses, for concentration on staying races of two miles or more will put off prospective breeders, while the horse might not have quite the speed for a sustained campaign over twelve furlongs. In this area between true middle-distance and true staying race the Yorkshire Cup fills a vital role, and the fact that since the distance was reduced it has been won by (apart from Ardross) the likes of Aunt Edith (1966: she won the King George VI and Queen Elizabeth Stakes later that season), Buoy (1974: winner of the Coronation Cup the following month), Bruni (1976: St Leger winner the previous year) and Moon Madness (1988: St Leger winner 1987) testifies to its value.

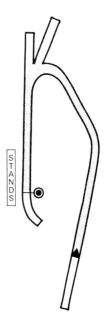

WINNERS SINCE 1980

1980 Noble Saint
L. Piggott 10–1 (8 ran)

1981 Ardross
L. Piggott 2–1 (6 ran)

1982 Ardross
L. Piggott 2–5 (6 ran)

1983 Line Slinger
E. Hide 33–1 (10 ran)

1984 Band
W. Carson 9–4 (9 ran)

1985 Ilium
R. Hills 5–1 (10 ran)

1986 Eastern Mystic
Pat Eddery 9–4 (7 ran)

1987 Verd-Antique
S. Cauthen 7–4 (7 ran)

1988 Moon Madness
Pat Eddery 6–5 (8 ran)

1989 Mountain Kingdom
S. Cauthen 2–1 (6 ran)

1990 Braashee
M. Roberts 11–8 (6 ran)

EPSOM SUMMER MEETING

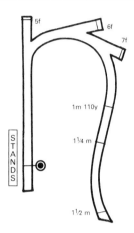

The runners on the twelve-furlong course go uphill after the start and take a mild right-hand bend before moving over to the opposite rail and continuing on the upgrade until they reach the top of Tattenham Hill, from where they make the steep left-handed descent to Tattenham Corner. The home straight is just under half a mile long, and runs gradually downhill from Tattenham Corner before going marginally uphill just before the line; an added complication is that the camber of the straight slopes away from the stands side. The five-furlong course is downhill practically all the way, and exceptionally fast.

The Epsom Summer Meeting is a pivotal moment of the season, for whichever horse wins the Derby, racing history has been made, and the future programme for that horse will set the mood for the rest of the campaign. The racing world is a significantly different place after this meeting than it was before.

As a meeting the Epsom Summer fixture is of course completely dominated by Derby Day, one of the world's great sporting occasions and steadfastly remaining so in spite of criticism levelled at the race itself. The special nature of THE DERBY and of the first Wednesday of June when it is run is described on the following few pages. The first day of the meeting includes one other Pattern race, the Group Three DIOMED STAKES, which commemorates the winner of the inaugural running of the Derby in 1780.

By Thursday the bedlam of Derby Day has faded, leaving the Downs strewn with litter — mostly betting tickets — and the racing to the purists, who have the Group One CORONATION CUP (pages 56–7) to appreciate. If there's a morning-after feel about Epsom Downs on Thursday, on Friday the hangover gets worse, though the feature race of the day, the NORTHERN DANCER HANDICAP over the full Derby course for four-year-olds and upwards, is always a keenly fought contest. But on the Saturday the tempo rises again with the second Classic of the meeting, THE OAKS (pages 58–61), which though not in the same league as the Derby as an occasion none the less brings a large crowd — and an appropriate influx of atmosphere — back to the course, and sometimes provides a more keenly anticipated contest than the more famous Epsom Classic.

The Derby

Epsom: 1½ miles

Group One: three-year-old colts and fillies

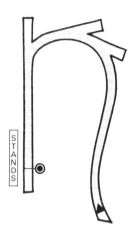

The trouble with the Derby, a head lad told the writer Jeffrey Bernard, is that 'the bastards are all trying'.

And well they might, for despite increasing competition from other big events in Europe and the USA, the Derby remains a race apart – the Flat race which every owner, trainer, jockey, breeder and stable lad or lass most wants to win. Its position as the world's greatest horse race rests not only with the frequently disputed notion that one and a half miles round Epsom provides the supreme test of the three-year-old, nor solely in the fact that winning the Derby will instantly increase the stud value of the victor to mind-boggling sums. The Derby is unique in British racing because it forms the focal point of the nation's greatest and most enduring popular celebration – Derby Day.

There is truly nothing like Derby Day. Hundreds of thousands of people – the exact number is impossible to calculate – congregate on Epsom Downs on the first Wednesday in June not just to be present at the running of the third Classic of the season but to revel in the experience of the day when traditionally the entire spectrum of British society gets together for an unofficial public holiday. The sight of this sociologist's dream spread out to all corners of the downs is one not to be forgotten, and many of the traditional elements of the day survive. There are the gypsies, who arrive at Epsom from round the country throughout the previous week and set up camp on the downs with their fortune-telling booths and their menageries of horses, ponies, goats and chickens. By Tattenham Corner there is the funfair, dominated by the Big Wheel, where merry-go-rounds and dodgems cram in among the side-shows. And inside the horseshoe shape of the course is a teeming mass of humanity. Down by the rails they are packed twenty deep, hoping to hold a position good enough to catch a glimpse of the race itself; beyond these are the open-topped buses weighed down with food, champagne and sozzled revellers, and beyond these the humbler fare offered by hundreds of booths dispensing food, drink, clairvoyance and the other essentials of a day at the races. Bands and other entertainment are liberally provided, and of course there are the bookmakers. Well away from the betting ring in Tattersalls where the serious transactions are taking place, the mass of bookies add their own special contribution to the glorious bedlam of London's big day out.

It was this notion of the inhabitants of London all engaged in the

In 1794 there were just four runners in the Derby.

same enterprise which caught the imagination of the American novelist Henry James in 1877:

> It was extremely low and rowdyish. But a stranger even of the most refined taste might be glad to have a glimpse of the popular revel, for it would make him feel he was learning something more about the English people. It would give a meaning to the old description of England as merry. It would remind him that the natives of that country are subject to some of the lighter of the human impulses, and that the decent, dusky vistas of the London residential streets are not a complete symbol of the complicated races that erected them.

The idea of Derby Day as an expression of quintessential Englishness lay behind the jingoistic description in the *Illustrated London News* in the same period – 'the most astonishing, the most varied, the most picturesque and the most glorious spectacle that ever was, or ever can be, under any circumstances, visible to mortal eyes'. With the wind thus in its sails, the journal changed tack: 'For once, people speak to other people to whom they have never been formally introduced, and positively hob and nob with those palpably inferior to them in station. It is clearly subversive of the proper distinctions which should always in a well-governed society exist between class and class.'

Subversive or not, the classlessness began on The Road to Epsom, a common theme for mid-Victorian writers, artists and illustrators who would enthusiastically depict the crowd clinging to carts, bumping along on stagecoaches, or – after the railway had reached Epsom in 1848 – cramming into railway carriages. In 1859 *Punch* offered some 'Laws of the Road on Derby Day', advising its readers 'to stand up in your carriage, to shout, to use your arms like a wild telegraph, and your legs like a pair of compasses, to talk, joke and laugh in the easiest and decidedly freest manner, with persons you would be ashamed of being seen to exchange a single word with on any other occasion than the Derby'. And the *Illustrated London News* helpfully advised the toffs that if the lower orders threw things at them, they should 'just throw them back' (but there were limits – 'oranges and lobster claws are just all right but not bags of flour or bad eggs'). One nineteenth-century Epsom character not in sympathy with the noble ideal of forgetting class distinctions for the day was Donkey Jemmy, who for sixpence would bray like a donkey: not for just anyone, though – 'I do the donkey to please the aristocracy, not the common people.'

Whatever their class, a large proportion of the masses saw little or nothing of the race, but once the overflowing revelry of Derby Day had become its *raison d'être* this shortcoming was irrelevant: *Bell's Life in London* remarked of the 1823 occasion that 'By one o'clock there must have been eighty thousand persons on the Downs – what they all went thither for is best known to themselves, but certainly not one twentieth of them saw the race, and the only other amusements were broiling on an arid heath beneath a mid-day sun, or sitting in booths crowded to suffocation amidst the fumes of tobacco and all sorts of hideous uproar.'

The idea of Derby Day as an unofficial public holiday was even supported in the corridors of power, for in the nineteenth century it was common practice for the sitting of the House of Commons to be suspended on that day so that MPs could attend the race. The first Member to move the adjournment was the great Turf reformer Lord George Bentinck in 1847, and the tradition continued for many decades. That particular tradition is defunct, but Derby Day still epitomizes more than any other sporting event that intangible which calls us from slumping in front of the television – atmosphere.

But what of the race itself? That horse racing takes place at all at Epsom we owe to one Henry Whicker, who during the drought of 1618 was having trouble finding water for his cattle. Chancing upon a small spring on the common between Ashtead and Epsom, he tried to refresh his herd, but they would have none of it. When Whicker himself sampled the water he discovered why: it tasted foul. But when he alerted the locals to this source of unpleasant water local physicians investigated, and found its properties useful for treating wounds. Over a decade later a group of labourers who drank from the spring were soon made aware of its excellent purgative effects, and gradually the medicinal benefits of Epsom water – and the Epsom salts which were taken from it – became famous. By the mid-seventeenth century Epsom had become a notable spa town (Samuel Pepys in 1667 drank four pints of the water 'and had some very good stools by it'), and the running of horse races on the Downs became part of the social activity of the place.

In 1773 Edward Stanley, aged twenty-one, leased from his uncle by marriage General Burgoyne a house on the outskirts of Epsom named The Oaks. Four years later Burgoyne commanded the British troops

HOW THEY RATE

Mill Reef *146*
Nijinsky *144*
Grundy *141*
Shergar *140*
Roberto *138*
Troy *136*
Reference Point *135*
Slip Anchor *135*
Snow Knight *135*
The Minstrel *135*
Golden Fleece *134*
Shahrastani *134*
Shirley Heights *132*
Nashwan *131*
Empery *130*
Henbit *128*
Teenoso *128*
Kahyasi *126*
Morston *126*
Secreto *126*

GRAHAM GOODE'S DAY OF THE YEAR

Derby Day stands head and shoulders above everything else in the Channel Four Racing year. it is the jewel in our crown, demanding more from every member of the team than any other event we cover.

The first Derby I called was Shergar's – not the most difficult to unravel, and I shall always be grateful to Walter Swinburn for making my job easier that day. Since then the drive to make each successive commentary better than the last brings an extra-special tension as the hour approaches. It's not the size of the world-wide audience which for those two and a half minutes will be hanging on my every word which sets the pulse racing, but the awareness that I have one chance and one chance only of getting it right. In many ways the Derby is an easy race for the commentator – the colours and names are familiar. It's the occasion, not the actual race itself, which is all-important.

Derby Day transcends whatever the weather can come up with – and in 1990 it came up with such foul conditions that in my commentary box perched precariously on top of the grandstand I was buffeted by the wind, lashed by the rain and frozen to the marrow, but still the adrenalin raced as I called home Quest For Fame in my tenth Derby commentary.

Derby Day is like that: of all the big events on Channel Four Racing it's the biggest by far. Every single year, rain or shine, that first Wednesday in June is very special.

All social classes mingle at the Derby: King George V and three of his subjects arrive for the 1920 event.

Amato, winner of the Derby in 1838, had never raced before his Epsom outing, and never raced afterwards.

who surrendered at Saratoga during the American War of Independence, and by the time he returned to his native country Stanley had succeeded his grandfather to become the twelfth Earl of Derby. Between them Burgoyne and the new Earl hatched a plan to stage at Epsom a new race for three-year-old fillies over one and a half miles which would follow the example of Anthony St Leger's race, first run three years earlier at Doncaster, in running young horses in a single contest – thus going against the common practice of the time of staging races in heats over distances of between two and four miles. The Oaks – the new race was named after the house – was an instant success, and at a dinner party on the night of that first running the Earl of Derby and Burgoyne discussed with their guests, who included the politician Charles James Fox, the playwright Richard Brinsley Sheridan and the prominent Turf figure Sir Charles Bunbury, the notion of inaugurating a similar race for three-year-old colts and fillies, to be run over one mile. Racing folklore has it that Derby and Bunbury tossed a coin to decide whose name this new race should bear; other accounts suggest that dice were thrown or cards drawn between all present. It was more likely to have been diplomatically agreed that the race would appropriately take the name of the host that evening – but however the decision was reached, it was as the Derby that the new contest was run on 4 May 1780.

The first Derby fulfilled the original intention of being run over a dog-leg mile which commenced to the west of the present Tattenham Corner (the distance was not increased to its present one and a half miles until 1784). It was won by Diomed, owned by Sir Charles Bunbury – some consolation for the race not bearing his name – and ridden by Sam Arnull, who was to win the Derby four times in all (one fewer than his brother John, and one more than his nephew William). Just nine of the thirty-six entries started, and this experimental event attracted little attention. Soon, however, the status of the race grew, and the 1788 running was witnessed by the Prince of Wales, for whom the Prince's Stand was specially built – though the opening stages of the race were obscured by woods: it was not until 1848 that the start was moved to within sight of the stands.

From those stuttering beginnings the Derby grew into the greatest horse race in the world. Scratch the surface of any running and you will find a story worth the telling, but in many years the race has produced tales of such drama, emotion, skulduggery or sensation that they have been woven into the fabric of Turf history:

1836

The winner Bay Middleton was ridden by Jem Robinson, his sixth victory in the race: this record was not bettered until Lester Piggott won his seventh Derby on Empery 140 years later. But the 1836 running contained an element of human tragedy: the Hon. Berkeley Craven, one of the big gamblers of the age, lost heavily and, unable to meet his debts, returned to his home in Connaught Terrace and shot himself.

1844

'The Dirtiest Derby'. First past the post was Running Rein – except that the horse was not the three-year-old Running Rein at all but a four-year-old named Maccabeus. The two had been switched in 1842 by the disreputable Levy Goodman, in whose London stables they were kept and whose attention to detail ran to ensuring that a scar on Maccabeus's leg following a minor injury was also to be found on Running Rein. The horse known as Running Rein made its racecourse debut at Newmarket in 1843 in a two-year-old race – though he was three! – and, backed down from 10–1 to 3–1, he duly brought off a substantial coup for Goodman. Suspicions had been aroused but the subsequent enquiry failed to prove the switch. Goodman decided brazenly to go for another touch in the following year's Derby, and although the Turf authorities (notably the zealous Lord George Bentinck) tried to have the horse examined before he ran, the Epsom stewards took the extraordinary line that Running Rein could take part, but if he won the stakes would be withheld pending an enquiry. Running in the name of the Epsom corn merchant Alexander Wood (who was probably not party to the fraud), Running Rein duly beat Orlando by three quarters of a length. Orlando's owner Colonel Peel immediately brought an action against Wood, and Running Rein was disqualified, the judge tartly commenting that 'if gentlemen condescended to race with blackguards, they must condescend to expect to be cheated'. The horse himself, who would have been conclusive evidence, could not be produced: he had disappeared, as had Goodman, who fled the country and was never brought to justice.

But the 1844 Derby saw other intrigues. The second favourite, Ratan, was got at the night before the race, and on Derby Day, according to contemporary report, 'his coat was standing like quills upon the fretful porcupine, his eyes were dilated and he shivered like a man with ague'. If that were not enough to scupper his chance, he was pulled in the race – that is, restrained to prevent his winning – by his jockey Samuel Rogers. His owner William Crockford died two days later. Also pulled was the favourite Ugly Buck, but a more unfortunate fate befell the German challenger Leander, who was struck into by Running Rein at the top of the hill and broke a leg: he was rapidly put down. Leander had aroused comment about his age before the race, and his lower jaw was removed and examined by a vet, who proclaimed him four. His owners the Lichtwald brothers, safely back in Germany, queried the competence of the vet, claiming that Leander was not four but six!

1848

Lord George Bentinck, probably the most influential individual in racing history, tried for decades to win the Derby. In 1846 he sold up his racing interests in order to concentrate on politics, and among the yearlings thus disposed of was Surplice. Two years later Surplice won the Derby by a neck from Springy Jack when even-money favourite,

> The last filly to be placed in the Derby was Nobiliary, runner-up to Grundy in 1975.

> Twice the Derby has ended in a dead-heat. In 1828 Cadland and The Colonel were inseparable, and Cadland won the run-off. In 1884 Harvester and St Gatien divided the prize money.

> Seven post-war Derby winners never raced again after victory at Epsom – Nimbus (1949), Galcador (1950), Crepello (1957), Psidium (1961), Morston (1973), Golden Fleece (1982) and Secreto (1984).

Four greys have won the Derby:
Gustavus (1821), Tagalie (1912),
Mahmoud (1936) and Airborne
(1946).

and the following day Benjamin Disraeli found Bentinck in the library of the House of Commons:

> He gave a sort of superb groan. 'All my life I have been trying for this, and for what have I sacrificed it?' he murmured. It was in vain to offer solace. 'You do not know what the Derby is,' he moaned out. 'Yes, I do, it is the Blue Ribbon of the Turf.' 'It is the Blue Ribbon of the Turf,' he slowly repeated to himself, and sitting down, he buried himself in a folio of statistics.

1865

The victory of the French colt Gladiateur, the 5–2 favourite, hurt British pride but caused raptures back in France: the colt was dubbed 'The Avenger of Waterloo'. He won the Triple Crown and then followed the now unthinkable course for a Classic winner of running in the Cambridgeshire: he carried nine stone twelve pounds but was unplaced, a result some accounts blame on his notoriously short-sighted jockey Harry Grimshaw for laying impossibly far out of his ground. Lord Palmerston is said to have declared that he would not survive to the end of the year if 'that damn'd French horse' won the Derby. He didn't.

1867

The race was won by the 1000–15 outsider Hermit, but the real interest of the 1867 Derby is human. In 1864 the Marquis of Hastings, an immensely rich man in his his early twenties and a gambler on a prodigious scale, eloped with Lady Florence Paget – the 'pocket Venus' – who was about to be married to Henry Chaplin. (One version of the story goes that a few days before the wedding Lady Florence had gone to shop in Oxford Street with Chaplin: she left him at the entrance to Marshall and Snelgrove, walked into the store and out of a side entrance where Hastings was waiting to whisk her away.) Chaplin, understandably miffed by this turn of events, sought distraction in racing: he 'bought horses as if he was drunk and betted as if he was mad'. Among the horses he purchased was Hermit, for whom the disappointed underbidder was Hastings. Chaplin punted heavily on Hermit for the 1867 Derby and Hastings laid even more heavily against him. Ridden by twenty-year-old Johnny Daley, Hermit came with a sweeping run in the straight to beat Marksman a neck. Hastings was the first man to greet the horse on his return to unsaddle, but he had lost over £120,000 on the result – some £20,000 of it to Chaplin, who generously sent word that payment could be deferred until convenient for the Marquis. The following year what has been described as Hastings's 'short and useless life' came to an untimely end: he was twenty-six, ruined and virtually friendless. Shortly before he died he proclaimed: 'Hermit's Derby broke my heart, but I didn't show it, did I?'

Sometimes even the weather joins
in the Derby fun. In 1867 heavy
snow fell on the course on Derby
Day, 22 May.

1880

Fred Archer, the greatest jockey of the age, won the Derby five times. His victory on Bend Or was not only his finest Classic victory but possibly the greatest of all his 2,748 winning rides. Less than a month before the Derby, a horse named Muley Edris, a vicious creature whom Archer had given fierce rides in several races, went for his revenge after a training gallop and savaged the jockey, severely injuring his arm. Archer was out of action while recovering from the injury and his weight – always a problem – started creeping up, so that he had to lose a stone in four days in order to take the mount on Bend Or, a bout of severe wasting that left him debilitated. Worse, the injury had not completely healed, and Archer went to the start with the arm strapped uselessly to a piece of iron inside his jacket. He rode a furious race on Bend Or, the 2–1 favourite, but a quarter of a mile out he still had two lengths to make up on the leader Robert The Devil. Forgetting his useless arm, Archer went for his whip and dropped it, but he was gradually making up the deficit and had his horse perfectly balanced. Robert The Devil was not stopping, though, and just as it seemed he would last home his jockey Rossiter made the fatal error of looking behind him: this unbalanced the horse and Bend Or in full cry would not be denied. He got up on the line to win by a head. When some years later Archer was asked by a journalist in America which was his most sensational victory he nominated without hesitation the 1880 Derby victory on Bend Or: 'It was right out of the fire, I can tell you, sir.'

> The longest price returned about a Derby winner was 100–1: Jeddah (1898), Signorinetta (1908) and Aboyeur (1913). The shortest was 9–2 on: Ladas in 1894. Terimon's 500–1 in 1989 – he was second – is the longest price at which a horse has been placed.

1909

The Prince of Wales had won the Derby with Persimmon in 1896 and with Diamond Jubilee in 1900. Now King Edward VII, he became the first (and to date the only) reigning monarch to own the Derby winner when Minoru beat Louviers by a short head to unleash probably the greatest reception ever seen at Epsom. By the time the race was run the following year the King was dead.

1913

There are two parts to the story of the extraordinary 1913 Derby – the suffragette and the disqualification. Emily Wilding Davison, one of the most militant members of the Women's Social and Political Union, positioned herself on the inside rail at Tattenham Corner and stepped out on to the course just after the main bunch of runners had

The Suffragette Derby of 1913: the collision of Anmer and Emily Wilding Davison.

Mahmoud's winning time of 2 minutes 33.8 seconds in 1936 remains the fastest in Derby history, though the quickest time recorded by the more accurate electrical method was that of Kahyasi in 1988: 2 minutes 33.84 seconds.

gone past. Avoiding the straggler Agadir, she made a grab for the reins of King George V's runner Anmer and was felled: she died four days later and was accorded a heroine's funeral by the suffragette movement (its only martyr), but exactly what she intended when she strode out into Anmer's path can only be a matter for surmise. At the business end of the race the 6–4 favourite Craganour beat the 100–1 outsider Aboyeur by a head after a barging match up the straight, but the Stewards objected to the winner and awarded the race to Aboyeur.

1935

Bahram was the last horse to win the Triple Crown before Nijinsky in 1970. Starting 5–4 favourite for the Derby, he was ridden by Freddy Fox to a two-length victory over Robin Goodfellow. He retired to stud at the end of his three-year-old career, the unbeaten winner of nine races.

1947

Tudor Minstrel, seven-length winner of the Two Thousand Guineas, went off the 7–4 on favourite – the shortest priced runner of the post-war period – but suffered a sensational defeat. He pulled very hard against jockey Gordon Richards, and his resolute refusal to settle was compounded by his lack of stamina to bring about one of the most notorious Derby results ever: he finished fourth behind Pearl Diver, Migoli and Sayajirao.

1949

Nimbus beat Amour Drake by a head, with Swallow Tail a further head away in third. Nimbus never raced again (though he did get a walkover in a small event at Haydock Park) and none of the first three is exactly a Turf legend, but the 1949 Derby has its place in history as the first occasion on which the photo-finish camera was used to decide the result.

1953

The Derby was run four days after the Coronation of Queen Elizabeth II in Westminster Abbey, and the new Queen had a first-rate chance of crowning the Coronation celebrations by leading in the Derby winner: her volatile colt Aureole was a 9–1 chance. Only Pinza and Premonition at 5–1 joint favourites started at shorter odds, but Pinza's jockey caused a division in the nation's loyalties. For this was Gordon Richards's twenty-eighth Derby: he had just been knighted, he was obviously coming towards the end of his career, and he had never ridden the winner of the Derby. In a race which overflowed with emotion and sentiment, only a dead-heat between Pinza and Aureole would have been perfect, but the event itself produced the next best thing, Pinza striding home four lengths clear of Aureole. Gordon Richards recalled the subsequent royal interview:

Her Majesty sent for me after the race, and there was no sign of disappointment in her face. Aureole had finished a gallant second, but the fact remains that – good horse though Aureole certainly is – he never had a chance with Pinza, who was one of the greats of all time.

Twenty-eighth time lucky: Sir Gordon Richards wins the 1953 Derby on Pinza.

Still, before the race everyone had thought that Aureole could win, and you know how hopeful an owner always is! But Her Majesty seemed to be just as delighted as I was with the result of the race.

After she had congratulated me, the rest of the Royal Family gathered round. We talked about the race, about Pinza, and about Aureole. The Duke of Edinburgh suddenly asked me if I was going to retire now that I had won the Derby. Before I had time to reply, the Queen answered him for me. She said: 'Of course not! He's going to ride for me in the Derby next year, on Landau.'

Landau did indeed run in the 1954 Derby (and was well beaten behind Never Say Die), but Gordon Richards was sidelined by injury and could not take the ride. Later in the 1954 season the Queen's filly Abergeldie reared and fell on him in the paddock at Sandown Park (see page 25), inflicting injuries that brought about his retirement from the saddle.

> During both World Wars the Derby was run on the July Course at Newmarket. It was first supported by commercial sponsorship in 1984, since when it has been run as the Ever Ready Derby.

1962

Seven horses fell on the descent to Tattenham Corner. One – King Canute II – had to be put down, and the others included the favourite Hethersett, who went on to win the St Leger. The race was won by Larkspur, trainer Vincent O'Brien's first Derby winner.

1965

Sea Bird II, ridden by Pat Glennon, won the race with such breathtaking ease that the performance stamped him as one of the greatest Derby winners ever. With over a furlong to go he sailed past the leader I Say and was eased down in the final few yards, allowing Meadow Court to get within two lengths of him. It was a high-class Derby field, but Sea Bird II was way above his rivals in a class of his own.

1972

The furious battle between Roberto and Rheingold will live for ever in the memory of anyone who saw it, primarily on account of the ferocity

Pat Eddery pushes Quest For Fame clear in the Ever Ready Derby in 1990.

John Forth in 1829 was over sixty when winning on Frederick.

BROADCASTING THE DERBY

The Derby was first broadcast on radio in 1927, and the first newsreel with sound of Derby Day was made by British Movietone News in 1929. In 1931 John Logie Baird televised the Derby to an invited audience in his studio in Long Acre, London, and the following year the race was transmitted to a larger audience in the Metropole Cinema in Victoria. The BBC began regular television broadcasts of the Derby in 1938, later sharing coverage with ITV until the mid-1970s. ITV had exclusive coverage from 1975 (though the 200th running in 1979 was shown on both sides). The race has been shown exclusively on Channel Four Racing since it took over midweek coverage in 1984.

LESTER PIGGOTT

Lester Piggott won the Derby nine times, though his fabled career in the event started inauspiciously. His first mount, Zucchero in 1951, went backwards as the tapes flew up, and though the fifteen-year-old Piggott eventually persuaded this notoriously wayward horse to set off and join his rivals, he could never get into the race with a chance. The following year Piggott finished second to Tulyar on Gay Time. Just beyond the winning post Gay Time slipped and unshipped his jockey, and then galloped off, evading capture for twenty minutes. When he was brought back to unsaddle, his jockey wanted to object to Charlie Smirke on Tulyar for leaning on Gay Time in the closing stages, but owner Mrs Rank declined to let Piggott do so.

When at the age of eighteen Piggott brought home 33–1 chance Never Say Die in 1954, he was the youngest jockey this century to win the Derby. (Walter Swinburn was an older eighteen when winning on Shergar in 1981.) His second victory came on Sir Victor Sassoon's Crepello in 1957, and it was in the same colours that he brought St Paddy home in 1960. His next three winners were all the result of his fabulously successful association with the Irish trainer Vincent O'Brien. Sir Ivor in 1968 was produced with one brief but deadly burst of speed in the final furlong to thwart Connaught, and Nijinsky in 1970 won with his jockey sitting quiet and supremely confident. But Piggott's next winning effort was in complete contrast, giving Roberto the full treatment to force him a short head in front of Rheingold in 1972. When the French-trained Empery sailed home three lengths ahead of Relkino in 1976 with the hot favourite Wollow failing to stay and finishing unplaced, Piggott's bottom was high in the air, always a signal that he was going very easily. But the following year it was back to the machine-gun whip action to get The Minstrel, unflinching under the severest pressure, past Hot Grove to win by a neck. His final victory came in 1983 on Teenoso, who set off for the line as soon as he rounded Tattenham Corner and never looked in danger of being caught, winning by three lengths from Carlingford Castle.

Lester Piggott's last Derby ride was on Theatrical in 1985: he finished seventh behind Slip Anchor. In all he rode in the race thirty-two times; in addition to his nine victories he was second on four occasions: with Gay Time (1952), Meadow Court (1965), Ribocco (1967) and Cavo Doro (1973). No jockey in the history of racing understood better than 'The Long Fellow' the peculiar nature of the Epsom course, where he also won the Oaks six times. But Lester Piggott was in his element in the top Classic. For more than three decades the casual punter needed no more information when picking a Derby choice than the identity of Piggott's mount, and his nine victories ran the whole extent of his riding repertoire. Derby Day is not quite complete without him in the race.

Shergar (Walter Swinburn) canters past the stands on his way to the start of the 1981 Derby.

of Lester Piggott's finish on Roberto. Never had he ridden a more powerful climax to a race, cracking away with his whip and practically lifting his horse over the line after Ernie Johnson on Rheingold had seemed to have his measure. But Piggott's victory was confirmed only after a Stewards' Enquiry, and even then victory was not widely popular, for he had got the ride on Roberto at the expense of Bill Williamson, who had been injured the previous month but made a speedy recovery and was declared fit to ride at Epsom: indeed, the two winners Williamson rode later in the afternoon were given more rousing receptions than the Derby victor.

1981

Shergar recorded the longest winning margin in the history of the race when scampering home ten lengths clear of Glint Of Gold in one of the most spectacular Derby victories of all. The outstanding quality of this performance only exacerbates the horror of the fate which befell Shergar in February 1983, when he was abducted from the Ballmany Stud in County Kildare, never to be heard of again.

1986

A recording of the controversial finish between Shahrastani and Dancing Brave is doubtless not very high on Greville Starkey's list of favourite videos. Starkey had the unbeaten Dancing Brave, 2–1 favourite on the strength of a brilliant victory in the Two Thousand Guineas, at the rear of the field as the runners came into the straight, and though he made up a staggering amount of ground in the final quarter of a mile he failed by half a length to get to Walter Swinburn and Shahrastani. Dancing Brave decisively beat his conqueror in two subsequent meetings, but Starkey's mount had been the subject of a huge gamble at Epsom, and the smell of burnt fingers pervades all recollection of a sensational running.

> Slip Anchor in 1985 became the only Derby winner since the Second World War who could boast a winner of the race both as his sire (Shirley Heights) and paternal grandsire (Mill Reef).

'God made the bees
The bees made the honey
The soldiers do the dirty work
And the bookies take the money'

Prince Monolulu, doyen of Derby
Day tipsters

'Anyone who doesn't consider the
Epsom Derby one of the greatest
sporting events in the world must
be out of his mind'

John Galbreath, owner of
Roberto, 1972

'The whole world was at Epsom
yesterday'

The Times, 1829

'On Derby Day, a population rolls
and surges and scrambles through
the place that may be counted in
millions'

Charles Dickens, 1851

1989

Nashwan's glorious victory in the 1989 Ever Ready Derby, when his
huge stride brought him home five lengths clear of his rivals, marked a
significant moment in modern racing history, for it was the first time
that the race had been won by a member of the Maktoum family.
Nearly a third of the 169 entries for the 1989 running were owned by
members of the family: Sheikh Mohammed entered thirty-six, but the
first prize went to his elder brother Hamdan Al-Maktoum. The terms
of Nashwan's stud syndication valued him at £18 million.

But why has the Derby reached the pre-eminence whereby its winner
can be worth such a sum? Once the Classic programme was
established early in the nineteenth century the Epsom race was, for
colts, the middle leg in a pattern which began with the Two Thousand
Guineas over one mile and ended with the St Leger over one and
three quarter miles; the Derby was thought suitable for Classic status
as the bizarre contours of the terrain over which it is run make it the
the ideal test of a three-year-old. For Lester Piggott, the supreme
Derby rider, 'You have to have speed and be able to stay one and a
half miles, and also to be able to gallop uphill and downhill.' Piggott
typically understates the problems which the course poses for horse
and jockey, for beyond dispute the Epsom twelve furlongs is one of the
trickiest trips of all the racecourses of the world. Immediately after the
start the runners go uphill into a right-hand bend, then move over to
the other rail and continue to gallop up rising ground to the top of
Tattenham Hill, where they start the left-handed descent towards
Tattenham Corner. They come into the straight just under half a mile
from home and then run downhill until the ground rises slightly inside
the final furlong, but the run for the line is not as simple as it sounds,
for the difficulties of Epsom are compounded for tired horses in the
closing stages by the ground's sloping in towards the far rail in the
straight, which causes some runners to hang in to their left. So to win
the Derby a horse must be speedy enough to stay handy through the
first half mile, agile enough to run uphill and then come down the hill
on the turn at breakneck speed, and then balanced enough and
blessed with the stamina to last home through the final half mile.

It's a tall order, but the rewards which await the winner are
immense – not just in terms of the prize money but in the future
breeding opportunities which will immediately endow him with
multi-million-pound stud value. Beyond such mercenary considera-
tions lie that Thoroughbred's place in the overall history of his breed,
for the horse that wins the Derby becomes a vital part of the future of
the bloodstock industry, as he will subsequently be employed in
attempts to produce offspring who will replicate his feat. The great
Italian breeder Federico Tesio elegantly summed up the true
importance of the Derby:

> The Thoroughbred exists because its selection has depended not on
> experts, technicians or zoologists but on a piece of wood: the winning
> post of the Epsom Derby.

And Nashwan worth eighteen million quid. No wonder the bastards
are all trying.

Opposite: Nashwan at the Nunnery
Stud, 1990.

Coronation Cup

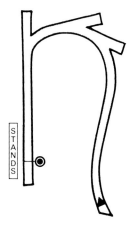

Epsom: 1½ miles

Group One: four-year-olds and upwards

The Coronation Cup is the first Group One race of the season for horses older than three. It was first run in 1902 to mark the coronation of Edward VII, a great supporter of the Turf and owner of three Derby winners, and before long was a natural target for the top middle-distance performers of the previous season's Classic generation. Because of its conditions – strict level weights, with fillies and mares getting an allowance – it almost always attracts very small fields: only six times in its history have there been ten or more runners.

Small but select the Coronation Cup has been from the beginning, and within a few years of its inauguration its roll of honour boasted

one of the very greatest names of racing history. Pretty Polly won the race twice, and her first victory – in 1905 – produced possibly the best performance of her life. She had only two opponents: Zinfandel provided a direct form link between Pretty Polly and Sceptre, whom he had beaten in the Coronation Cup the previous year, and the third runner was the French horse Caius, winner of many big races in his native country. Caius set a very fast pace but Otto Madden on Pretty Polly was not perturbed, closing up with over a furlong to run and striding away to win with contemptuous authority, setting a new course record as she did so. The correspondent for the *Illustrated Sporting and Dramatic News* missed the key moment: 'Zinfandel was leading by three lengths when someone's hat got in my way and when I could see again suddenly Pretty Polly was three lengths ahead.' Pretty Polly won the race again a year later, with the 1904 Derby winner St Amant back in third, and the next two runnings saw another dual winner, The White Knight. Lemberg in 1911 was the first Derby winner to take the Coronation Cup, a feat emulated by Pommern in 1916, when the race was run at Newbury on account of the war.

In more recent times the race has maintained its status and continued to attract many of the very best horses kept in training. Petite Etoile became the third dual winner (1960 and 1961) and Triptych – 'The Iron Lady' – the fourth, Tony Cruz pushing her past Rakaposhi King in 1987 and Steve Cauthen in 1988 coaxing her through an extraordinary performance. In the early stages she seemed totally ill at ease on the firm ground and began to lose interest in the proceedings, getting farther and farther adrift of her three opponents, but once she found herself safely down the hill she consented to put her best foot forward and eased into the lead, then stuck her head in the air as if finding the whole business distasteful. She won by three quarters of a length from Infamy. (She had also been beaten a short head by 20–1 outsider Saint Estephe in 1986.)

When you contemplate the list of winners since 1970 (see panel), and consider that during the previous two decades it had been won by such horses as Aureole (1954), Ballymoss (1958), Exbury (1963), Relko (1964), Charlottown (1967), Royal Palace (1968) and Park Top (1969), the status of the Coronation Cup is plain enough.

Triptych capping a remarkable performance in the 1988 Hanson Coronation Cup by going past Infamy and Moon Madness.

WINNERS SINCE 1970

1970 Caliban
      A. Barclay 8–1 (4 ran)

1971 Lupe
      G. Lewis 5–2 (6 ran)

1972 Mill Reef
      G. Lewis 2–15 (4 ran)

1973 Roberto
      L. Piggott 4–9 (5 ran)

1974 Buoy
      J. Mercer 4–1 (5 ran)

1975 Bustino
      J. Mercer 11–10 (6 ran)

1976 Quiet Fling
      L. Piggott 5–2 (6 ran)

1977 Exceller
      G. Dubroeucq 13–8 (6 ran)

1978 Crow
      Pat Eddery 9–4 (5 ran)

1979 Ile De Bourbon
      J. Reid 4–6 (4 ran)

1980 Sea Chimes
      L. Piggott 5–4 (4 ran)

1981 Master Willie
      P. Waldron 1–2 (5 ran)

1982 Easter Sun
      B. Raymond 20–1 (8 ran)

1983 Be My Native
      L. Piggott 8–1 (6 ran)

1984 Time Charter
      S. Cauthen 100–30 (6 ran)

1985 Rainbow Quest
      Pat Eddery 8–15 (7 ran)

1986 Saint Estephe
      Pat Eddery 20–1 (10 ran)

1987 Triptych
      A. Cruz 4–5 (5 ran)

1988 Triptych
      S. Cauthen 11–8 (4 ran)

1989 Sheriff's Star
      R. Cochrane 11–4 (9 ran)

1990 In The Wings
      C. Asmussen 15–8 (6 ran)

The Oaks

Epsom: 1½ miles

Group One: three-year-old fillies only

The Oaks is the second oldest Classic, three years younger than the St Leger and a year older than the Derby.

When 'Gentleman Johnny' Burgoyne, who was to be instrumental in founding the Derby (see pages 45–6), returned to England in disgrace after commanding the defeated troops at Saratoga, he went to stay with his nephew by marriage Edward Stanley (by then Lord Derby) at the house near Epsom which he had leased to Stanley – The Oaks. Burgoyne advised Derby on bloodstock, and between them the two men decided to stage an experiment on Epsom Downs: a race for three-year-old fillies which would be modelled on the the new-fangled event which Colonel Anthony St Leger had instituted at Doncaster in 1776, and the race would be run over one and a half miles (half a mile shorter than the original St Leger). That first year there were seventeen subscribers at fifteen guineas each. Twelve horses started, and the race was won by the Earl's own filly Bridget. She was ridden by Richard Goodisson, who proceeded to win the next two runnings.

Once the Derby became established not only as the principal Classic of the season but as the high point of the whole racing year, the Oaks tended to fall under its shadow, and as an occasion Oaks Day is not remotely in the same league as the pandemonium of Derby Day three days earlier. But for the purists the race itself is highly important, for although fillies may run in the Derby they very rarely do so, and the Oaks is their race, requiring all the qualities of stamina, speed and agility which make the Derby such a searching test of a colt. The two races are not exactly parallel, for fillies develop at a different rate from colts, and it is not unusual for some of the top fillies of the generation not to be forward enough to win at Epsom: given the sun on their backs, they often mature well after the running of the Oaks in early June, so a certain amount of precocity – or at least forwardness – is required in an Oaks winner.

Yet despite the fact that plenty of good fillies will blossom later in the summer, the history of the Oaks is the history of most of the best staying fillies to grace the British racing scene. As early as 1801 Eleanor became the first filly to win the Oaks and the Derby. Owned by Sir Charles Bunbury, who had been so influential in setting up the first Derby, she was a grand-daughter of Eclipse. Shortly before the Derby, Eleanor's trainer Cox was taken mortally ill. A parson was called for and Cox indicated that he wished the holy man to hear his final words. As the parson craned to hear the deathbed message, Cox

The Oaks was first supported by commercial sponsorship in 1984, since when it has been run as the Gold Seal Oaks.

whispered, 'Depend on it, that Eleanor is the hell of a mare,' before breathing his last. Cox was right, for she won the Derby when 5–4 favourite and the next day won the Oaks at 2–1 on. Whether the parson had the double up is not recorded. The next winner of both Epsom Classics was Blink Bonny in 1857: she won the Derby at 20–1 and two days later the Oaks at 5–4 on. Then there was Signorinetta in 1908: breeding legend insists that she was the result of a true love match between her sire Chaleureux and dam Signorina, whose paddock in Newmarket the sire would pass every morning when being exercised. The two horses formed a deep attachment, and the result was Signorinetta. She gave little indication of her true ability in her two-year-old days and started at 100–1 when winning the Derby before taking the Oaks at 3–1. The fourth Oaks-Derby winner was Fifinella in 1916, who won wartime substitute races at Newmarket.

That quartet hold a special place in racing records, but in terms of ability were surpassed by the two fillies who dominated the sport in the very early years of the century. Sceptre won the Oaks in 1902 at 5–2, two days after finishing fourth in the Derby, the only Classic which she did not win. And in 1904 it was the turn of Pretty Polly. She started at 100–8 on (the shortest price ever returned in an English Classic) to beat three opponents at Epsom. That there were only four runners from an original entry of 211 is just another tribute to Pretty Polly's quality, for it was pointless to oppose her. She came to Epsom unbeaten in ten races and was clearly queen of her generation. Led around the paddock by her travelling companion Little Missus, Pretty Polly impressed all who saw her: 'She was cool and well and had done a preparation which made her look harder, cleaner and finer drawn than she has ever done before', reported William Allison in *The Sportsman*. In the race she was never out of a canter, and won with her ears pricked by three lengths from Bitters.

Pretty Polly went on to win the St Leger and thus land what some insist on calling the fillies' Triple Crown, a feat not repeated until Sun Chariot in 1942 won the three Classics for King George VI in the wartime races at Newmarket. The next filly to win the three was Meld in 1955. Her Epsom victory saw in a purple patch in the history of the Oaks, and one dominated by French-trained runners: Sicarelle (1956), Bella Paola (1958), Never Too Late (1960) and Monade (1962) all took the prize across the Channel, and the gaps between these four notable Gallic victories were all filled by significant home-trained winners. The 1957 heroine Carrozza, ridden by Lester Piggott, was leased by the National Stud to Queen Elizabeth II and provided her first Classic victory. The 1959 race went to the great Petite Etoile: she started at 11–2 in a field that included Cantelo, who would win the St Leger later that year, but won with great ease by three lengths and went on to prove herself one of the finest fillies of all time. And in 1961 Sweet Solera added to her One Thousand Guineas triumph when beating Ambergris by one and a half lengths. Two years later Noblesse turned in a sensational performance to win by ten lengths from Spree; she raced only once more, finishing fourth in the Prix Vermeille, before being retired to stud, but at Epsom she was as great a filly as the Oaks has seen in modern times.

The Queen won the race again with Dunfermline in 1977, a highly

The 1911 Oaks winner Cherimoya won a Classic on the only racecourse appearance of her life. Ridden by Fred Winter (father of the great jump jockey and trainer) and owned by the American Broderick Cloete (who in 1915 was drowned when the *Lusitania* was torpedoed by a German submarine), she started at 25–1 and won by three lengths from Tootles.

WINNERS SINCE 1970
with ratings (see page 13)

1970 Lupe *130*
   A. Barclay 100–30 (16 ran)

1971 Altesse Royale *134*
   G. Lewis 6–4 (11 ran)

1972 Ginevra *126*
   A. Murray 8–1 (17 ran)

1973 Mysterious *124*
   G. Lewis 13–8 (10 ran)

1974 Polygamy *133*
   Pat Eddery 3–1 (15 ran)

1975 Juliette Marny *130*
   L. Piggott 12–1 (12 ran)

1976 Pawneese *133*
   Y. Saint-Martin 6–5 (14 ran)

1977 Dunfermline *130*
   W. Carson 6–1 (13 ran)

1978 Fair Salinia *120*
   G. Starkey 8–1 (15 ran)

1979 Scintillate *120*
   Pat Eddery 20–1 (14 ran)

1980 Bireme *125*
   W. Carson 9–2 (11 ran)

1981 Blue Wind *126*
   L. Piggott 3–1 (12 ran)

1982 Time Charter *123*
   W. Newnes 12–1 (13 ran)

1983 Sun Princess *129*
   W. Carson 6–1 (15 ran)

1984 Circus Plume *123*
   L. Piggott 4–1 (15 ran)

1985 Oh So Sharp *130*
   S. Cauthen 6–4 (12 ran)

1986 Midway Lady *124*
   R. Cochrane 15–8 (15 ran)

1987 Unite *125*
   W. R. Swinburn 11–1 (11 ran)

1988 Diminuendo *128*
   S. Cauthen 7–4 (11 ran)

1989 Aliysa *122*
   W. R. Swinburn 11–10 (9 ran)

1990 Salsabil –
   W. Carson 2–1 (8 ran)

appropriate result as the race was run at the very height of the Jubilee celebrations. But the occasion was marred by the accident which befell Lester Piggott and the favourite Durtal as they cantered back past the paddock prior to crossing the downs to reach the start. Durtal had been very keyed up and tried to bolt as Piggott brought her past the stands; her saddle slipped, Piggott came off, and she collided with the rails. She was withdrawn from the race and was never the same again.

The list of winners in the 1980s includes some exceptional fillies: Time Charter, Sun Princess (who went on to win the St Leger), the triple Classic winner Oh So Sharp (who beat Triptych six lengths), the One Thousand Guineas winner Midway Lady (who never ran again)

and Diminuendo. The Oaks has been enjoying another purple patch, stained only by the controversy over Aliysa's decisive triumph in 1989, after which she failed the routine dope test when traces of a derivative of the prohibited substance camphor were detected in her urine: how it got there had not been resolved by the time the next running came around, so that the 1990 Oaks was run before the 1989 had been decided. Any cloud which this bizarre situation cast over the race was blown away by the brilliant triumph of the One Thousand Guineas winner Salsabil, who stormed home by five lengths to give Willie Carson his fourth Oaks victory and went on to a unique Classic treble in the Irish Derby.

HOW THEY RATE

Altesse Royale *134*
Pawneese *133*
Polygamy *133*
Dunfermline *130*
Juliette Marny *130*
Lupe *130*
Oh So Sharp *130*
Sun Princess *129*
Diminuendo *128*
Blue Wind *126*
Ginevra *126*
Bireme *125*
Unite *125*
Midway Lady *124*
Mysterious *124*
Circus Plume *123*
Time Charter *123*
Aliysa *122*
Fair Salinia *120*
Scintillate *120*

Time Charter winning the 1982 Oaks from Slightly Dangerous and Last Feather (hooped sleeves).

ROYAL ASCOT

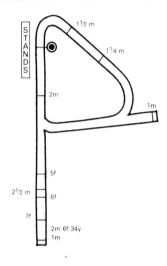

The course is about one and three quarter miles round. The Old Mile and the straight New Mile start on chutes: the start of the Old Mile is in Swinley Bottom, at the furthest point of the round course, and climbs gradually to the straight, where the course continues uphill before levelling out shortly before the winning post; the New Mile is quite straight and undulates a little before joining the round course less than three furlongs out. After the winning post the course rises slightly and then sweeps sharply downhill to Swinley Bottom.

Love it or hate it, Royal Ascot is undeniably the high point of the Flat season in terms of the sheer quality of racing. However irritating to the true racing fan it may be to have thousands of top-hatted socialites getting in the way, however terminal the week is for the battalions of Scotch salmon, lobsters, turkeys, chicken, ducks and other unfortunates who are sacrificed so that the toffs and would-be toffs have something substantial to go with the ten thousand bottles of vintage champagne and ten thousand pounds of strawberries (won't they be sick?), Royal Ascot is simply the best.

The traditional first race of the meeting is the QUEEN ANNE STAKES, a Group Two event on the straight mile which commemorates the monarch who founded Ascot in 1711. The other highlights on the Tuesday are the ST JAMES'S PALACE STAKES (opposite), the Group Two PRINCE OF WALES'S STAKES over ten furlongs, the Group Three COVENTRY STAKES (six furlongs) for two-year-olds and the Group Two KING EDWARD VII STAKES over one and a half miles for three-year-olds. Wednesday sees the CORONATION STAKES (pages 65–6) and the ROYAL HUNT CUP (page 67) as well as the Group Three QUEEN MARY STAKES (five furlongs) for two-year-old fillies and the Group Three JERSEY STAKES for three-year-olds over seven furlongs. Although the GOLD CUP (pages 68–9) has lost much of its status the Thursday – Ladies' Day – remains the pinnacle of the meeting, and also features the Group Two RIBBLESDALE STAKES for three-year-old fillies (one and a half miles), the Group Three six-furlong sprint the CORK AND ORRERY STAKES, and the Group Three NORFOLK STAKES for two-year-olds over five furlongs. The final day of the Royal Meeting includes the Group Two HARDWICKE STAKES, a top-class twelve-furlong race for older horses, the Group Two KING'S STAND STAKES, one of the most prestigious five-furlong sprints of the year, the six-furlong WOKINGHAM STAKES – a fiercely competitive handicap – and the traditional final race of the Royal week, the marathon QUEEN ALEXANDRA STAKES over two miles six furlongs.

St James's Palace Stakes

Ascot: 1 mile

Group One: three-year-olds colts and fillies

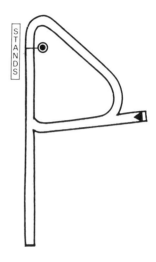

Raised to Group One status in 1988 in recognition of the high-class fields it invariably attracts, the St James's Palace Stakes is nowadays the most valuable race run at the Royal Meeting. It was first run over the straight New Mile in 1934 and carried a prize of 100 sovereigns. Traditionally it was the last race on the programme on the first day of the meeting, but was shifted to the centre of the programme in 1980: it was too good a race to miss for the sake of a quick getaway.

Although today the race is primarily the target for horses who are being campaigned at around a mile, it was not always so, and until the Second World War often went to the winner of the Derby, including two great horses owned by the Duke of Westminster, Bend Or (1880) and his son Ormonde (1886), Iroquois (1881), Common (1891), the Triple Crown winner Rock Sand (1903), Minoru (1909), Captain Cuttle (1922), Coronach (1926), Cameronian (1931) and another Triple Crown winner, Bahram (1935). (Sceptre, who won every

---

─ JOHN TYRREL'S DAY OF THE YEAR ─

At seven o'clock on a sunny June morning, the first day of Royal Ascot, there's a little dew remaining on the rose plucked in the garden for the buttonhole. I take tea to my wife. She has been planning her outfit for three months and has yet to decide exactly what to wear, but at eleven o'clock an elegantly coutured vision descends and I stow the champagne safely into the car. The limousines on the M3 sport rear-window shelves cluttered with expensive millinery. Soon we are making a happy rendezvous with friends and the champagne eases the exquisite discomfort of the inescapable picnic.

In the Royal Enclosure the grass is fresh and eager and the barmaids likewise, and shortly before the first race the Royal Procession passes the stands with a pomp and circumstance unequalled anywhere in the world. Leaning over the balcony rail as the runners go to post for the Queen Anne Stakes in commemoration of the monarch who founded Ascot in 1711, and gazing at the elegant scene below, it is easy to hear Imperial echoes and reflect upon England's past – of which Ascot remains an enduring fragment.

Five races later, the temperature has risen to ninety in the shade. In the High Street, foreign tourists gawp in amazement at our formal garb as we return to the car. They think we're mad, and they may be right. But 'though the English are effete, they're quite impervious to heat' – and we ease gently into the traffic for the drive home.

Classic except the Derby, took the St James's Palace in 1902.) Since the war the race has become the province of the specialist milers and no Derby winner has taken part, though it is a common target for horses who have run prominently in the Two Thousand Guineas at Newmarket or the Irish Two Thousand Guineas at The Curragh: the Newmarket-Ascot double has been achieved in the post-war period by Tudor Minstrel (1947), Palestine (1950), Nearula (1953), Right Tack (1969), Brigadier Gerard (1971), Bolkonski (1975) and To-Agori-Mou (1981). To-Agori-Mou's victory over King's Lake was one of the most thrilling mile races of recent years, the tension sharpened by the needle between the two jockeys, Greville Starkey and Pat Eddery, after their clash in the Irish Two Thousand: King's Lake had beaten To-Agori-Mou a neck but the two had brushed each other repeatedly throughout the final furlong, and the course Stewards awarded the race to Starkey's mount. On appeal the Stewards of the Turf Club reversed the decision and gave the race back to King's Lake, but a mighty controversy was stirred up which was still bubbling away by Royal Ascot. This time To-Agori-Mou beat King's Lake by a neck, and the slow-motion replay on thousands of video machines was used over and over in attempts to decide the exact sentiments behind the gesture which Greville Starkey seemed to direct at Pat Eddery as the two flashed past the post. King's Lake won the next bout – the Sussex Stakes at Goodwood – by a head, and the two met again in the Prix Jacques le Marois at Deauville, where To-Agori-Mou finished a nose in front of King's Lake but five lengths behind North Jet.

Among the familiar names beaten in the Two Thousand Guineas at Newmarket but successful at the Royal Meeting are Major Portion (1958), Silly Season (1965), Petingo (1968), Kris (1979), Posse (1980), Chief Singer (1984) and Bairn (1985). Shaadi (1989) was beaten at Newmarket but won the Irish Two Thousand Guineas and the St James's Palace Stakes.

There is obviously a very close link between the St James's Palace Stakes and the first English Classic, but the courses on which they are run are not at all alike. Newmarket is dead straight and in the closing stages runs steeply down and then up. The Old Mile at Ascot is a very different proposition, but no less demanding and just as exciting. The runners climb uphill for the first five furlongs or so until negotiating the sweeping turn into a short straight and continuing on the upgrade until the ground levels out close to the winning post. Such a trip demands the speed to lay up handy, for with a such a short straight Ascot is no place to have too much ground to make up once the field has turned for home – as Lord Florey discovered in 1990 when vainly trying to catch the front-running Shavian.

'Look, Reggie! Two jockeys with the same colours!' Royal Ascot, 1989. (Ronald Frain)

'Goggles down – and October here we come!' Work on the Al Bahathri Gallop, Newmarket, 1989. (Lesley Sampson)

'In my Easter bonnet.' Studying form at Kempton Park, Easter Monday, 1988. (Mel Fordham)

'Miss Tic-tac.' (Ronald Frain)

The Shadwell Estates Private Sweepstakes, Ascot, 29 September 1989. *Above:* 'I've got a steamer!' *Left to right:* Jimmy Lindley, Richard Pitman, Bill Smith, Brough Scott, John McCririck, John Oaksey, John Francome. *Below:* 'Fooling the bookies.' (Jack Knight)

'Close finish at Kempton.' Lonely Street (Nicky Adams, right) beats Dawn's Delight (Ray Cochrane) by a short head in the Quail Stakes at Kempton Park, 4 April 1988. (Mel Fordham)

Graham McCourt on Norton's Coin (left) fights out the finish of the Tote Cheltenham Gold Cup with Mark Pitman on Toby Tobias, 15 March 1990. (Edward Whitaker)

'I know it's the Chair, but you didn't have to sit on it.' William Crump (Simon McNeill, left) and Proverity (Philip Fenton) come to grief in the John Hughes Memorial Trophy at Liverpool, 6 April 1989. (Colin Turner)

Pat Eddery and friend at Deauville, 1989. (Jack Knight)

'Stevie and me at the pictures.' Steve Cauthen and friend, Windsor, 1989. (Ronald Frain)

'Jumping for joy.' Willie Carson dismounts from Nashwan after winning the Ever Ready Derby at Epsom, 7 June 1989. (Mel Fordham)

'Back to barracks'. Desert Orchid after winning the Racing Post Chase at Kempton Park, 24 February 1990. (Ronald Frain)

'You'd think the bucket would be gold after the races I've won.' Nashwan after winning the King George VI and Queen Elizabeth Diamond Stakes at Ascot, 22 July 1989. (Ronald Frain)

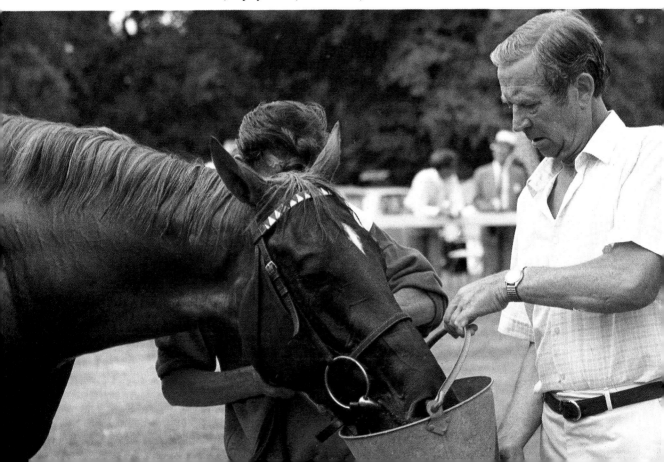

'Let me know if you ever decide to go public, Mr Griffiths!' Queen Elizabeth the Queen Mother presents the Tote Cheltenham Gold Cup to Sirrell Griffiths after Norton's Coin's triumph, 15 March 1990. (Bernard Parkin)

'Hi, Mum – we won again!' Sheikh Mohammed at Sandown Park, 29 April 1989. (Mel Fordham)

'Morning greetings.' Sprinter Padre Pio unwinds after morning work, 1988. (Mel Fordham)

Coronation Stakes

Ascot: 1 mile

Group One: three-year-old fillies only

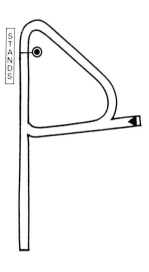

The Coronation Stakes, the fillies' equivalent of the St James's Palace Stakes, is run on the second day of the Royal Meeting and was first held in 1840, named in honour of the coronation of Queen Victoria. Like its brother race it was upgraded to Group One in 1988, normally attracts small but highly select fields, and boasts results similarly dominated by Guineas winners.

It was won in 1904 by Pretty Polly, who twelve days after her victory in the Oaks started at 5–1 on, despite conceding a stone to six of her seven rivals and more to the seventh. She won in a canter by three lengths. The 1927 running went to Viscount Astor's Book Law, who had come second in the One Thousand Guineas and was only beaten by a head in the Oaks. Later in 1927 she won the St Leger, but her real contribution to racing history came at stud: mated with Nearco, she produced Archive, a horse who never won but who sired one who would make a name for himself in a sphere far removed from Royal Ascot – Arkle.

Since the war the race has been won no fewer than eight times by the winner of the One Thousand Guineas at Newmarket, and between 1951 and 1955 Belle Of All, Zabara, Happy Laughter, Festoon and Meld all lifted both. The next dual winners were Fleet in 1967, Humble Duty in 1970 and One In A Million, who in 1979 benefited from the controversial disqualification of Buz Kashi, the 33–1 outsider who interfered with the beaten Lightning Record as she made her run, with the result that jockey Paul Cook was suspended for careless riding and One In A Million, who took no part in the incident, was spared an embarrassing defeat.

Throughout the 1980s the race displayed fillies of the highest class. Cairn Rouge (1980) went on to take the Champion Stakes, Sonic Lady (1986) the Sussex Stakes, and Milligram (1988) handed out a famous defeat to Miesque when returning to Ascot for the Queen Elizabeth II Stakes in September. But perhaps the best Coronation Stakes still fresh in the memory was that of 1984. Three of the ten runners were Group One winners: Pebbles had won the One Thousand Guineas at Newmarket, Katies the Irish One Thousand at The Curragh, and Desirable the top two-year-old fillies' race of the season, the Cheveley Park Stakes, the previous year. Pebbles, who since her Guineas victory had been sold by Captain Marcos Lemos to Sheikh Mohammed, went off the 11–4 favourite, with Katies, for whom Terry Ramsden had reputedly paid around half a million pounds after she had finished third in the Princess Elizabeth Stakes at the Epsom Spring Meeting, at twice those odds. These two fine fillies had far too much pace for their rivals, and as they drew clear in the straight it seemed as if Pebbles would prevail. She had taken the lead and was keeping up her gallop resolutely, but though she still had the advantage inside the final furlong Philip Robinson on Katies had more in hand, and when he asked her to go past Pebbles she lengthened her already raking stride: pushed out, she came home a length and a half to the good. The pair were six lengths ahead of the third horse, So Fine.

Royal Hunt Cup

Ascot: 1 mile

Handicap: three-year-olds and upwards

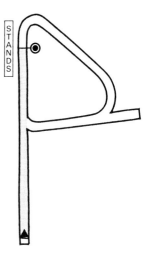

The Royal Hunt Cup is the biggest betting race of the Royal Meeting. First run in 1843, it was named after the Royal Buckhounds, whose master was in charge of Ascot racecourse from its foundation in 1711 until the accession of Edward VII. In that first running Knight Of The Thistle beat twenty-three opponents, and since then this most competitive of handicaps has seen large fields thundering out of the stalls just in front of the magnificent Golden Gates and up the Ascot straight.

Not that this great sight meant much to the financier and gambler James White in 1919. He owned Irish Elegance, co-favourite for the race despite a crushing burden of nine stone eleven pounds, and had backed the horse to win £100,000, causing the odds to tumble from 50–1 a few days before the race to his starting price of 7–1. But White, miffed at not being able to gain entrance to the Royal Enclosure, did not attend the race. In his absence his horse won with great ease.

Occasionally the field will include a future Group horse, such as the 1982 winner Buzzards Bay. Bought for a mere 880 guineas as a yearling and supposedly a mulish character, on his day he was a top-notch miler, and when Joe Mercer brought him wide of his rivals in the closing stages of the Hunt Cup he appreciated the solitude and won very handily at 14–1. Three months after his victory he returned to Ascot to win the Queen Elizabeth II Stakes at 50–1. In 1984 there ran in the Royal Hunt Cup an even better horse, and one whose genuineness was not in doubt – Teleprompter. Trying to emulate Irish Elegance's feat of carrying nine stone eleven to victory and equipped for the first time on a racecourse with what was to become the most familiar pair of blinkers in racing, Teleprompter failed by a length to get to Hawkley. Never mind: the following year he would win the Arlington Million and enter Turf legend.

Opposite: Two Group One winners for Steve Cauthen at Royal Ascot, 1990. *Above:* Shavian in the St James's Palace Stakes on the Tuesday; *below:* Chimes of Freedom in the Coronation Stakes on the Wednesday.

WINNERS SINCE 1980

1980 Tender Heart
  J. Mercer 13–2 (22 ran)

1981 Teamwork
  G. Starkey 8–1 (20 ran)

1982 Buzzards Bay
  J. Mercer 14–1 (20 ran)

1983 Mighty Fly
  S. Cauthen 12–1 (31 ran)

1984 Hawkley
  T. Williams 10–1 (18 ran)

1985 Come On The Blues
  C. Rutter 14–1 (27 ran)

1986 Patriach
  T. Quinn 20–1 (32 ran)

1987 Vague Shot
  S. Cauthen 10–1 (25 ran)

1988 Governorship
  J. Reid 33–1 (26 ran)

1989 True Panache
  Pat Eddery 5–1 (27 ran)

1990 Pontenuovo
  G. Bardwell 50–1 (32 ran)

Gold Cup

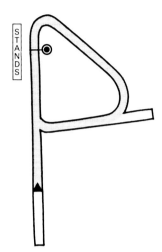

Ascot: 2½ miles

Group One: four-year-olds and upwards

The Ascot Gold Cup is the only Group One race in Britain for stayers, and as the breeding and training of racehorses has concentrated more and more on middle-distance performers the race has lost a great deal of its status. Once it was the natural target for the previous year's Classic horses who had remained in training: now they will be aimed at the King George and the Arc, leaving the Gold Cup to those unfashionable stayers. A sign of the times is that the runners in the 1990 Gold Cup were competing for a first prize of £83,501, as opposed to £112,383 for the St James's Palace Stakes and £102,438 for the Coronation Stakes, the two other Group One races of the meeting.

The Gold Cup was first run in 1807 and won by Master Jacky, one of the few three-year-olds to win the race (which is now confined to four-year-olds and upwards). That first running was attended by the Prince of Wales, soon to become the Prince Regent: he acceded to the throne as George IV in 1820 and in 1829 came to Ascot for the last time to see one of the best fields ever to contest a Gold Cup – two winners of the Derby, one winner of the St Leger, one of the Oaks, and the previous year's Gold Cup winner Bobadilla. George IV, desperate to win the Gold Cup, could have bought Zinganee for 2,500 guineas on the morning of the race but decided against, only to see the horse beat the 1827 Derby winner Mameluke by a length.

In 1844 Czar Nicholas I paid a state visit to Britain and attended Ascot with Queen Victoria and Prince Albert. That year's Gold Cup was won by an unnamed colt by Defence; his owner, Lord Albemarle, courteously renamed the horse The Emperor in honour of the distinguished visitor, who had already made it known that he would give £500 a year for a cup to be run at Ascot. So from 1845 the Gold Cup became the the Emperor's Plate. This state of extreme cordiality and international friendliness did not survive the clash of sport and politics once hostilities broke out between England and Russia in the Crimean War, and in 1854 the race was the Gold Cup again, won by the first colt to have taken the Triple Crown, West Australian. Two other Triple Crown winners would win the Ascot Gold Cup – Gladiateur (1866) and Isinglass (1895) – and throughout the nineteenth century the race maintained its status, with dual winners such as Touchstone (1836 and 1837), The Hero (the 1847 and 1848 Emperor's Plates), the remarkable Fisherman, whose victories in 1858 and 1859 were among his seventy wins from 121 races, and Isonomy (1879 and 1880). Other nineteenth-century winners whose names are

Lester Piggott rode the winner of the Ascot Gold Cup eleven times: on Zarathustra (1957), Gladness (1958), Pandofell (1961), Twilight Alley (1963), Fighting Charlie (1965), Sagaro (1975, 1976, 1977), Le Moss (1979) and Ardross (1981, 1982).

woven into the fabric of Turf legend are The Flying Dutchman (1850), St Simon (1884) – who beat Tristan by twenty lengths and ran on for a mile before he could be pulled up – and Persimmon (1897).

From the turn of the century until the Second World War the race kept its place as the top contest of the season for horses over three, and it produced some famous races. In 1906 Bachelor's Button threw the racing world into mourning by beating Pretty Polly – 'Alas, and again Alas! Pretty Polly beaten!', moaned the *Sporting Life*. And the 1936 renewal produced what is still considered by many to be the most exciting race ever run in England. The two market leaders were Omaha, who had come to England to be trained by Captain Cecil Boyd-Rochfort after winning the Triple Crown in the USA in 1935, and Quashed, winner of the 1935 Oaks by a short head (and subsequently third in the Cesarewitch carrying eight stone nine pounds). Early in the straight the two drew away from their rivals: Quashed was leading but Omaha looked to have her measure, and with just over a furlong to run ranged alongside the filly. She would not give in, and though Omaha headed her briefly she fought back with great courage to win by a short head.

The post-war history of the Gold Cup reflects the emergence of the specialist stayer. Ocean Swell, who took the 1945 race a year after winning the wartime subsitute Derby at Newmarket, was the last British Classic winner to go on to win the Gold Cup, and four years later the hugely popular Alycidon beat the 1948 St Leger winner Black Tarquin by five lengths to announce himself a stayer of exceptional merit. The 1950s saw the race go to such horses as Pan II (1951), Elpenor, who beat two St Leger winners (Premonition and Talma II) in the 1954 running, the brilliant Italian horse Botticelli (1955), the Irish Derby and Irish St Leger winner Zarathustra (1957) and the great Irish mare Gladness (1958). Fighting Charlie in 1965 and 1966 was the first horse to win the race in successive years since Trimdon (1931 and 1932), a feat repeated subsequently by Le Moss (1979 and 1980), Ardross (1981 and 1982), Gildoran (1984 and 1985) and Sadeem (1988 and 1989): Sadeem's first win was on the sensational disqualification of Royal Gait, whose jockey Cash Asmussen was controversially judged to have ridden carelessly after Tony Clark was unseated from pacemaker El Conquistador early in the straight. But the horse with perhaps the most unenviable place in the history of the Ascot Gold Cup is Rock Roi: in both 1971 and 1972 he was first home, and both times he was disqualified – for failing the dope test in 1971 and for interfering with Erimo Hawk in 1972.

Only one horse has ever won the Gold Cup three times. Sagaro's third victory, in 1977, saw him saunter home under Lester Piggott five lengths clear of a high-class field: second was Buckskin, who had beaten Sagaro in three big staying races in France earlier in the season; third, Citoyen, another top-notch French stayer; fourth, the 1975 St Leger winner Bruni; fifth, the Yorkshire Cup winner Bright Finish; and last, Centrocon, who would herself find a place in racing history as the dam of Time Charter. Sagaro was a great horse, and his performance that day showed that whatever the vagaries of breeding fashion, the Ascot Gold Cup still deserves its special place in the racing year.

WINNERS SINCE 1970

1970 Precipice Wood
J. Lindley 5–1 (6 ran)

1971 Random Shot
G. Lewis 11–1 (10 ran)

1972 Erimo Hawk
Pat Eddery 10–1 (8 ran)

1973 Lassalle
J. Lindley 2–1 (7 ran)

1974 Ragstone
R. Hutchinson 6–4 (6 ran)

1975 Sagaro
L. Piggott 7–4 (8 ran)

1976 Sagaro
L. Piggott 8–15 (7 ran)

1977 Sagaro
L. Piggott 9–4 (6 ran)

1978 Shangamuzo
G. Starkey 13–2 (10 ran)

1979 Le Moss
L. Piggott 7–4 (6 ran)

1980 Le Moss
J. Mercer 3–1 (8 ran)

1981 Ardross
L. Piggott 30–100 (4 ran)

1982 Ardross
L. Piggott 1–5 (5 ran)

1983 Little Wolf
W. Carson 4–1 (12 ran)

1984 Gildoran
S. Cauthen 10–1 (9 ran)

1985 Gildoran
B. Thomson 5–2 (12 ran)

1986 Longboat
W. Carson evens (11 ran)

1987 Paean
S. Cauthen 6–1 (8 ran)

1988 Sadeem
G. Starkey 7–2 (13 ran)

1989 Sadeem
W. Carson 8–11 (8 ran)

1990 Ashal
R. Hills 14–1 (11 ran)

Northumberland Plate

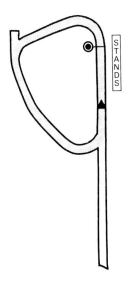

The Northumberland Plate course is mainly flat, though there is a slight rise once the runners have turned into the straight, less than half a mile out. The bends are easy, so long-striding animals are not disadvantaged.

Newcastle: 2 miles

Handicap: three-year-olds and upwards

The 'Pitmen's Derby', as the Northumberland Plate is popularly known (or 'The Plate', as it is referred to locally), was first run in 1833. For that first running £100 was added to stakes of £15 per runner, and its arrival on the Newcastle programme was timely, for the course was in something of a decline. When considering the 1833 season on the Town Moor (the course did not move to its present site of Gosforth Park until 1882) *The New Sporting Magazine* wrote: 'We have before adverted to the falling off of sport at Newcastle with regret not unmingled with the hope of better things. The chief improvement in the list for the present year consists in the establishment of a handicap plate.'

Before long that 'handicap plate' was the highlight of the racing year in the north-east, attracting high-class competitors. In 1863 and 1864 it went to Caller Ou, an exceptionally tough filly who won fifty-one of her 101 races, including the 1861 St Leger by a head from the Derby winner Kettledrum; and the previous decade the Plate had been won three times by Underhand. By this time the race had become established as one of the biggest betting events in the calendar, and it fell prey to the sharp practice of horses being scratched very shortly before the race was due to be run, through collusion between owners and bookmakers and with no comeback for punters. 'The meeting at Newcastle', wrote Van Driver in *Baily's Magazine*, 'certainly eclipses all others for the unblushing and disreputable robberies perpetuated upon the public by the owners of the animals engaged in the Northumberland Plate. Although nearly a score of horses had been in the betting, the event proved that not more than three or four were really meant.' Sometimes owners ran their horses but wished they had not: *The Sporting Review* described how in the 1847 race Inheritress 'disappointed her party by winning when they did not expect her to, whereas at Ascot she lost when she should have won.' That's racing . . .

The second running of the Plate at Gosforth Park in 1883 saw one of the greatest victories in its history when Barcaldine humped nine stone ten pounds to victory over Shrewsbury: Barcaldine's jockey Fred Archer described him as one of the best horses he ever rode, which is saying something. But by the early part of the twentieth century the race no longer attracted the calibre of horse it once had, though its local appeal was still very strong. Winners of note since the Second World War include Souepi, who followed his 1952 Newcastle victory with short-head triumphs in both the Ascot Gold Cup and the

Goodwood Cup the following year, Peter O'Sullevan's little battler Attivo (1974), the dual winner Tug Of War (1977 and 1978) and the 1989 winner Orpheus, the first horse since Joe Chamberlain in 1900 to win the race as a three-year-old. There have also been some notable losers of late: John Cherry (1975), Sea Pigeon (1977 and 1978) and Nicholas Bill (1979) were all beaten favourites.

The Northumberland Plate usually sees a big field, and always a highly competitive race in which some of the best staying handicappers in training take each other on. It may not be what it was in the nineteenth century, but it stills forms the highlight of the Flat racing year at Newcastle.

Richard Fox brings Orpheus to a three-length victory in the 1989 Newcastle 'Brown Ale' Northumberland Plate.

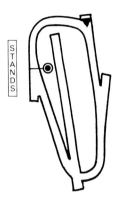

Course description on page 22.

Eclipse Stakes

Sandown Park: 1¼ miles

Group One: three-year-olds and upwards

The Eclipse Stakes has produced some of the best moments in the history of racing in Britain, and is always one of the most keenly awaited contests of the year. The reasons are not far to seek, for the Eclipse is the first event of the season when the top middle-distance three-year-olds meet the cream of their elders, and thus is the first real opportunity for that fascinating exercise of comparing one generation of racehorses with another. Just think of some of the clashes – not only between generations but among the very best of the same age – which the race has brought about: Ard Patrick, Rock Sand and Sceptre; Royal Palace, Taj Dewan and Sir Ivor; Sadler's Wells and Time Charter; Pebbles and Rainbow Quest; Mtoto and Reference Point.

The Eclipse Stakes was the first £10,000 race run in England, and in its inaugural year of 1886 was worth more than twice the value of the Derby. That first race set a standard which would slacken only rarely: the six-year-old Bendigo beat Candlemas and the 1884 Derby winner St Gatien. In 1892 Orme, who had missed the Two Thousand Guineas and the Derby as a result of a mysterious and nearly fatal poisoning (he had probably been got at), beat Orvieto by a neck after a long-drawn-out struggle up the straight. The following year he won again, beating La Fleche, winner in 1892 of the One Thousand

Willie Carson on Elmaamul wins the 1990 Coral-Eclipse Stakes from Michael Roberts on Terimon.

Guineas, Oaks and St Leger. In 1900 the Eclipse went to Diamond Jubilee, who would win the Triple Crown that year, and in 1903 another horse came to Sandown Park in July having won the Two Thousand Guineas and Derby and destined to add the St Leger.

This was Rock Sand, who started 5–4 favourite despite facing two horses who between them had taken all five Classics in 1902. Sceptre had won the Two Thousand Guineas, the One Thousand Guineas, the Oaks and the St Leger, and in the Derby had run fourth to Ard Patrick. Sceptre started at 7–4 in the Eclipse, with Ard Patrick at 5–1 and the other two runners quite unconsidered. If ever there was a clash of titans this was it: three horses who had won seven Classics (with an eighth to come). They provided a suitably memorable race. Rock Sand was going nicely early in the straight, but once let down he could find little, and as Sceptre and Ard Patrick drew away the crowd sensed that they were in for something special. And so they were, for although the beloved Sceptre took a narrow lead and seemed to be going on to win, Otto Madden on Ard Patrick would not be flustered. Inside the final quarter of a mile the two were running neck and neck, with neither giving way, and with a hundred yards to go Madden conjured a little extra out of the colt – enough for Ard Patrick to get home by a neck. He never ran again.

Seven years later the race saw another famous finish. Neil Gow had beaten Lemberg a short head in the Two Thousand Guineas but finished fourth behind him in the Derby; in the Eclipse the two great rivals were inseparable, running a dead-heat.

Between the wars three Derby winners took the Eclipse – Coronach (1926) and Blue Peter (1939) as three-year-olds, and Windsor Lad (1935) at four – and since the race resumed in 1946 (run that year at Ascot) after its wartime hiatus it has consistently maintained its importance. Migoli, who in the 1947 Eclipse beat the great miler Tudor Minstrel, went on to take the Prix de l'Arc de Triomphe in 1948, and in 1952 the Eclipse again went to the Derby winner: Tulyar. Ballymoss, second in the Derby and winner of the St Leger in 1957, included the Eclipse in his glorious haul as a four-year-old in 1958, and the quality of the fields held up throughout the 1960s, with Derby winner St Paddy taking the 1961 race, Ragusa winning in 1964, and the Queen's Canisbay just getting the better of Roan Rocket by a short head in a desperate finish in 1965. Busted in 1967 was one of those horses – Mtoto was another – whose true potential had not been visible at three and whose performance as a four-year-old in the Eclipse proclaimed arrival in the highest class: second to Busted in the Eclipse was Great Nephew, and eight years later their respective sons Bustino and Grundy would produce a finish at Ascot which would be dubbed 'The Race of the Century'.

The 1968 Eclipse Stakes provided a contest which for class and excitement could be set alongside the 1903 running, and as on the earlier occasion it offered a clash of the very best of two generations: indeed, it was the first time since Ard Patrick took on Rock Sand that two Epsom Derby winners had opposed each other in the race. This time Sir Ivor represented the younger generation: he had won the Derby with a superb burst of speed but since then had been beaten by Ribero in the Irish Derby. Ribero had been ridden that day by Sir

WINNERS SINCE 1970

1970 Connaught
   A. Barclay 5–4 (3 ran)

1971 Mill Reef
   G. Lewis 5–4 (6 ran)

1972 Brigadier Gerard
   J. Mercer 4–11 (6 ran)

1973 Scottish Rifle
   R. Hutchinson 15–8 (6 ran)

1974 Coup De Feu
   Pat Eddery 33–1 (12 ran)

1975 Star Appeal
   G. Starkey 20–1 (16 ran)

1976 Wollow
   G. Dettori 9–4 (9 ran)

1977 Artaius
   L. Piggott 9–2 (10 ran)

1978 Gunner B
   J. Mercer 7–4 (9 ran)

1979 Dickens Hill
   A. Murray 7–4 (7 ran)

1980 Ela-Mana-Mou
   W. Carson 85–40 (6 ran)

1981 Master Willie
   P. Waldron 6–4 (7 ran)

1982 Kalaglow
   G. Starkey 11–10 (9 ran)

1983 Solford
   Pat Eddery 3–1 (9 ran)

1984 Sadler's Wells
   Pat Eddery 11–4 (9 ran)

1985 Pebbles
   S. Cauthen 7–2 (4 ran)

1986 Dancing Brave
   G. Starkey 4–9 (8 ran)

1987 Mtoto
   M. Roberts 6–1 (8 ran)

1988 Mtoto
   M. Roberts 6–4 (8 ran)

1989 Nashwan
   W. Carson 2–5 (6 ran)

1990 Elmaamul
   W. Carson 13–2 (7 ran)

ECLIPSE

Reputedly the best horse ever to have raced in England, Eclipse was bred by the Duke of Cumberland (a son of George II) and foaled in 1764. The Duke died when the horse was a yearling and so never knew that he had bred a phenomenon. Eclipse did not race until he was five, and by the time of his first contest – at Epsom in May 1769 – his reputation had preceded him: he started 4–1 on in the first of three four-mile heats and in the second heat landed the famous bet 'Eclipse first, the rest nowhere' for the Irish gambler Dennis O'Kelly, who had predicted that Eclipse would 'distance' (finish more than 240 yards in front of) his rivals. O'Kelly later bought a half-share in Eclipse from his owner William Wildman, and subsequently bought the horse outright. A striking chestnut with a white blaze and one white stocking, Eclipse was unbeaten in eighteen races, and at stud proved as phenomenal a success as he had when racing: he sired three of the first five winners of the Derby, and the great majority of modern Thoroughbreds trace back to him.

Ivor's Epsom partner Lester Piggott, but Piggott was back on Sir Ivor at Sandown, and the pair went to post favourite at 5–4 on. The main danger seemed to be Royal Palace, winner of the Two Thousand Guineas and the Derby in 1967 and already successful three times as a four-year-old. Third favourite was the French-trained Taj Dewan, narrowly beaten by Royal Palace in the Two Thousand Guineas and fresh from victory in the Prix Ganay. Yves Saint-Martin on Taj Dewan made his move early in the straight – so often the best Sandown Park tactic – and seemed to have the legs of his main rivals, for Sir Ivor was not making progress and Royal Palace, try as he might, could not make any appreciable dent in the French horse's advantage. Then Sandy Barclay went for a final effort from Royal Palace and this gallant horse's response started to bring him closer to the leader: Taj Dewan still had a good lead with fifty yards to go but Royal Palace was flying now, and the two passed the post locked together, with Sir Ivor three-quarters of a length back in third. The bookmakers in the ring bet as low as 8–1 on Taj Dewan getting the verdict, but when the announcement came the winner was Royal Palace, by a short head.

The following year Wolver Hollow gave 26-year-old Henry Cecil his first big-race success (in his first season of training), though he was widely regarded as an extremely lucky winner: Geoff Lewis on the great mare Park Top managed to get into all sorts of traffic problems up the straight despite there being only seven runners, and by the time Park Top had been extricated to mount her challenge, Lester Piggott on Wolver Hollow was home and hosed.

The Eclipse was won by by Mill Reef (1971) and Brigadier Gerard, but it cannot be said that The Brigadier's victory in 1972 was one of his more spectacular efforts. The race was run in foul rainy conditions which the great horse was known to hate, and in the betting he drifted from 6–1 on to his starting price of 11–4 on. He won by a length from Gold Rod. This was the last Eclipse Stakes to be run in front of the old Sandown Park grandstand, and the 1973 renewal (which went to Scottish Rifle) was held at Kempton Park while the new Sandown stand was being built. Later in the 1970s the roll of honour includes Star Appeal, who started at 20–1 in 1975 and won with a stunning burst of acceleration; perhaps even more stunning was the fact that by the time Star Appeal took the field for the Arc later that year most people had forgotten that the horse was capable of such speed. Those with better memories were rewarded when he took the Longchamp race at 119–1. In 1976 the Two Thousand Guineas winner Wollow was awarded the Eclipse on the disqualification of the French challenger Trepan, found to have traces of the prohibited substance theobromine in his urine.

In the 1980s five horses went on from Sandown to win the country's most prestigious race for three-year-olds and over, the King George VI and Queen Elizabeth Diamond Stakes at Ascot: Ela-Mana-Mou (1980); Kalaglow (1982); Dancing Brave (1986), whose Eclipse victory in 1986 over Triptych and Teleprompter did something to erase the memory of his controversial defeat by Shahrastani in the Derby; Mtoto, who won the King George in 1988 three weeks after his second successive Eclipse victory; and Nashwan, whose gigantic

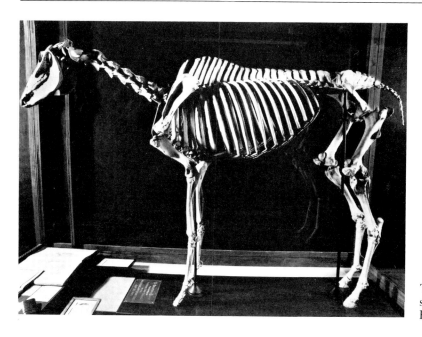

This one's run up a bit light: the skeleton of Eclipse in the National Horseracing Museum, Newmarket.

stride brought him thundering home five lengths clear of Opening Verse and Indian Skimmer in 1989, with a below-par Warning in arrears. Other notable winners in the decade were Sadler's Wells, who beat Time Charter by a neck in 1984 and on retiring to stud at the end of that season rapidly became one of the most successful sires of the modern age, with Old Vic and Salsabil in his first two crops; and Pebbles, the first filly ever to win the race when beating Rainbow Quest in 1985.

But for the essence of the Eclipse Stakes we can single out the 1987 race. Here was the clash of the generations: the Derby winner Reference Point pitched against the likes of the durable Triptych, now five, and Mtoto, who had recently won the Prince of Wales's Stakes at Royal Ascot with a devastating turn of foot. Here was the clash of tactics: Reference Point the front-runner against Triptych and Mtoto, the horses with finishing speed. As expected, Reference Point led from the off, and swept into the straight with most of his rivals at full stretch. It looked as though the Derby winner would hold on to his lead, but Mtoto set off after him halfway up the straight and with a furlong to go had all but caught up. The two went for the line with tremendous resolution, but Mtoto was just the stronger and edged ahead, and despite a last-gasp effort from Reference Point had an advantage of three quarters of a length at the post. It had been, in its way, a quintessential Eclipse Stakes, a complete vindication of the original impulse behind its foundation over a century earlier – that a ten-furlong race between three-year-olds and older horses at Sandown Park will sort out the very best.

NEWMARKET JULY MEETING

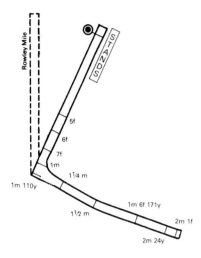

The July Course and the Rowley Mile course are the same for the first mile or so. Then before the Devil's Dyke the July Course branches off and runs downhill until the ground rises appreciably through the final furlong. Like the Rowley Mile, the course is dauntingly wide.

The July Course is sheer delight. John Tyrrel, in his book Racecourses on the Flat, *puts his finger on how the personality of the Bunbury Mile (the formal name of the last mile of the course) differs from that of the Rowley Mile course across the Heath: 'The Rowley is thrusting and purposeful, like those lantern-jawed gentlemen who leap over battlements to give ladies boxes of chocolates, while the Bunbury is easy-going, casual and would simply put the chocolates in the post.'*

The July Meeting is the major event on the course, though Newmarket racing moves over here from the Rowley Mile for the whole summer before returning across the Heath in the autumn, and it provides a stark contrast in mood to Royal Ascot a few weeks before. The essence of the July Meeting is informality, a mood helped immeasurably by the course itself. Here in the height of summer the horses are led around among the trees before being taken into the parade ring, and racegoers can cool themselves in the shade while casting an eye over their fancy. The stands are old but sturdy. The weighing-room sports a thatched roof. The whole place breathes relaxation.

Not for the participants, though, for the July Meeting contains some excellent sport. The peak of the week is the JULY CUP (pages 78–9) for sprinters, and there is an important middle-distance race in the PRINCESS OF WALES'S STAKES (opposite). But beyond these there is a feast of racing, including the Group Three CHERRY HINTON STAKES (six furlongs) for two-year-old fillies, won in 1987 by subsequent Oaks winner Diminuendo; the BUNBURY CUP, a keenly contested seven-furlong handicap; the Group Two CHILD STAKES (one mile) for fillies of three and over, won in recent years by such as Royal Heroine (1983), Al Bahathri (1985) and Sonic Lady (1986 and 1987); and the Group Three JULY STAKES (six furlongs), first held in 1786 and the oldest two-year-old race still run.

Princess of Wales's Stakes

Newmarket (July Course): 1½ miles

Group Two: three-year-olds and upwards

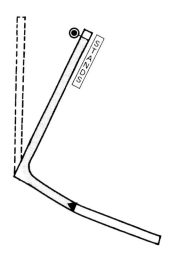

First run in 1894 and named after the then Princess of Wales, who as consort of King Edward VII was to become Queen Alexandra (and was thus great-grandmother of Queen Elizabeth II), the Princess of Wales's Stakes is the first Group event of the season when three-year-olds can take on their elders over the classic middle distance of one and a half miles. The first running went to Isinglass, who the previous season had become the sixth colt to win the Triple Crown: at Newmarket he won by a head from Bullingdon, with that year's Derby winner Ladas back in third. Both Derby winners owned by Edward VII himself when he was Prince of Wales met defeat in the race: Persimmon in 1896 and Diamond Jubilee in 1900 and 1901. But Ard Patrick restored the fortunes of Derby winners when taking the 1903 running, and that year's Triple Crown winner Rock Sand won in 1904.

Between the wars winners of the Princess of Wales's Stakes included Blandford (1922), Solario (1925), Colorado (1927, when he beat the 1926 Derby winner Coronach by eight lengths) and Fairway (1929). Airborne, the last grey horse to win the Derby, took the race a few weeks after his Epsom triumph in 1946, and two years later the three-year-old Alycidon started at 100–8 and beat the 1947 St Leger winner Sayajirao by two lengths.

In the last twenty years the race has served the important purpose of bringing together good-class horses in a race often seen as a stepping-stone to the more intense competition to come later in the season. Winners during the period include 1970 Oaks heroine Lupe (1971: she never ran again), 1980 St Leger winner Light Cavalry (1981), Nashwan's dam Height of Fashion (1982), Petoski (winner in 1985 before landing the King George), Shardari, Celestial Storm and Unfuwain (1986, 1987 and 1988 respectively: all three were second in the King George), and Carroll House, who went on to win the Arc.

WINNERS SINCE 1980

1980 Nicholas Bill
   P. Waldron 12–1 (9 ran)

1981 Light Cavalry
   L. Piggott 11–4 (8 ran)

1982 Height Of Fashion
   W. Carson 4–1 (4 ran)

1983 Quilted
   W. Newnes 7–2 (11 ran)

1984 Head For Heights
   L. Piggott 100–30 (9 ran)

1985 Petoski
   W. Carson 8–1 (5 ran)

1986 Shardari
   W. R. Swinburn 5–2 (6 ran)

1987 Celestial Storm
   R. Cochrane 13–8 (8 ran)

1988 Unfuwain
   W. Carson 6–4 (5 ran)

1989 Carroll House
   W. R. Swinburn 10–1 (5 ran)

1990 Sapience
   Pat Eddery 11–2 (7 ran)

July Cup

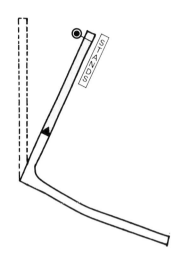

Newmarket (July Course): 6 furlongs

Group One: three-year-olds and upwards

The centrepiece of the July Meeting, the July Cup was promoted from Group Two to Group One in 1978, just over a century after the first running in 1876. In its very early days it had been won by middle-distance Classic winners such as Melton, who won in 1886 after landing the previous year's Derby, and Memoir, the 1890 Oaks winner who took the July Cup as a four-year-old. Sundridge was the only horse to win three times (1902, 1903 and 1904, on each occasion carrying ten stone two pounds, at that time the weight allotted to four-year-olds and over), and since the early part of the century the race has become very much the province of the specialist sprinters, including Spanish Prince (1912, 1913), Diadem (1919, 1920) and Myrobella (1933).

The best sprinter of the late 1940s, the flying grey Abernant, won in 1949 and 1950, and was soon followed by other famous names:

JIM MCGRATH'S DAYS OF THE YEAR

There's a carnival atmosphere at the July Meeting. Most patrons – unlike many of those who attend the Derby at Epsom or Royal Ascot – are there out of enthusiasm for the racing, and they get the sport at its best. Season after season promising two-year-olds begin their racing careers here, and the competition for older horses is top-class. The July Cup, over six furlongs on the final day, is Britain's most prestigious sprint prize, usually attracting established sprinters and frequently a target for horses reverting to sprinting after racing over a mile. Often a reputation dented in the Guineas has been restored in this race, the roll of honour of which in recent years has included such as Habibti, Chief Singer, Soviet Star and – most recently – Royal Academy.

But the July Meeting is about more than just the racing, and if you've never attended, think on: granted a fine day, with the weather high, a steel band in full swing and good horses on view, it's a great day out. Lounge against the rails in one of the tree-shaded paddocks used before and after saddling; or, if you fancy a break from the serious business of racing, just 'take the rays, man' and sit around, Pimms in hand, sampling the delight of the English high summer. (Note, though, that the July Meeting on a humid, rainy afternoon when the place is invaded by thunderflies and the quaint but antiquated stands offer little but claustrophobia is a somewhat different proposition!)

Three wonderfully enjoyable days, and the Channel Four Racing team are paid to be there: no wonder our enthusiasm shines through!

Vilmoray (1954), Matador (1956), Right Boy (1958 and 1959) and Tin Whistle, who walked over for the race in 1960. In the 1970s the July Cup remained one of the key targets for the best sprinters, falling to Thatch in 1973 and to Time Charter's sire Saritamer in 1974. In 1975 the brilliant filly Lianga provided Daniel Wildenstein with his first victory in Britain with a horse trained in France; she was later beaten a neck and a head by Bolkonski and Rose Bowl in the Sussex Stakes. Lochnager (1976) and Gentilhombre (1977) kept up the standard, though the latter got the race only on the disqualification of Marinsky. Ridden by Lester Piggott and trained by Vincent O'Brien, Marinsky ran in a muzzle at Newmarket, for he had disgraced himself when savaging Relkino on Tattenham Hill during the running of the Diomed Stakes on Derby Day. He won the July Cup easily but had bumped Gentilhombre when making his challenge and although it was acknowledged that the interference was accidental he was demoted to second. O'Brien undertook that the horse would not run in England again: a few weeks later Marinsky died of a twisted gut.

For the 1978 running the arrival of sponsorship gave the July Cup a boost which complemented its upgrading, and its first running as the William Hill July Cup went to one of the very best sprinters of the age. Like Marinsky, Solinus was trained by Vincent O'Brien and ridden by Lester Piggott, and he brought them consolation for the previous year's disqualification, though he had to work hard for it. He took the lead early on and in the closing stages was attacked first by Double Form, whose challenge in the Dip he repelled, and then by the fast-finishing Sanedtki. Solinus held on by a neck. He went on to win the William Hill Sprint Championship and finish second to Sigy in the Prix de l'Abbaye, only the second defeat of his ten-race career.

Throughout the 1980s the July Cup went to top-notch sprinters. In 1980 the race provided the first real evidence that Moorestyle was an exceptional horse when Lester Piggott brought him home ahead of Vaigly Great and Sharpo: that year he was the first sprinter ever to be voted Horse of the Year. Sharpo's own turn came in 1981, and meanwhile the July Cup had been won in 1982 by the filly Marwell, who stormed up the hill to beat Moorestyle by three lengths. Another filly, the brilliantly fast Habibti, took the 1983 running from Soba, whom she beat again in the Vernons Sprint Cup at Haydock and the Prix de l'Abbaye. Chief Singer, runner-up to El Gran Senor in the Two Thousand Guineas, won in 1984, and the following year Never So Bold easily went clear of Committed, only to hobble into the unsaddling enclosure in extreme discomfort: he had been in the same condition after winning the King's Stand Stakes at Royal Ascot, but on both occasions the lameness disappeared within a few minutes. For the rest of the decade the race belonged to two of the Maktoum brothers. The 1986 running went to another Two Thousand Guineas runner-up, Green Desert (owned by Maktoum Al-Maktoum), and in 1987 to Ajdal (Sheikh Mohammed), whose previous race had been over twice the distance in the Derby. Sheikh Mohammed's French-trained Soviet Star (1988) and Maktoum Al-Maktoum's Cadeaux Genereux (1989) produced performances which confirmed the race's status alongside the Nunthorpe Stakes and the Prix de l'Abbaye as one of the three peaks of the European sprinting year.

WINNERS SINCE 1970

1970 Huntercombe
A. Barclay 8–13 (4 ran)

1971 Realm
B. Taylor 11–2 (8 ran)

1972 Parsimony
R. Hutchinson 16–1 (5 ran)

1973 Thatch
L. Piggott 4–5 (6 ran)

1974 Saritamer
L. Piggott 11–4 (9 ran)

1975 Lianga
Y. Saint-Martin 10–1 (13 ran)

1976 Lochnager
E. Hide 3–1 (10 ran)

1977 Gentilhombre
P. Cook 10–1 (8 ran)

1978 Solinus
L. Piggott 4–7 (14 ran)

1979 Thatching
L. Piggott 2–1 (11 ran)

1980 Moorestyle
L. Piggott 3–1 (14 ran)

1981 Marwell
W. R. Swinburn 13–8 (14 ran)

1982 Sharpo
Pat Eddery 13–2 (16 ran)

1983 Habibti
W. Carson 8–1 (15 ran)

1984 Chief Singer
R. Cochrane 15–8 (9 ran)

1985 Never So Bold
S. Cauthen 5–4 (9 ran)

1986 Green Desert
W. R. Swinburn 7–4 (5 ran)

1987 Ajdal
W. R. Swinburn 9–2 (11 ran)

1988 Soviet Star
C. Asmussen 15–8 (9 ran)

1989 Cadeaux Genereux
Paul Eddery 10–1 (11 ran)

1990 Royal Academy
J. Reid 7–1 (9 ran)

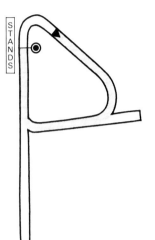

Course description on page 62.

Only three horses over the age of four have won the King George: Aggressor (1959), Park Top (1969) and Mtoto (1988), all of whom won at five.

King George VI and Queen Elizabeth Diamond Stakes

Ascot: 1½ miles

Group One: three-year-olds and upwards

For sheer nerve-tingling excitement, nothing in the racing year is quite like those few seconds which bring the runners in the King George VI and Queen Elizabeth Diamond Stakes swinging round the final turn into the short Ascot straight. The bell rings out, and with less than three furlongs to run England's top middle-distance race is up for grabs. Whether the next half a minute brings Ribot or Nijinsky or Shergar to dominate his field, or a pulsating battle between Grundy and Bustino or Nashwan and Cacoethes or Belmez and Old Vic, the very stuff of racing history is about to be made.

The King George is one of the major races of the world for several reasons. It comes at a time of the year when the three-year-olds should have sorted themselves out: the best of that generation will be ready to take on the cream of the older horses (and some will already have done so in the Eclipse). The trip of one and a half miles is the classic European middle distance, and the Ascot course is one of the fairest and most testing in the country. And not least, the prize money is – by British standards – huge.

The race owes its existence to Sir John Crocker Bulteel, Clerk of the Course at Ascot from 1946 until his death ten years later, who devised the plan for a top-class international race which was first held to mark the Festival of Britain in 1951. The King George VI and Queen Elizabeth Festival of Britain Stakes attracted a field of nineteen (of which six were from France) – the largest in the history of the race – which included the 1951 Derby winner Arctic Prince; the 1950 Prix de l'Arc de Triomphe hero Tantieme, who would win the Arc again in 1951 and had already lifted the Coronation Cup; the 1950 St Leger winner Scratch II; Sir Winston Churchill's great grey Colonist II; the temperamental Zucchero, mount of fifteen-year-old Lester Piggott; both that season's Guineas winners, Belle Of All and Ki Ming; and Wilwyn, who the following year would win the first running of the Washington International. But that first King George went to a three-year-old who had not run in the Classics but had taken three races earlier in the season: Supreme Court, ridden by Charlie Elliott and starting at 100–9, won from Zucchero. He did not race again.

In 1952 the Derby and Eclipse winner Tulyar, ridden by Charlie Smirke, beat Gay Time – second to him at Epsom – by a neck. This time there were seven raiders from France and one from Germany:

already the international appeal of the race was strong, and throughout the 1950s its stature held up. In 1953 Pinza and Aureole were the first two home, as they had been in the Derby; Pinza did not run again, and Aureole's turn came the following year. Vimy in 1955 became the first French-trained winner of the race, with Derby winner Phil Drake back in sixth: Vimy was the fourth of the first five King George victors not to race again after Ascot. In 1956 the great Italian horse Ribot sploshed home by five lengths in dreadful going, and 1957 proved a benefit for the French, with Montaval beating Al Mabsoot by a short head with their compatriots Tribord and Saint Raphael third and fourth. Ireland joined the roll of honour in 1958 when Ballymoss, trained by Vincent O'Brien, cruised in three lengths clear of the Queen's Almeria, with Derby winner Hard Ridden well beaten in sixth, but the home team scored in 1959 with Alcide, trained at Newmarket by Cecil Boyd-Rochfort, who beat the wonderful Irish mare Gladness. By the end of the decade the King George and Queen Elizabeth Stakes was firmly established as the most prestigious English race in the calendar.

Its tenth running produced one of the most notorious upsets in post-war racing history when 5–2 on favourite Petite Etoile, one of the best fillies of the century, failed to get a clear run in the straight and could not find her devastating speed on the rain-softened ground: she went down by half a length to Aggressor, and vilification rained down on her jockey, Lester Piggott, for getting her boxed in at the crucial moments. In 1961 French-trained Right Royal V beat the previous year's Derby winner St Paddy, and the following year Match III took the race across the Channel for the fourth time. It went to Ireland again with Ragusa in 1963, and in 1964 looked a complete certainty to stay there: Santa Claus, winner of the Derby and the Irish Derby, started at 13–2 on – the shortest-priced runner in the history of the race – to beat just three rivals, but failed to peg back the French-trained front-runner Nasram II. In 1965 the real star turn was for once missing, as Sea Bird II, who had won the Derby with insolent ease, was not at Ascot. In his absence Meadow Court, runner-up at Epsom, gave Lester Piggott his first King George, with Classic winners Niksar (1965 Two Thousand Guineas), Homeward Bound (1964 Oaks) and Indiana (1964 St Leger) well behind. Piggott won again in 1966 on Aunt Edith, trained at Newmarket by Noel Murless, who also sent out the 1967 winner Busted and Jim Joel's colt Royal Palace, who in 1968 became the first horse to add the King George to victories in the Two Thousand Guineas and Derby (1967) and Eclipse Stakes (1968). The 1960s was rounded off with another Piggott victory, on Park Top.

The early 1970s saw three quite exceptional horses racing in Europe, and all of them won the King George. Nijinsky in 1970 and Mill Reef in 1971, both three-year-olds, simply underlined their excellence, but for Brigadier Gerard in 1972 the race – sponsored for the first time by the De Beers diamond company – represented a venture into unknown territory. Unbeaten in fourteen races, the Brigadier was without doubt one of the greatest horses of the modern period, but at Ascot he would race for the first time over a distance beyond ten furlongs. Would he stay one and a half miles? Among

The 1986 King George: Dancing Brave holds off Shardari, with Triptych third and Shahrastani a remote fourth.

those determined to test him to the full were four other Classic winners – Riverman (Poule d'Essai des Poulains), Steel Pulse (Irish Sweeps Derby), Gay Lussac (Italian Derby) and Parnell, winner in 1971 of the Irish St Leger and now one of the best long-distance horses in Europe. Brigadier Gerard started favourite at 13–8 on but many thought he might not stay, not least owner John Hislop, who wrote in his book *The Brigadier*:

> There was a grave chance that the Brigadier might meet his first defeat. But I have always contended that owners in this country place too much emphasis on defeat and not enough on proving horses thoroughly; and that to be beaten honourably carries more merit than preserving an undefeated record by avoiding the issue.

Willie Carson drove the confirmed stayer Parnell into the lead after five furlongs, and at the turn into the straight he was two lengths clear of the favourite, who had been brought easily through the field by Joe Mercer and was now poised to come through and take the leader. Halfway up the straight the Brigadier, on the outside, collared Parnell, but then veered in towards the far rail, appearing to hamper Parnell. Though at the limit of his stamina Brigadier Gerard kept going, and at the line had the verdict by one and a half lengths, but it was no great surprise when a Stewards' Enquiry was announced. Thirteen anxious minutes followed while the Stewards deliberated, but the head-on film satisfied them, and the result stood.

In 1973 the betting for the King George was dominated by Rheingold and Roberto, who had fought out a furious finish for the Derby in 1972. Rheingold, beaten a short head at Epsom, was 13–8 favourite, but had no answer to an extraordinary burst of acceleration from the French-trained filly Dahlia, who just a week earlier had won the Irish Guinness Oaks at The Curragh. She was ridden to victory that year by Bill Pyers, but Lester Piggott had the mount in 1974 when she beat the Queen's filly Highclere to become the only horse ever to have won the King George twice.

A year later Dahlia started at 6–1 to take the race for a third time, but she was never playing more than a small supporting role to the two horses preferred to her in the betting for the 1975 King George – the first running for which the sponsorship of De Beers was marked by adding 'Diamond' to the race's title. Favourite at 5–4 on was Grundy, ridden by Pat Eddery and trained by Peter Walwyn: Grundy had won the Derby and the Irish Derby in the manner of an exceedingly good horse. Second favourite was the 1974 St Leger winner Bustino, who in his only race as a four-year-old had beaten Ashmore in the Coronation Cup. Trained by Dick Hern and ridden by Joe Mercer, Bustino was the horse with undoubted stamina, and a strategy was hatched whereby not one but two pacemakers – Kinglet and Highest – would set a scorching pace in the early stages of the race in order to draw the sting of fast-finishing Grundy. The pacemakers performed effectively, and by the turn into the straight Bustino had set sail for home with all of his rivals bar one toiling behind. The one who would not be beaten off was Grundy, who came to pass Bustino early in the straight. Bustino would not capitulate, and the two ran neck and neck for the winning post. Then Grundy forged ahead, but Bustino rallied and fought back inside the final furlong, making a desperate effort to claw back the length which his younger rival had taken off him, but just before the line he faltered, and Grundy got home by half a length in what was generally agreed to be the greatest race of modern times.

Follow that! In 1976 Oaks heroine Pawneese, ridden by Yves Saint-Martin, led all the way and held on from the 1975 St Leger winner Bruni and Orange Bay, who the following year went down by a short head to the Derby winner The Minstrel, with the likes of Exceller, Bruni and Crow behind. After Ile De Bourbon had beaten Acamas and Hawaiian Sound in 1978, the 1979 King George again fell to the Derby winner when Troy cosily beat Gay Mecene, and the horse well beaten in third place that day came good in 1980, when Ela-Mana-Mou defeated Mrs Penny and Gregorian.

Through the rest of the 1980s the King George produced wonderful performances. Shergar won by four lengths at 5–2 on in 1981. Kalaglow beat Assert in a rousing finish in 1982. In 1983 the previous year's Oaks winner Time Charter charged up the outside to cut down Diamond Shoal and Sun Princess, who had won the Oaks that year and would win the St Leger. Lester Piggott won his seventh and last King George when riding the 1983 Derby hero Teenoso to a brilliant tactical victory in 1984. In 1985 Oh So Sharp came to Ascot from victory in the One Thousand Guineas and the Oaks but was thwarted a neck by the finishing surge of Petoski.

The 1986 running contained an element of that special rivalry which adds such spice to the anticipation of a big race, for second favourite Dancing Brave had a score to settle with the market leader Shahrastani, who had controversially beaten him in the Derby. Dancing Brave's jockey Greville Starkey had been fiercely criticized for giving the colt too much to do at Epsom, but had made some amends with victory in the Eclipse Stakes. Meanwhile Shahrastani had won the Irish Derby. Starkey was out of action for the Ascot race and Pat Eddery took over on Dancing Brave, who once he had swept into the lead halfway up the straight never looked like being beaten. Behind him came Shardari, Triptych and Shahrastani.

Reference Point in 1987 led from the start to beat Celestial Storm, with Triptych again third, and in 1988 Mtoto produced a terrific burst of acceleration to brush aside Unfuwain in the closing stages. The 1989 King George seemed to be a benefit for the unbeaten Nashwan, who had already that season won the Two Thousand Guineas, the Derby and the Eclipse Stakes. At Ascot he started at 9–2 on but a tough race in the Eclipse may have left its mark, for he had to call on untapped reserves of resolution to hold off the dogged challenge of Cacoethes.

That Nashwan was the twelfth Derby winner to lift the King George in its comparatively short life-span is yet further evidence of its supreme quality, further enhanced by the furious 1990 finish between Sheikh Mohammed's two colts, the three-year-old Belmez and the four-year-old Old Vic. There is no more eloquent testimony of the importance of the race than its runners and winners over the last four decades – which is why when that bell rings as the field sweeps round the Ascot home turn, the racing world knows that something special is only a few seconds away.

HOW THEY RATE

Brigadier Gerard *146*
Mill Reef *146*
Nijinsky *144*
Dahlia *141*
Dancing Brave *141*
Grundy *141*
Shergar *140*
Troy *136*
Ile De Bourbon *135*
Reference Point *135*
The Minstrel *135*
Teenoso *135*
Petoski *134*
Kalaglow *133*
Pawneese *133*
Mtoto *131*
Nashwan *131*
Ela-Mana-Mou *130*
Time Charter *128*

Grundy and Bustino at the climax of their battle for the 1975 King George.

GOODWOOD JULY MEETING

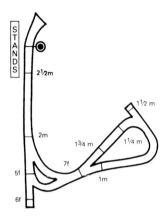

Goodwood has perhaps the weirdest configuration of any track in Britain. The six-furlong course is practically straight and mostly downhill. To it is attached a loop around which the runners race right-handed, joining the straight course at one of two junctions depending on the distance of the race. The course is very undulating and the further turn into the straight is notably sharp, so Goodwood favours a nimble and well-balanced type of horse.

The morning suit and the topper are put away as soon as Royal Ascot finishes. For Glorious Goodwood, out come the blazer and the panama. That at least is the traditional approach to the Goodwood July Meeting, but the ambiance of the Edwardian garden party at this most wonderfully scenic of all English racecourses has received something of a bashing in recent years as the more modern yet very diverse social phenomena of corporate hospitality and lager loutishness have, according to many traditionalists, altered irrevocably the nature of the meeting. But from whatever social standpoint the sport is viewed, the racing is – for the most part – indeed glorious.

The first day features the STEWARDS' CUP (opposite) and the twelve-furlong Group Three GORDON STAKES, an important race for three-year-olds and often a significant pointer to the St Leger: in the 1980s Commanche Run (1984) and Minster Son (1988) have won the race before going on to take the final Classic. Wednesday features the SUSSEX STAKES (pages 86–7), the meeting's richest race, the Group Two RICHMOND STAKES for two-year-olds and the GOODWOOD STAKES, a two-mile handicap which in times past was one of the highlights of the meeting and was won three times by the famous Goodwood performer Predominate (1958, 1959, 1960). Thursday has the GOODWOOD CUP, a two-and-a-half-mile Group Three contest which with the equivalent races at Ascot and Doncaster forms what is informally known as the Stayers' Triple Crown; the Group Three KING GEORGE STAKES, a manic sprint down Goodwood's five-furlong course; and the SCHWEPPES GOLDEN MILE, a valuable one-mile handicap first run in 1987 and now of the the biggest betting races of the meeting. On Friday is run the Group Three MOLECOMB STAKES (five furlongs) for two-year-olds, and Saturday's big event is the NASSAU STAKES, a ten-furlong Group Two race for three-year-old and older fillies which usually attracts some of the best middle-distance fillies in training.

And even as Glorious Goodwood is in full swing, at some remote part of the country the National Hunt season grinds back into action.

Stewards' Cup

Goodwood: 6 furlongs

Handicap: three-year-olds and upwards

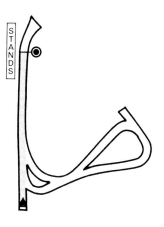

Not all the great sights of the racing year occur towards the climax of the big events. The contribution of the Stewards' Cup to the select list of visual high-points comes shortly after the start of the race, when the large field, spread out across the course, appears on the brow of the hill at the far end of the Goodwood straight before commencing the hectic charge down towards the stands. When the horses thunder past the winning post about a minute later and wheel to the right before pulling up, some hefty gambles will have been won and lost, for this is one of the big betting races of the year: the victory of Rotherfield Greys in 1988 is reputed to have relieved the bookmakers of not much short of a million pounds, for owner Tony Gleeson and his family had been backing the horse, who started at 14–1, at odds as long as 40–1.

The Stewards' Cup was first run under that name in 1840, though its true history goes back a little further: in 1834 a custom was begun whereby the senior of the two stewards of the meeting gave a cup for a race of his choosing, and the 1840 prize was donated by the two stewards of the previous year.

Twenty years after that inaugural running Goodwood saw a demonstration of extraordinary versatility when the three-year-old Sweetsauce won the Stewards' Cup on the Tuesday at 20–1 and two days later the marathon Goodwood Cup. In recent years the race has gone to some familiar names, notably the indefatigable Soba, who as a three-year-old in 1982 took the Cup in a season when she won eleven races. Ante-post favourite until a trapped nerve put her participation in jeopardy less than three weeks before, Soba recovered well enough to take part but market support for her had dwindled, and, carrying eight stone four pounds, she started at 18–1 to beat twenty-nine rivals. They hardly saw which way she went, for she led from the moment the stalls opened and never looked like being caught, winning by two and a half lengths in course record time. The following season she was back at Goodwood to take a Pattern race in the King George Stakes, and in 1982 she was also second in three Group One sprint races. Some 18–1 shot! Another good-class winner fresh in the memory is Petong, who set a weight-carrying record for the race when taking the 1984 running under nine stone ten pounds and went on to win the Group Two Vernons Sprint Cup at Haydock Park from Habibti and Never So Bold.

WINNERS SINCE 1980

1980 Repetitious
    A. Clark 15–1 (28 ran)

1981 Crews Hill
    G. Starkey 11–1 (30 ran)

1982 Soba
    D. Nicholls 18–1 (30 ran)

1983 Autumn Sunset
    W. Carson 6–1 (23 ran)

1984 Petong
    B. Raymond 8–1 (26 ran)

1985 Al Trui
    M. Wigham 9–1 (28 ran)

1986 Green Ruby
    J. Williams 20–1 (24 ran)

1987 Madraco
    P. Hill 50–1 (30 ran)

1988 Rotherfield Greys
    N. Day 14–1 (28 ran)

1989 Very Adjacent
    D. Gibson 12–1 (22 ran)

1990 Knight of Mercy
    B. Raymond 14–1 (30 ran)

Sussex Stakes

Goodwood: 1 mile

Group One: three-year-olds and upwards

The Sussex Stakes, first run in 1841, is the first Group One event of the year when the top three-year-old milers can meet their elders, though it was not always thus: from 1860 until 1959 the race was confined to three-year-olds, and from 1960 until 1974 to three- and four-year-olds.

The Sussex Stakes has long been one of the most prestigious one-mile races of the season, and the list of winners since the war testifies to its importance. In the period between 1946 and the final running of the race confined to three-year-olds in 1959 it was won on three occasions by horses which had taken Classics earlier in the season: Two Thousand Guineas winners My Babu (1948) and Palestine (1950) and the One Thousand and Oaks winner Petite Etoile (1959). Other noteworthy winners of that period include the Queen's Landau (1954); Quorum (1957), second to Crepello in the Two Thousand Guineas and later to sire Red Rum; and Jim Joel's Major Portion (1958), second to Pall Mall in the Two Thousand.

In the 1960s the race went to the likes of Romulus (1962), Roan Rocket (1964), Reform (1967) and Petingo (1968), though after Petite Etoile in 1959 the Sussex Stakes did not fall to another Classic winner until One Thousand Guineas heroine Humble Duty in 1970. The following year the race went to one of the very greatest horses to take part in it when Brigadier Gerard (whose sire Queen's Hussar had won in 1963) beat Faraway Son by five lengths after leading throughout the race and drawing away from his rivals in the final quarter mile – the first time front-running tactics had been used on this outstanding horse. Other Two Thousand Guineas winners to take the Sussex Stakes since Brigadier Gerard were Carlo d'Alessio's pair Bolkonski and Wollow (1975 and 1976), and On The House in 1982 had won the One Thousand earlier in the season – too much earlier for some people's memories, for she started at 14–1 at Goodwood, and those who had faith in the old tenet that Classic form is always the best form were well rewarded.

But the Sussex Stakes is often an ideal contest for a horse whose supremacy does not truly become apparent until after the running of the early Classics, and in recent times several horses who failed to win at Newmarket have succeeded at Goodwood: Kris (1979), Posse (1980) and Chief Singer (1984) had all been second in the Two Thousand, and Sonic Lady (1986) third in the One Thousand. Warning (1988) was forced to miss the Two Thousand through injury yet proved himself in the top bracket in the Sussex Stakes, and Zilzal

Opposite: Zilzal (Walter Swinburn) scorches home in the 1989 Swettenham Stud Sussex Stakes.

(1989) did not set foot on a racecourse until more than three weeks after the running of the Classic but then developed into a miler of the highest class, coming to Goodwood unbeaten and storming clear of Green Line Express and Markofdistinction, with a below-par Warning well in arrears.

Warning's attempt to win the race as a four-year-old went against the statistical grain, for in only six of the thirty-one runnings between 1960 (the first year when four-year-olds could take part) and 1990 has it gone to an older horse – the six-year-old Noalcoholic in 1983 and the four-year-olds Le Levanstell (1961), Jimmy Reppin (1969), Ace Of Aces (1974), Rousillon (1985) and Distant Relative (1990). So the winner is likely to be a three-year-old. What other qualities might it have? Above all it will need the speed to stay handy in what is usually a fast-run race, and then the ability to quicken further towards the end of the race which is the hallmark of only top-class horses; it must also possess the balance required of any horse asked to tear along Goodwood's undulations and round its bends. The winner is likely to be a horse which has announced its class already, and it is no coincidence that ten of the twenty-one winners of the race between 1970 and 1990 have been favourite (in one case joint favourite), and that during the same period only three winners started at odds longer than 9–2.

Or, to put it another way: the Sussex Stakes is a top-class race and it takes a top-class horse to win it.

WINNERS SINCE 1970

1970 Humble Duty
D. Keith 11–8 (5 ran)

1971 Brigadier Gerard
J. Mercer 4–6 (5 ran)

1972 Sallust
J. Mercer 9–2 (3 ran)

1973 Thatch
L. Piggott 4–5 (7 ran)

1974 Ace of Aces
J. Lindley 8–1 (10 ran)

1975 Bolkonski
G. Dettori 1–2 (9 ran)

1986 Wollow
G. Dettori 10–11 (9 ran)

1977 Artaius
L. Piggott 6–4 (11 ran)

1978 Jaazeiro
L. Piggott 8–13 (6 ran)

1979 Kris
J. Mercer 4–5 (7 ran)

1980 Posse
Pat Eddery 8–13 (9 ran)

1981 King's Lake
Pat Eddery 5–2 (9 ran)

1982 On the House
J. Reid 14–1 (13 ran)

1983 Noalcoholic
G. Duffield 18–1 (11 ran)

1984 Chief Singer
R. Cochrane 4–7 (5 ran)

1985 Rousillon
G. Starkey 2–1 (10 ran)

1986 Sonic Lady
W. R. Swinburn 5–6 (12 ran)

1987 Soviet Star
G. Starkey 3–1 (7 ran)

1988 Warning
Pat Eddery 11–10 (9 ran)

1989 Zilzal
W. R. Swinburn 5–2 (8 ran)

1990 Distant Relative
W. Carson 4–1 (7 ran)

YORK AUGUST MEETING

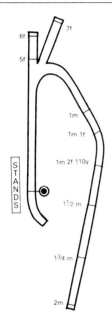

Course description on page 38.

The York August Meeting would be ringed in the calendar of anyone's racing year, for in terms of atmosphere and racing quality it can hardly be bettered in the whole Flat season. Shorn of the social complications which entangle Royal Ascot, the big York meeting can concentrate on the sport.

Each of the three days features a Group One race – the INTERNATIONAL STAKES (opposite) on Tuesday, the YORKSHIRE OAKS (pages 91–2) on Wednesday and the NUNTHORPE STAKES (pages 94–5) on Thursday, and the rest of the racing is of a very high order, with the EBOR HANDICAP (page 93) and several other Pattern races sustaining interest. The Group Two GREAT VOLTIGEUR STAKES for three-year-olds over a mile and a half was first run in 1950 and commemorates Voltigeur, whose match against The Flying Dutchman in 1851 was the most famous race ever run at York: Voltigeur went down by a length in front of a crowd of a hundred thousand people. The Great Voltigeur is a notable trial for the St Leger: Premonition (1953), Alcide (1958), St Paddy (1960), Hethersett (1962), Ragusa (1963), Indiana (1964), Athens Wood (1971), Bustino (1974) and Reference Point (1987) all won the York race en route to victory at Doncaster, while other famous winners are Arc heroes Alleged (1977) and Rainbow Quest (1984). The Group Two GIMCRACK STAKES for two-year-old colts and geldings over six furlongs is named after another famous horse, though ironically the diminutive grey Gimcrack was beaten on both his runs at York; the owner of the winner has the privilege of giving the main speech at the annual dinner of the Gimcrack Club in December, a task which fell to Paul Mellon in 1970 after his colt Mill Reef had cruised home by ten lengths in appalling going, since when only Nebbiolo (1976) has gone on to win an English Classic the following year. The Group Two LOWTHER STAKES is the fillies' equivalent race: it boasts many famous names among its winners over the last two decades, including Devon Ditty (1978), Mrs Penny (1979), Habibti (1982) and Al Bahathri (1984), though the last Lowther winner to go on and lift the One Thousand Guineas was Enstone Spark, winner in 1977 at 33–1 and at Newmarket the following spring at 35–1.

International Stakes

York: 1 mile 2½ furlongs

Group One: three-year-olds and upwards

Beforehand it all seemed so simple. The first running of the Benson and Hedges Gold Cup, on 15 August 1972, was a one-horse race, and that one horse was Brigadier Gerard, unbeaten in fifteen outings. In his most recent race he had for the first time attempted a trip of one and a half miles in the King George VI and Queen Elizabeth Stakes at Ascot, and had come through with his record intact (see page 81–2): the Benson and Hedges should be a doddle.

His four opponents did not seem to pose much of a problem. True, Roberto and Rheingold had engaged in that thrombotic finish in the Derby – Lester Piggott forcing Roberto home by a short head – but since then Roberto had been beaten in the Irish Derby, finishing well behind Steel Pulse, whom Brigadier Gerard had given five pounds more than weight-for-age and a five-length beating at Royal Ascot. Rheingold had enhanced his reputation by taking the Grand Prix de Saint-Cloud, and started second favourite in the Benson and Hedges: Brigadier Gerard was 3–1 on, with Rheingold at 7–2, Roberto at 12–1, Gold Rod (second to Brigadier Gerard in the Eclipse) at 33–1 and Bright Beam at 300–1. Were further evidence needed of the lack of confidence in Roberto, it was supplied by Lester Piggott's decision to desert the Derby winner in favour of Rheingold; Bill Williamson, who had lost the Derby ride to Piggott, was not available, so the Panamanian jockey Braulio Baeza was brought over from the USA for his first ride in Britain.

Roberto could not have started quicker had one of the stalls handlers clamped a firecracker under his tail, and he screeched off into a commanding lead. Before three furlongs were covered Gold Rod was being scrubbed along, and by the home turn Bright Beam was beating a retreat. Rheingold could make no impression, but Brigadier Gerard was keeping effortlessly in touch. Three furlongs to go, and Roberto, contrary to the script, was not stopping. Two furlongs out, and Joe Mercer on Brigadier Gerard drew his whip: well, it would be a hard-fought victory for the Brigadier rather than a canter. But Baeza and Roberto had other ideas, and a furlong out the unthinkable was happening. The Brigadier was beaten. Try as he might, he could not get to the Derby winner, who maintained his furious pace into the closing stages as Mercer dropped his hands and eased Brigadier Gerard. Roberto won by three lengths in course record time.

It was the Brigadier's only defeat in a career which consisted of eighteen races, and it set the tone for the history of the race which remained the Benson and Hedges Gold Cup until 1985: it became the Matchmaker International in 1986, the International Stakes in 1988 and then the Juddmonte International Stakes. Whatever its title, sensational defeat has never been far away. In the second running – 1973 – the odds-on Rheingold could only finish third behind 14–1 chance Moulton, a result which must have brought a particular satisfaction to Yves Saint-Martin: for Saint-Martin had been booked to ride Rheingold, only to be replaced by Piggott on the day of the race when Roberto, Piggott's intended mount, was withdrawn, at which point Piggott decided he would like to ride Moulton – until he was offered the ride on Rheingold! Order was restored in 1974 when Piggott rode the great filly Dahlia (15–8 on) to beat Imperial Prince and the Derby winner Snow Knight, but in 1975 sensation was back with a vengeance. Favourite at 9–4 on was Grundy, who just over three weeks earlier had prevailed in that famous race for the King George at Ascot (see page 82). But that epic struggle with Bustino had taken more out of Grundy than was realized at the time, and in the Benson and Hedges he could only trail in a dispirited fourth behind Dahlia, the first horse to win the race twice.

The fifth running (1976) went to the Two Thousand Guineas winner Wollow, with Trepan, who had beaten Wollow in the Eclipse only to have the race taken away from him after the result of the dope test became known, last. Another odds-on favourite was turned over in 1977 when Artaius was second to 33–1 outsider Relkino, and in 1978 Hawaiian Sound gained some recompense for narrow defeat by Shirley Heights in the Derby. In 1979 Troy won at 2–1 on to complete a notable sequence of Derby, Irish Derby, King George and Benson and Hedges.

In the 1980s upsets continued: in 1985 Oh So Sharp had won the One Thousand Guineas and Oaks before coming to York, where she started at 5–2 on and was thwarted by one of Lester Piggott's most brilliant rides on Commanche Run. Two years of comparative calm followed with victories for favourites Shardari and Triptych, then in 1988 Persian Heights beat Roberto's course record when finishing in front of Shady Heights and Indian Skimmer – only to have the race taken away from him for interfering with Indian Skimmer and given to Shady Heights. And in 1989 Cacoethes, fresh from nearly lowering the colours of Nashwan in the King George, started at 5–2 on but could not peg back his 16–1 stable companion Ile De Chypre.

That the International Stakes comes at an awkward time for horses who have been campaigned in the top middle-distance races through mid-summer may explain in part its habit of bringing about the downfall of odds-on favourites, but despite – or because of? – its catalogue of tales of the unexpected it remains one of the most absorbing contests of the racing year.

Yorkshire Oaks

York: 1½ miles

Group One: three-year-old fillies

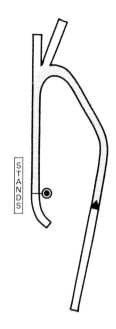

The Yorkshire Oaks is the third and last Group One race in Britain, after the two fillies' Classics, to be confined to three-year-old fillies. In its long and distinguished history – it was first run in 1849 – it has always attracted good-class fields, but since the end of the war has increased in status, so that in recent years it has become the natural target for fillies who have been campaigned in the Oaks at Epsom and its Irish equivalent at The Curragh.

The first filly in the post-war period to pull off the Epsom–York double was Frieze, who beat three opponents in 1952, and seven years later Petite Etoile followed suit when showing her customary turn of foot to go clear of just two rivals. Small but high-class fields remained the norm through the 1960s, when winners included West Side Story (1962: a short-head second to Monade in the Oaks), the 1964 Oaks winner Homeward Bound, and Mabel (1965: second to Long Look in

DEREK THOMPSON'S DAYS OF THE YEAR

It's the smell that gets to me first. As I arrive at the Knavesmire, the aroma from the Terry's chocolate factory near the racecourse sets off the annual anticipation of the York August Meeting. This fixture has the lot: one of the very best handicaps of the year, three Group One events and some of the most absorbing two-year-old races of the season. The York August Meeting is about enjoyment and relaxation, for nowhere in the racing year is the tone as laid-back as here. This is real Yorkshire hospitality – no frills – and the friendliness pervades the place from the moment you walk in.

For me York is the best racecourse in the world. The sport is top-class, the amenities are superb, and they don't fleece the punters. Best of all, it's so well arranged that even at the August Meeting you don't have to use your elbows to get around: there's room for everyone.

And of all the races on these magical three days I have a particularly soft spot for the International Stakes – and not only because way back in 1972, when I was previewing the inaugural running of the Benson and Hedges Gold Cup for Radio Four's Today *programme, I was the only racing journalist to suggest that the mighty Brigadier Gerard would get turned over by the Derby winner Roberto! He did, but the York crowd swallowed their disappointment and gave Roberto a great reception – typical of the sporting atmosphere of the occasion.*

The York August Meeting is simply the best. You can't say fairer than that.

the Oaks); and in 1970 Lupe came to York with a career record of three races, three wins, including the Oaks, and beat Highest Hopes and Christine without fuss.

Sometimes, though, the Yorkshire Oaks goes to a horse who has developed too slowly to be a serious contender at Epsom early in June but has matured sufficiently by mid-August to announce her class at York. Such a filly was Attica Meli, who was still a maiden halfway through her three-year-old season in 1972 but then came good in no uncertain fashion, winning the Yorkshire Oaks before going on to take the Park Hill Stakes at Doncaster and the Princess Royal Stakes at Ascot. Mysterious, winner of the One Thousand Guineas and the Oaks, won the Yorkshire Oaks in 1973, and the following year few begrudged Dibidale her victory, for at Epsom she had been one of the unluckiest Classic losers ever, Willie Carson's saddle slipping under her belly two furlongs out and the weight-cloth flying off in her wake: Carson rode her bareback into third place behind Polygamy, but she was of course disqualified as she had not carried the correct weight throughout the race. She received some compensation when winning the Irish Oaks at The Curragh, and in the Yorkshire Oaks scrambled home from Mil's Bomb.

May Hill, a daughter of the 1965 winner Mabel, had Oaks and Irish Oaks winner Juliette Marny back in third when winning in 1975, but three years later Fair Salinia, ridden by Greville Starkey, pulled off a remarkable treble. She had won the Oaks in a breathtaking finish with Dancing Maid, and had then been controversially awarded the Irish Guinness Oaks on the disqualification of Sorbus. Despite that record she started 5–1 third favourite at York, with Relfo – behind her at The Curragh – and Sorbus preferred in the betting, but Starkey pushed her into the lead at halfway and she would not be caught, coming home a length and a half clear of Sorbus to become the first filly to win the Oaks, the Irish Oaks and the Yorkshire Oaks. Shoot A Line in 1980 was another to go on from victory at The Curragh to win at York.

The 1981 running was won with a late surge by the Irish filly Condessa, but is also remembered for the horrific accident in which Silken Knot fell on the home turn and broke both forelegs, jockey Willie Carson sustaining injuries which kept him out of action for many months. The 1980s saw three more horses complete the Epsom–York double: Sun Princess (1983), who went on to win the St Leger; Circus Plume (1984); and Diminuendo (1988), who had also dead-heated in the Irish Oaks.

Classic form obviously has a great bearing on this race, but it does not necessarily work out: between 1975 and 1989 six horses won the Irish Oaks but were beaten at York – Juliette Marny (1975), Godetia (1979), Give Thanks (1983), Helen Street (1985), Colorspin (1986) and Alydaress (1989). Yet defeat at York does not always spell gloom: the Queen's Dunfermline, third in the Yorkshire Oaks after winning at Epsom, went on the following month to beat Alleged in the St Leger.

Ebor Handicap

York: 1¾ miles

Handicap: three-year-olds and upwards

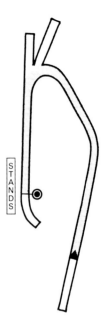

That the York August Meeting is sometimes popularly known as the 'Ebor Meeting' reflects the importance of the great handicap whose title reflects the Roman name for the city – Eboracum. For many the race is still the centrepiece of the three days and often proves the best-class Flat handicap of the year.

The Ebor was first run in 1843, and soon boasted some notable winners: The Hero (1849) had twice won the Ascot Gold Cup – or Emperor's Plate, as it was known at that period; Nancy (1851) had won the Chester Cup and Goodwood Cup; Lily Agnes (1875), who won twenty-one races, was the dam of Ormonde; and Isonomy (1879) had won the Ascot Gold Cup earlier in the season and would win it again in 1880. Brown Jack won the race in 1931 carrying nine stone five pounds.

In more recent memory the Ebor's greatest performance was perhaps that of the Vincent O'Brien-trained mare Gladness, who in 1958 carried nine stone seven pounds to a six-length victory; before York she had won the Ascot Gold Cup and the Goodwood Cup, and the following year finished second to Alcide in the King George VI and Queen Elizabeth Stakes. Or perhaps it was in 1979, when the extraordinary Sea Pigeon at the age of nine beat Gladness's weight-carrying record when lugging ten stone to a short-head verdict over Donegal Prince, to whom he conceded forty pounds. Sea Pigeon's two victories in the Champion Hurdle were still ahead of him then, though he had finished second to Monskfield at Cheltenham in 1978 and 1979. Other notable Ebor winners in the last two decades include Sir Montagu, who in 1976 won by eight lengths from future Cheltenham Gold Cup winner Alverton and went on to win the Prix Royal Oak (the French St Leger); Protection Racket (1981) who proceeded to win the Doncaster Cup and the Irish St Leger; Jupiter Island, who won the Ebor as a four-year-old in 1983 and three years later capped a wonderfully consistent career with victory in the Japan Cup (see page 183); Crazy (1984), who the next month finished fourth to Commanche Run in the St Leger; the unbeaten Kneller (1988), who subsequently won the Doncaster Cup and the Jockey Club Cup before having to be put down; and Sapience (1989), second to Michelozzo in the St Leger.

WINNERS SINCE 1980

1980 Shaftesbury
  G. Starkey 12–1 (16 ran)

1981 Protection Racket
  M. Birch 15–2 (22 ran)

1982 Another Sam
  B. Rouse 16–1 (15 ran)

1983 Jupiter Island
  L. Piggott 9–1 (16 ran)

1984 Crazy
  W. R. Swinburn 10–1 (14 ran)

1985 Western Dancer
  P. Cook 20–1 (19 ran)

1986 Primary
  G. Starkey 6–1 (22 ran)

1987 Daarkom
  M. Roberts 13–2 (15 ran)

1988 Kneller
  Paul Eddery 9–1 (21 ran)

1989 Sapience
  Pat Eddery 15–2 (18 ran)

1990 Further Flight
  M. Hills 7–1 (22 ran)

Nunthorpe Stakes

York: 5 furlongs

Group One: two-year-olds and upwards

Nunthorpe is a village some fifty miles north of York. Although there was a Nunthorpe Selling Stakes run at York from 1903 to 1921, the Nunthorpe Stakes as we know it today was first staged in 1922. (We had to call the race the William Hill Sprint Championship from 1976 to 1989 before it reverted to its original title with new sponsorship from the Keeneland Association in Kentucky.) Its status was raised from Group Two to Group One in 1984 in recognition of the high quality of sprinter which it regularly attracts, and it is now firmly established with the July Cup (pages 78–9) and the Ladbroke Sprint Cup (pages 96–7) as one of the three peaks of the British racing year for sprinters. It is the only Group One race in Britain over five furlongs, and (like the Ladbroke) is an opportunity for speedy two-year-olds to take on their elders.

The quality of the race was set early on in its life, for the third running in 1924 went to Mumtaz Mahal, one of the fastest horses ever seen in England. She won the Nunthorpe by six lengths, and was then retired: at stud her idiosyncrasies included an aversion to bullocks, whom she would chase if they were put in the paddock with her. Highborn II in 1926 and 1927 was the first horse to win the race twice, followed from 1928 to 1930 by Tag End, one of only two horses to score three times.

Soon after the Second World War the Nunthorpe fell to another of the century's great sprinters, Abernant, who won in 1949 and 1950. Beaten a short head by Nimbus in the Two Thousand Guineas of 1949 (the first time the photo-finish was used to determine the result of an English Classic), Abernant reverted to sprint distances and won the King's Stand Stakes, the July Cup and the King George Stakes before starting at 11–2 on at York against three opponents and striding in by three lengths. In 1950 he was beaten by Tangle in the King's Stand but won the King George Stakes by five lengths before making all the running to beat two rivals once more in the Nunthorpe at odds of 100–7 on. He did not run again, and was sorely missed from the sprinting scene, for unlike many of the Turf's speed merchants Abernant was a real character. Gordon Richards recalled him at the start of his first Nunthorpe:

He was a great favourite of mine, a horse of pronounced personality with a character quite unlike any other sprinter I have ever ridden. He was a kind horse, absolutely placid although he took a great interest in all that was going on around him. He would canter quietly down to the

Opposite: Last Tycoon, ridden by Yves Saint-Martin, wins the William Hill Sprint Championship in 1986.

start, and then when he got to the other side of the gate he would give a great big sigh, prop himself lazily on three legs, and have a look round at everything and everybody. One day at York, three or four kids were on their knees, playing on the ground quite near the start. Abernant had propped himself up as usual, but he suddenly saw the children and he started to stare at them. He kept on staring at them, and I could not make out what was the matter. But soon he made his thoughts quite clear: he began to scrape his foot on the ground. I am prepared to swear that all he wanted to do was to get down and play with those kids. He was just like a big, faithful old dog.

Since then most of the top sprinters have won the Nunthorpe, though no horse since Ennis in 1956 has won as a two-year-old. Royal Serenade in 1951 and 1952 and Right Boy in 1958 and 1959 were further dual winners, and during the 1960s the race went to such as Floribunda (1961), Polyfoto (1965), So Blessed (1968) and Tower Walk (1969). Lochnager in 1976 became the first horse since Abernant in 1949 to win the big York sprint after taking the King's Stand and July Cup – though he won not the Nunthorpe Stakes but the William Hill Sprint Championship: bookmakers William Hill had wanted to stage a new £30,000 sprint at the York August Meeting in 1976 but their request was turned down by the Jockey Club, who allowed the company instead to give £20,000 towards the Nunthorpe (making the race the most valuable all-aged sprint run that year in Britain) and do away with its name. Under its William Hill banner the race added many familiar names to its list of winners, including Solinus (1978) and Never So Bold (1985) – who both followed Lochnager in adding the York race to the King's Stand and the July Cup – and Sharpo, whose victories in 1980, 1981 and 1982 made him the only horse apart from Tag End to win thrice. These were all great sprinters, as were Habibti (1983) and Last Tycoon (1986).

With the demotion of the King's Stand Stakes to Group Two and the raising of the Ladbroke Sprint Cup to Group One and with all eyes then on the Prix de l'Abbaye, the York race is no longer the culmination of the sprinting year but an important step along the way. And like all the great sprints, it demands of its participants that most glorious attribute of the racehorse, never better illustrated than by Dayjur's record-breaking victory in 1990 – speed.

WINNERS SINCE 1970

1970 Huntercombe
  A. Barclay 6–4 (3 ran)

1971 Swing Easy
  L. Piggott 2–1 (9 ran)

1972 Deep Diver
  W. Williamson 100–30 (7 ran)

1973 Sandford Lad
  A. Murray 4–1 (8 ran)

1974 Blue Cashmere
  E. Hide 18–1 (12 ran)

1975 Bay Express
  W. Carson 100–30 (10 ran)

1976 Lochnager
  E. Hide 4–5 (11 ran)

1977 Haveroid
  E. Hide 10–1 (8 ran)

1978 Solinus
  L. Piggott 1–2 (9 ran)

1979 Ahonoora
  G. Starkey 3–1 (10 ran)

1980 Sharpo
  Pat Eddery 3–1 (11 ran)

1981 Sharpo
  Pat Eddery 14–1 (9 ran)

1982 Sharpo
  S. Cauthen evens (11 ran)

1983 Habibti
  W. Carson 13–8 (10 ran)

1984 Committed
  B. Thomson 5–1 (8 ran)

1985 Never So Bold
  S. Cauthen 4–6 (7 ran)

1986 Last Tycoon
  Y. Saint-Martin 7–2 (8 ran)

1987 Ajdal
  W. R. Swinburn 2–1 (11 ran)

1988 Handsome Sailor
  M. Hills 5–2 (12 ran)

1989 Cadeaux Genereux
  Pat Eddery 11–10 (11 ran)

1990 Dayjur
  W. Carson 8–11 (9 ran)

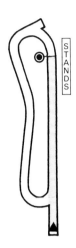

The Haydock Park straight six furlongs is flat, wide and completely fair, though in testing conditions there is some advantage of sticking to the stands rails, so high numbers in the draw may benefit.

Ladbroke Sprint Cup

Haydock Park: 6 furlongs

Group One: two-year-olds and upwards

The early years of what is now the Ladbroke Sprint Cup belong to Peter O'Sullevan's wonderful sprinter Be Friendly. He won the first running of the Vernons November Sprint Cup – sponsored by the pools company – on 5 November 1966 to bring his owner an experience that, as described in O'Sullevan's *Calling the Horses*, seemed 'an extravagant dream':

> The dream contained such improbable ingredients as a fine and exuberantly athletic two-year-old named Be Friendly, carrying my undistinguished black and yellow colours, ridden by an apprentice who could not claim his allowance, striding clear of the season's acknowledged top senior sprinters inside the final furlong – according to my BBC TV commentary – to win the richest all-aged race ever staged in Britain by a comfortable two lengths and to receive a generous ovation in the process. The dream further included such unlikely embellishment as Be Friendly at 15–2 (10–1 to early customers) landing the O'Sullevan nap and becoming the middle leg of a 57–1 *Daily Express* treble completed by another swift-rising young star, Persian War, at Sandown where the gallant Freddie won the Gallaher Gold Cup.

It was no dream. At that time the race was run on the old six-furlong course at Haydock, where the race started on a chute off the round course and the runners had to negotiate a sharp turn into the straight. But the apprentice jockey Colin Williams on the two-year-old Be Friendly reaped the benefit of walking the course before racing and went for the better ground up the stands rail to score from Green Park and Dondeen. The following year Be Friendly, who had meanwhile won the King's Stand Stakes and the Ayr Gold Cup, was back for another crack. Ridden this time by his usual partner Scobie Breasley, Be Friendly prevailed by a neck after a thrilling tussle with Mountain Call. In that period the Vernons was run on the final day of the Flat season, and the 1968 running promised to be a very special occasion, for not only was Be Friendly – who had recently won the Prix de l'Abbaye at Longchamp – going for a third win, the race would take place on the last day of Scobie Breasley's distinguished riding career. But the weather intervened: fog descended on Haydock Park, and the race could not be run.

During the 1970s the Vernons Sprint Cup was moved from November to September to bring it into a more central position in the pattern of the major sprint races, and was taken by several familiar names: the French-trained filly Lianga won in 1975 from the gigantic Roman Warrior; Lady Beaverbrook's popular gelding Boldboy took the 1977 running at the age of seven; the grey Absalom started at 20–1 in 1978 and beat Sanedtki and Vaigly Great; and the following year Double Form beat Ahonoora and Devon Ditty – giving Geoff Lewis his final riding victory in Britain – and then went on to win the Prix de l'Abbaye. The three-year-old Moorestyle, ridden by Lester Piggott, maintained the quality in 1980, with Habibti taking the 1983 running, Green Desert the 1986, and Ajdal the 1987 race. These were horses of the highest class, and it came as no surprise when in 1988, following the installation of a straight six-furlong course at Haydock, the race was upgraded to Group One. That first Group One running – won by Khalid Abdullah's Dowsing – was the last under Vernons' sponsorship, and when Danehill took the 1989 race in the same colours the race had found a new sponsor and become the Ladbroke Sprint Cup.

The only Group One race run at Haydock Park, the Ladbroke Sprint Cup does not yet enjoy the status of the other top sprint races such as the July Cup (pages 78–9) or the Nunthorpe Stakes (pages 94–5). But with its promotion to Group One status it is guaranteed to fill an important position between the York race and the Prix de l'Abbaye and consolidate its place as one of the cornerstones of the European sprinting year.

WINNERS SINCE 1970
1970 Golden Orange *J. Lindley* 10–1 (5 ran)
1971 Green God *L. Piggott* 7–4 (7 ran)
1972 Abergwaun *L. Piggott* 11–10 (10 ran)
1973 The Blues *R. Marshall* 10–1 (8 ran)
1974 Princely Son *J. Seagrave* 8–1 (11 ran)
1975 Lianga *Y. Saint-Martin* 2–1 (7 ran)
1976 Record Token *Pat Eddery* 3–1 (8 ran)
1977 Boldboy *W. Carson* evens (7 ran)
1978 Absalom *M. Thomas* 20–1 (14 ran)
1979 Double Form *G. Lewis* 11–4 (8 ran)
1980 Moorestyle *L. Piggott* 8–13 (8 ran)
1981 Runnett *B. Raymond* 6–1 (6 ran)
1982 Indian King *G. Starkey* 3–1 (9 ran)
1983 Habibti *W. Carson* 8–13 (6 ran)
1984 Petong *B. Raymond* 11–1 (9 ran)
1985 Orojoya *B. Thomson* 11–1 (8 ran)
1986 Green Desert *W. R. Swinburn* 5–4 (8 ran)
1987 Ajdal *W. R. Swinburn* 8–11 (8 ran)
1988 Dowsing *Pat Eddery* 15–2 (10 ran)
1989 Danehill *Pat Eddery* 3–1 (9 ran)

The 1986 Vernons Sprint Cup: Green Desert (*left*) beats Hallgate by a neck.

DONCASTER SEPTEMBER MEETING

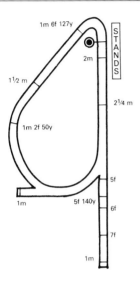

Doncaster is one of the fairest Flat tracks in the country, its gradual sweeping turn and long wide straight favouring the long-striding horse with plenty of stamina. It is practically flat, apart from a slight rise and fall on the far side.

Dominated by the running of the final Classic of the year, the ST LEGER (pages 100–3), the Doncaster September Meeting has about it an air of the Flat season about to commence its descent, though there are two more months of the season to go and plenty of big races still to be run.

Maybe the St Leger Meeting (as it is popularly known) is not what it once was, but the funfair still appears on Town Moor and after years of having its back to the wall the Classic itself has regained some of its status – though it could have done without the shenanigans of 1989. And the four days of the meeting provide a feast of Flat racing matched in the North only by York's August fixture. The PARK HILL STAKES is a Group Two race for three-year-old fillies over the full St Leger distance of 1 mile 6 furlongs and 127 yards. Named after the home of Colonel Anthony St Leger, it was first run in 1839 and has gone to some notable fillies, including the 1975 winner May Hill, who has a race at the meeting named in her honour: the MAY HILL STAKES is a Group Three race over one mile for two-year-old fillies, and boasts Nashwan's dam Height Of Fashion (1981, the inaugural running) and the dual Classic heroine Midway Lady (1985) among its winners. More of a betting proposition is the highly competitive PORTLAND HANDICAP (5 furlongs, 140 yards).

The Group Three DONCASTER CUP (two and a quarter miles) is the third leg of what is informally known as the Stayers' Triple Crown (the other legs being the Ascot Gold Cup and the Goodwood Cup), pulled off in recent years by Le Moss (1979 and 1980) and Longboat (1986), while the seven-furlong KIVETON PARK STAKES was upgraded from Listed status to Group Three in 1986. The CHAMPAGNE STAKES (see opposite) has a long and distinguished history, and the five-furlong FLYING CHILDERS STAKES for two-year-olds commemorates a horse foaled in 1714 and agreed by most historians to be the first truly great racehorse, though he ran only twice: the race was downgraded from Group One to Group Two in 1979 but has been won since then by several top-class horses, including Marwell (1980), Superlative (1983) and Green Desert (1985).

Champagne Stakes

Doncaster: 7 furlongs

Group Two: two-year-old colts and geldings

The Champagne Stakes dates back to 1823 and has long been one of the best two-year-old races of the year. Rock Sand won in 1902 and landed the Triple Crown the following year. Pretty Polly beat five opponents – including the next year's Derby winner St Amant – in 1903: she went off the 11–10 favourite, the last time she started at odds against. The 1912 race went to Craganour, who the following June ensured an unwelcome place for himself in Turf history when disqualified from first place in the Derby after his bumping match with Aboyeur.

The day before that notorious Derby there had run at Epsom a two-year-old of phenomenal speed and extraordinary colour – grey with white splodges all over. This was The Tetrarch, who blazed through the 1913 season like a meteor: nicknamed 'The Rocking Horse' and then 'The Spotted Wonder', he came to Doncaster for the Champagne Stakes unbeaten in six races, and slaughtered his two opponents. The intention to run him again that season was baulked when he rapped a fetlock joint in a gallop, and the planned three-year-old campaign was scrapped in spring 1914 when the injury recurred, so the Champagne Stakes proved to be his last race. As a stallion one of his more awkward quirks was a distinct indifference to sex, problematic for one in such a calling: he sired only 130 foals during his stud career in County Kildare before settling down to a quieter life being ridden down to the post office to mail the letters.

But two of The Tetrarch's limited offspring made their mark on the Champagne Stakes. In 1919 his colt Tetratema won, and the following spring took the Two Thousand Guineas; Tetratema's daughter Myrobella won in 1932. And in 1923 the Champagne Stakes fell to The Tetrarch's brilliant daughter Mumtaz Mahal.

Two winners from the inter-war period went on to take the Derby: Coronach (1925) and Mahmoud (1936). Since the Second World War that feat has been repeated only by Grundy (1974), though My Babu (1947, when he was known as Lerins), Palestine (1949), Darius (1953), Our Babu (1954), Wollow (1975) and Don't Forget Me (1986) all won the Two Thousand Guineas the following year.

But perhaps the greatest performance in the race in recent memory came from a horse who did not run again in England. In 1976 J. O. Tobin, ridden by Lester Piggott, turned in a stunning display to beat Durtal by four lengths. On his next outing he was beaten by Blushing Groom in France and subsequently raced in the USA, where he was the first horse to defeat the Triple Crown winner Seattle Slew.

WINNERS SINCE 1980

1980 Gielgud
   J. Mercer 11–2 (10 ran)

1981 Achieved
   Pat Eddery 11–4 (8 ran)

1982 Gorytus
   W. Carson 8–13 (5 ran)

1983 Lear Fan
   A. Clark 1–4 (4 ran)

1984 Young Runaway
   G. Starkey 5–2 (6 ran)

1985 Sure Blade
   B. Thomson 5–4 (5 ran)

1986 Don't Forget Me
   Pat Eddery 6–1 (9 ran)

1987 Warning
   Pat Eddery evens (4 ran)

1988 Prince Of Dance
   W. Carson 1–2 (7 ran)

1989 abandoned – course unsafe

St Leger

Doncaster: 1 mile 6 furlongs 127 yards

Group One: three-year-old colts and fillies

What are we to make these days of the traditional notion of the St Leger forming the culmination of a Classic programme which identifies the best three-year-old? In so many years it is patently not the case. Take the 1980s: in 1989 Nashwan sidestepped the St Leger, when the Triple Crown was there for the taking, in order to go for a supposedly easier preliminary race for the Prix de l'Arc de Triomphe; in 1986 Dancing Brave's participation was never seriously considered. True, Reference Point in 1987 became the first horse since Nijinsky to win the St Leger after having taken the Derby and the King George VI and Queen Elizabeth Stakes, but he was the first Derby winner to attempt the Doncaster race since Shergar in 1981 (who had finished a deflated fourth and did not run again). In the twenty runnings of the final Classic between 1970 and 1989 only three winners of the Derby at Epsom have run in the Doncaster race: so how can it be said to throw up the best?

On the other hand, the 1980s saw the St Leger drag itself out of the doldrums into which it had sunk to such an extent that calls were heard in some quarters for it to be opened up to older horses and thus made a more competitive and interesting race – a temptation to which the Irish equivalent succumbed. The middle of the decade saw the Oaks winner Sun Princess bravely thwart Esprit du Nord and Carlingford Castle (second to Teenoso in the Derby) in 1983; Commanche Run provide Lester Piggott with his record-breaking twenty-eighth Classic victory in 1984; and Oh So Sharp add a third Classic to her One Thousand Guineas and Oaks triumphs in 1985. Two years later it was Reference Point, and then in 1988 another Oaks winner narrowly failed when Diminuendo went down by a length to Minster Son after a stirring battle. Then just when it seemed safe for the St Leger to hold its head its head up again came the problems of 1989. On the first day of the meeting three horses fell in the closing stages of the Portland Handicap, and when on the Friday a two-year-old came down at approximately the same point on the course, subsidence of the turf was discovered and the track declared unfit for racing; the rest of the meeting was abandoned and the St Leger run the following week at Ayr (the first time a Classic had been run north of the border). It was one of the most awkward moments in the history of the race.

That history stretches back to 1776. The St Leger is the oldest of the Classics, three years the senior of the Oaks and four years older than the Derby, and owes its existence to Colonel Anthony St Leger, a noted soldier (and later Governor of Saint Lucia) who lived at Park Hill, near Doncaster. He had become intrigued by the running of races for three-year-olds – something of a novelty in the mid-eighteenth century – and came to the opinion that a two-mile race for three-year-old colts and fillies would provide competitive sport. The race of St Leger's devising was first run on 24 September 1776 on Cantley Common, near the present site of the Doncaster racecourse, Town Moor. Six horses ran; the winner of the unnamed race was an unnamed filly owned by Lord Rockingham, subsequently given the name Alabaculia (which has been spelt in several different ways since). A year later the race – still without a title – took place again, after which it was decided that the contest should bear the name of the man who had dreamt it up, and in 1778 it was run as the St Leger. That year the race was moved from Cantley Common to the Town Moor, where it has since remained, except when forced to move through unanticipated circumstances such as subsidence (1989) or war (1915–18, 1940–5). It took place at Newmarket from 1915 to 1918, Thirsk in 1940, Manchester in 1941, Newmarket again between 1942 and 1944 and York in 1945; the 1939 running was cancelled due to the outbreak of hostilities. It continued to be run over two miles until 1813; its distance was then reduced to one mile, six furlongs, 193 yards, and then to one mile, six furlongs, 132 yards in 1826. Another five yards were lopped off the trip in 1969.

In its very early years the St Leger remained something of a curiosity, and it was not until Champion in 1800 became the first Derby winner to take the race that it caught the national attention. As the Classic pattern began to evolve through the early nineteenth century, following the foundation of the Two Thousand Guineas in 1809 and the One Thousand in 1814, the St Leger became a race of the first importance, and the ideal of the three-year-old Thorough-bred as a horse who would have the speed to win over one mile at Newmarket in the spring, the agility and increasing stamina to go on to one and a half miles at Epsom in early summer and then the more extreme staying power to win at Doncaster over a distance in excess of one and three-quarter miles in the autumn was established.

The St Leger had become one of the key moments of the racing year, and in the latter half of the nineteenth century was won by most of the great horses of the time: the first Triple Crown winner West Australian (1853); Blair Athol (1864); Gladiateur (1865); Formosa (1868); Hannah (1871); Apology, the filly whose third Classic victory in 1874 supposedly set off cheering which could be heard at York Minster; Iroquois (1881); Ormonde (1886), the last of Fred Archer's six wins in the race; La Fleche (1892); Isinglass (1893); and Persimmon (1896). The last-named was owned by the Prince of Wales, who won again with Diamond Jubilee in 1900. Two years after that Sceptre beat Rising Glass by three lengths to become the only horse ever to win four Classics outright. Then it was Rock Sand, Triple Crown winner in 1903, and the following year Pretty Polly came to Doncaster unbeaten in twelve races and, starting at 5–2 on, won with ease. Two days later she took the Park Hill Stakes at 25–1 on. Between the wars the race went to Derby winners Coronach (1926), Trigo (1929), Hyperion (1933) and Windsor Lad (1934) as

> The St Leger was first sponsored in 1984, by Holsten Pils – who in 1989 announced that this support would not continue beyond that year's running. In the event the removal of the 1989 race to Ayr caused the premature withdrawal of the sponsorship.

well as the One Thousand Guineas heroine Tranquil (1923) and Triple Crown winner Bahram (1935).

After the Second World War, Airborne (1946), Tulyar (1952), Never Say Die (1954) and St Paddy (1960) went on from victory in the Derby to win at Doncaster and Meld added the St Leger to the One Thousand Guineas and Oaks in 1955 before Nijinsky, starting at 7–2 on in 1970, became the latest horse to land the Triple Crown. But by the time of Nijinsky's victory the emphasis of the race had changed, and his participation was an example of this shift in attitude: his running at Doncaster was not simply to prove him the complete three-year-old racehorse, it was also a preparation race for the Prix de l'Arc de Triomphe at Longchamp three weeks later, the highlight of the European racing year whose growth in status had caused that of the St Leger to decline. Nijinsky's failure in Paris led to some heart-searching as far as the Doncaster Classic was concerned: was it too demanding a race too close to the Arc? The three runnings of the St Leger after Nijinsky's triumph each went to a horse significantly remote from the highest class: Athens Wood (1971), Boucher (1972) – and Peleid (1973), who in his previous run had finished fourth in the Ebor Handicap and was a 28–1 outsider in the Classic. But class reasserted itself with Bustino in 1974, Bruni in 1975 and Crow in 1976.

Things got even better when the 1977 running produced one of the greatest races of recent memory. Favourite at 7–4 on was Alleged, trained by Vincent O'Brien and ridden by Lester Piggott and fresh from a contemptuously easy victory in the Great Voltigeur Stakes at

York. Alleged was simply tuning up for the Arc, but he had reckoned without the Queen's Oaks winner Dunfermline. After a hard-fought victory at Epsom Dunfermline had managed only third in a slowly run Yorkshire Oaks, and was an easy-to-back 10–1 chance in the St Leger. But under an inspired ride from Willie Carson she battled with Alleged up the Doncaster straight and worried the Irish challenger out of it close home to score a vastly popular Royal victory by one and a half lengths. (Alleged went on to win the Arc, and then repeated the feat in 1978.) It was a marvellous race, and proved that the St Leger could still produce the goods.

But how often can it do so? The shape of European racing has shifted, and the St Leger is just one more important race on the way to the rich pickings at Longchamp – and, latterly, beyond, in the Breeders' Cup races in the USA. Furthermore, the demands of the breeding industry militate against the St Leger, for the drive continues towards producing horses to compete at the middle distances of ten and twelve furlongs, and the sort of staying blood which the traditional type of St Leger winner will pass on is deemed far from desirable. The race will still sometimes go to a top-class horse, but for many it is too difficult a distraction at a time of the year when the Thoroughbred's programme is being geared towards future events which will prove more eye-catching for potential breeders: Reference Point is the only St Leger winner to have been declared the top three-year-old since the International Classifications were introduced in 1977. The St Leger still has an important role in the racing year, but its pre-eminence belongs in the past.

HOW THEY RATE
Nijinsky *144*
Bruni *138*
Bustino *137*
Boucher *134*
Crow *130*
Cut Above *130*
Dunfermline *130*
Oh So Sharp *130*
Athens Wood *129*
Sun Princess *129*
Julio Mariner *127*
Light Cavalry *127*
Son Of Love *126*
Touching Wood *126*
Commanche Run *125*
Minster Son *125*
Moon Madness *125*
Peleid *125*
Michelozzo *123*
Reference Point *123*

Reference Point (Steve Cauthen) wins the 1987 Holsten Pils St Leger.

Ayr Gold Cup

Ayr: 6 furlongs

Handicap: three-year-olds and upwards

The Ayr Gold Cup provides one of the most prestigious prizes a sprint handicapper can gain.

It was not always thus. The date usually given for the founding of the race is 1804, but the Gold Cup that year was competed for in two heats of two miles each, and the runners had to be bred and trained in Scotland. The first running went to Chancellor (who later in the afternoon finished second in a race run in four heats of four miles each); he won again in 1805, after which the practice of running the race in heats was dropped, though the distance remained at two miles. It was not until 1855 that the Ayr Gold Cup became a handicap, and in 1872 Fred Archer made his first visit to the course, winning the Gold Cup on Alaric. In those days the Ayr racecourse was situated at Bellisle, with a circuit as small and tight as Chester. The course moved to its present site in 1907, and the following year the Gold Cup was run for the first time over its current distance of six furlongs.

Nowadays it is highly unlikely that the Ayr Gold Cup field will contain a high-class sprinter, but in the last thirty years four notable horses have won the race.

Be Friendly, whose exploits in the Vernons Sprint Cup are described on page 96, came to Ayr in 1967 an improving three-year-old who earlier in the season had won the Two Thousand Guineas Trial at Kempton Park and the King's Stand Stakes at Royal Ascot. In the Gold Cup – one of thirty-three runners, the biggest field in the history of the race – he carried eight stone nine pounds and started at 100–8, with Forlorn River, winner of the July Cup and Nunthorpe Stakes, favourite at 7–1. Ridden by Geoff Lewis, Be Friendly cruised in by two lengths from Go Shell and Relian.

In 1973 Blue Cashmere, a three-year-old trained by Michael Stoute, carried eight stone two and drew clear of Parbleu to win by three lengths. The following year he won the Nunthorpe Stakes at York and the Temple Stakes at Sandown Park.

The 1975 field included some very good horses indeed. The favourite was the three-year-old Lochnager, who developed the following year into the best sprinter in Europe, and his opponents included the Stewards' Cup winner Import and Roman Warrior. Trained at Ayr by Nigel Angus, the four-year-old Roman Warrior was an enormous horse, but he would need all his strength to carry successfully the crushing burden of ten stone. In the closing stages Import was racing up the stands rails as Roman Warrior gradually got the better of Lochnager on the far side. Separated by the width of the

The straight six furlongs at Ayr is wide and relatively flat.

White-faced Roman Warrior (Johnny Seagrave) heads Lochnager (third) in the 1975 Ayr Gold Cup.

course, Import and Roman Warrior hammered through the final hundred yards, and at the line it was impossible to tell which had won. The photograph showed that Roman Warrior had got home by a short head, setting a record for the highest weight carried to victory in the race. But this heroic effort left no scar, for six days later Roman Warrior dead-heated with Swingtime in the Diadem Stakes at Ascot.

Three years later came another remarkable weight-carrying performance when the three-year-old Vaigly Great started 5–1 favourite and hardly came under pressure to win, ears pricked, under nine stone six pounds. Later that year he ran third to Absalom and Sanedtki in the Vernons.

The presence of such horses may be rare, but the qualities which make the Ayr Gold Cup the highlight of the course's Western Meeting – and thus the peak of the Flat season in Scotland – are to be found elsewhere: in the intense fascination of a huge field of closely handicapped sprinters and the sheer excitement of a race which usually produces a very closely fought finish.

WINNERS SINCE 1980

1980 Sparkling Boy
  J. Lowe 15–1 (24 ran)

1981 First Movement
  M. Miller 14–1 (21 ran)

1982 Famous Star
  Paul Eddery 13–2 (14 ran)

1983 Polly's Brother
  K. Hodgson 11–1 (28 ran)

1984 Able Albert
  M. Birch 9–1 (29 ran)

1985 Camps Heath
  W. Woods 14–1 (25 ran)

1986 Green Ruby
  J. Williams 25–1 (29 ran)

1987 Not So Silly
  G. Bardwell 12–1 (29 ran)

1988 So Careful
  N. Carlisle 33–1 (29 ran)

1989 Joveworth
  J. Fortune 50–1 (29 ran)

ASCOT SEPTEMBER MEETING

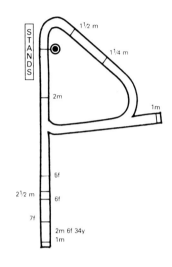

Course description on page 62.

The three days of Ascot's September Meeting have three very different moods, each to be relished. Thursday is a day for the purists to reflect and to look forward. The CUMBERLAND LODGE STAKES, a Group Three contest for three-year-olds and upwards over one and a half miles, is often used as a prep race for the Arc or an outing for a late-developing three-year-old whose true ability has not yet become apparent. The GORDON CARTER HANDICAP (two miles) is an excellent Cesarewitch preparation (Double Dutch won in 1989 and then went on to take the Newmarket marathon) and the BLUE SEAL STAKES is a fascinating race for two-year-old fillies who have not run before the beginning of September, and often pinpoints a future Classic filly – spectacularly so in the case of Noblesse (1962), who won the Oaks the following year by ten lengths.

The Friday is Ascot's annual charity day, when a good programme of racing is complemented by various other activities bent on raising money for a nominated charity. A special event on the 1989 card was the Shadwell Estates Private Sweepstakes, which pitched three ex-jockeys from the BBC TV racing team (Jimmy Lindley, Bill Smith and Richard Pitman) against three from Channel Four (John Oaksey, John Francome and Brough Scott; John McCririck could not do the weight). Sheikh Hamdan Al-Maktoum provided all six runners and a substantial donation to the Mental Health Foundation and the Ex-Services Mental Welfare Society, and the race produced one of the finest finishes of the day, Jimmy Lindley on Wabil short-heading Bill Smith on Polemos. John Oaksey (whose unorthodox means of travel to the paddock is illustrated in the colour section) was third on Hateel.

Saturday is the Festival of British Racing, an annual showcase of the sport and a day unique in the year in staging two Group One races – the QUEEN ELIZABETH II STAKES (pages 107–8) and the FILLIES' MILE (pages 109–10). It also has the Group Two ROYAL LODGE STAKES (page 111) and the Group Three DIADEM STAKES, a six-furlong sprint for three-year-olds and upwards. If the Thursday is for quiet appreciation and the Friday for digging deep into the pocket for charity, the Saturday is for celebration of the best of British racing.

Queen Elizabeth II Stakes

Ascot: 1 mile

Group One: three-year-olds and upwards

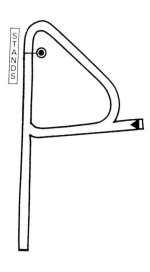

First run in 1955, when 9–4 favourite Hafiz II, trained in France by Alec Head and ridden by Roger Poincelet, beat seven opponents, the Queen Elizabeth II Stakes has ever since been one of the most important one-mile races of the year. The first three runnings went to France, with Cigalon in 1956 and Midget II following in the hoofprints of Hafiz; in 1958 the home team at last notched up a win with Major Portion, winner of the St James's Palace Stakes and the Sussex Stakes, coming home by a head from Babur.

Through the 1960s the status of the race was upheld, and the list of winners includes great milers such as Romulus (1962) and the Paddy Prendergast-trained Linacre, who beat Derring-Do in 1964. Derring-Do gained consolation by winning in 1965. The 1966 race went to Hill Rise, then trained by Noel Murless after a distinguished career in the USA which had seen him win twelve races and finish a narrow second to Northern Dancer in the Kentucky Derby, and the 1967 to that fine miler Reform.

In the early 1970s the Queen Elizabeth II Stakes went twice to Brigadier Gerard. As a three-year-old in 1971 he faced just two opponents and won as an 11–2 on chance should, striding home hard held by eight lengths. A year later Brigadier Gerard returned in need of rehabilitation after his reputation had been somewhat dented by the defeat by Roberto at York (see page 89). Had he gone off the boil, or over the top? Only emphatic victory would satisfy Brigadier Gerard's legion of fans, and he did not disappoint them, scything down Sparkler with a furlong to run and finishing six lengths clear in course record time. It was one of his very best performances.

A pulsating finish to the 1980 Queen Elizabeth II Stakes: Known Fact (*near side*) just gets the better of Kris.

In 1974 the course was waterlogged and the race abandoned, but the next two years saw another dual winner in Rose Bowl. In 1975 she beat Gay Fandango by two lengths, with Two Thousand Guineas winner Bolkonski well in arrears, and the following year doubled the distance of her 1975 victory when cruising home in a canter. Willie Carson, who rode Rose Bowl in both those victories, went on to notch up four in a row with 20–1 outsider Trusted (1977) and Homing (1978).

The 1979 race went to Kris, one of the very best milers of the post-war period, who won by five lengths and came back the following year to face a high-class field which included the three-year-old Known Fact, winner of the Two Thousand Guineas on the disqualification of Nureyev. The race which Kris and Known Fact produced was probably the finest in the history of the Queen Elizabeth II Stakes. A tremendous pace was set by Star Way, and by the time the field had completed the climb out of Swinley Bottom and approached the turn into the straight most of the runners had had enough. Joe Mercer pushed the 2–1 favourite Kris into a two-length lead coming round the home turn and the strapping chestnut set off for home. But Willie Carson on Known Fact was soon getting down to his famous pump-action finish, and with a furlong and a half to go Known Fact was in full pursuit of Kris. Known Fact got to his rival, and there ensued a desperate struggle. Kris was a great battler but Known Fact just had the legs of him, and near the line the Guineas winner edged ahead to win by a neck.

In 1981 the race again went to the Two Thousand Guineas winner: To-Agori-Mou. Then came a real shock when the unpredictable handicapper Buzzards Bay took the 1982 running at 50–1.

In the late 1980s class reigned, with Two Thousand Guineas winner Shadeed streaking home in 1985 and Sure Blade adding the race to his St James's Palace Stakes in 1986. Then in 1987 the race was accorded Group One status and formed the centrepiece of the inaugural Festival of British Racing. Typically for this race, the 1987 field was small but highly select, with the brilliant French filly Miesque, beaten only once in six outings that season (and that defeat was by Indian Skimmer in the Prix de Diane) looking unbeatable and going off the 4–1 on favourite. On 6–1 were the four-year-old Sonic Lady, winner of the Child Stakes at the Newmarket July Meeting, and Milligram, who had turned the Coronation Stakes at Royal Ascot into a procession and had most recently won the Waterford Crystal Mile. Milligram took up the running on the home turn about a length clear of Miesque, who pursued her from there to the post but could not make up the deficit, Milligram staying on so well that she won by two and a half lengths.

The next two runnings of the Queen Elizabeth II Stakes as a Group One race did nothing to suggest that its elevation was not highly justified: Warning produced a blistering turn of foot to win in 1988, and in 1989 Zilzal came right away from Polish Precedent in such a manner that he shared with Old Vic the highest rating in that year's International Classification. But it was the last time he would be seen on a British racecourse, for after failing in the Breeders' Cup Mile at Gulfstream Park he remained in the USA to take up stud duties.

Fillies' Mile

Ascot: 1 mile

Group One: two-year-old fillies

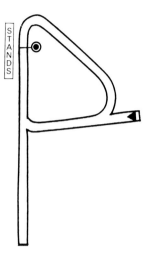

The race which in 1990 was named the Brent Walker Fillies' Mile began life in 1973 as the Green Shield Stakes, won by Lester Piggott on the Queen's filly Escorial. The following year the race could not be run because the course was waterlogged; it resumed as the Argos Star Fillies' Mile from 1975 to 1977. In 1978 Hoover took over sponsorship, and the race was promoted from Group Three to Group Two with the 1986 running, achieving Group One status in 1990.

The gradual upgrading of the race through the three Group categories proclaims its success as a vital opportunity for two-year-old staying fillies with Classic pretensions, and in its short life it has already proved its worth. Dunfermline, winner in 1977 of the Oaks and St Leger, came second to Miss Pinkie in 1976. Scintillate, fourth in 1978, won the Oaks the next year. The 1979 winner Quick As Lightning took the One Thousand Guineas the following spring, and Vielle, second at Ascot, was runner-up to Bireme in the 1980 Oaks. Leap Lively, winner in 1980, was third to Blue Wind at Epsom. In 1981 the Queen scored a second victory in the race with Height Of Fashion (dam of Nashwan), and the 1982 winner Acclimatise was second to Sun Princess at Epsom the following June. In 1983 Circus Plume could only finish third behind Nepula and Nonesuch Bay but went on to land the Oaks and the Yorkshire Oaks in 1984.

If by the very nature of the race the true worth of each running of the Fillies' Mile becomes apparent only when the participants engage in Classic competition the following year, the 1984 running marked a high point in its fortunes. For the first two home in a field of eight were to make a substantial mark on the 1985 season. Oh So Sharp came to Ascot unbeaten in her two previous races, a maiden event at Nottingham and the Solario Stakes at Sandown Park. Helen Street was also unbeaten, having won the Virginia Water Stakes at Ascot in July and then run away with the Prix du Calvados at Deauville, which brought her a four-pound penalty for the Fillies' Mile: she had to give weight away to her seven opponents, and Oh So Sharp started a hot favourite at 6–5. Rounding the home turn Oh So Sharp quickened up to take the lead, and though Helen Street made a determined challenge on her outside she was never going to get to the favourite, who won by a length and a half. The quality of the the first two became fully apparent in 1985 when Oh So Sharp won the One Thousand Guineas, Oaks and St Leger, and Helen Street the Irish Oaks.

WINNERS SINCE 1973

1973 Escorial
   L. Piggott 7–4 (11 ran)

1974 abandoned – waterlogged

1975 Icing
   C. Roche 5–1 (6 ran)

1976 Miss Pinkie
   L. Piggott 5–1 (8 ran)

1977 Cherry Hinton
   L. Piggott 10–11 (8 ran)

1978 Formulate
   J. Mercer 5–4 (9 ran)

1979 Quick As Lightning
   W. Carson 9–1 (9 ran)

1980 Leap Lively
   J. Matthias 9–2 (7 ran)

1981 Height Of Fashion
   J. Mercer 15–8 (8 ran)

1982 Acclimatise
   A. Murray 3–1 (8 ran)

1983 Nepula
   B. Crossley 3–1 (8 ran)

1984 Oh So Sharp
   L. Piggott 6–5 (8 ran)

1985 Untold
   W. R. Swinburn 6–4 (9 ran)

1986 Invited Guest
   S. Cauthen 8–11 (12 ran)

1987 Diminuendo
   S. Cauthen 2–1 (7 ran)

1988 Tessla
   Pat Eddery 5–2 (8 ran)

1989 Silk Slippers
   M. Hills 10–1 (8 ran)

The 1985 winner Untold took second behind Midway Lady in the 1986 Oaks and third in the Irish Oaks before winning the Yorkshire Oaks. Then in 1987, three years after Oh So Sharp's Ascot victory, another filly owned by Sheikh Mohammed and trained by Henry Cecil won the Fillies' Mile. Diminuendo had won three races (including the Cherry Hinton Stakes at Newmarket) and started 2–1 favourite: she thrust her way past Haiati inside the final furlong to win by two lengths, with Ashayer – who eight days later won the Prix Marcel Boussac at Longchamp on Arc day – third. The impression at the time that this was another high-class running of the Ascot race was confirmed when Diminuendo won the Oaks and Yorkshire Oaks in 1988, and dead-heated with Melodist for the Irish Oaks.

The essence of the Fillies' Mile is to sort out which of the supposedly top-ranking two-year-old fillies have the stamina to become contenders for the Oaks the next year, and in that role the race's record shows it to be conspicuously successful. Ascot's Old Mile will show up any flaws in stamina and determination, and the filly that wins this race can immediately go on the short-list for the Epsom Classic some eight months later.

The 1984 Hoover Fillies' Mile: Oh So Sharp (Lester Piggott) beats Helen Street.

Royal Lodge Stakes

Ascot: 1 mile

Group Two: two-year-old colts and geldings

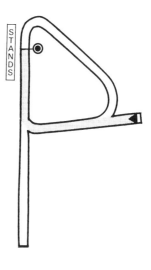

Named after the Royal Lodge built in Windsor Great Park for the Prince of Wales (later King George IV) and in recent times the Windsor residence of the Queen Mother, the Royal Lodge Stakes was held over five furlongs on its first two runnings in 1945 and 1946. But as soon as the distance was moved up to one mile it became a significant pointer to the following year's Derby: Swallow Tail, winner in 1948, was third, a head and the same behind Nimbus and Amour Drake, in the 1949 Epsom Classic. The 1958 winner Cantelo won the St Leger in 1959, shortly after which St Paddy won the Royal Lodge Stakes and went on to become the first Derby winner to have landed the race. Since then Royal Palace (1966) and Shirley Heights (1977) have provided the ultimate justification of the Royal Lodge Stakes as a signal of Derby potential by going on to win at Epsom.

But many of the runners in the Royal Lodge Stakes are two-year-olds as yet unexposed to the full heat of racing in the top class, and it would be too much to expect the form of the race to be solidly replicated the following season. Often a horse beaten at Ascot will mature over the winter and make Classic waves the next year. In 1976, for instance, the Royal Lodge was won by Gairloch, but the subsequent exploits of those behind him are better remembered: Pampapaul (second) won the Irish Two Thousand Guineas in 1977, and Hot Grove (third) was denied the 1977 Derby only by the inspired finish of Lester Piggott on The Minstrel. Hawaiian Sound was third to Shirley Heights in the 1977 Royal Lodge and beaten a whisker by the same horse in the Derby. And Troy in the 1978 Royal Lodge was caught inside the final furlong by Ela-Mana-Mou and beaten three-quarters of a length, but come the following June the Ascot winner was well beaten off as Troy thundered to a six-length Derby triumph. As a four-year-old Ela-Mana-Mou himself was in the top bracket, winning the Eclipse Stakes and the King George, while another King George winner to have run in the Royal Lodge as a two-year-old was Petoski, unplaced favourite in 1984. Julio Mariner, unplaced in 1977, won the 1978 St Leger.

---WINNERS SINCE 1980---

1980 Robellino
   J. Matthias 4–1 (8 ran)

1981 Norwick
   J. Mercer 12–1 (9 ran)

1982 Dunbeath
   L. Piggott 5–2 (9 ran)

1983 Gold And Ivory
   S. Cauthen 25–1 (5 ran)

1984 Reach
   T. Quinn 15–2 (8 ran)

1985 Bonhomie
   S. Cauthen 2–1 (7 ran)

1986 Bengal Fire
   M. Roberts 14–1 (9 ran)

1987 Sanquirico
   S. Cauthen 8–11 (10 ran)

1988 High Estate
   M. Roberts 4–6 (5 ran)

1989 Digression
   Pat Eddery 4–1 (9 ran)

NEWMARKET OCTOBER MEETING

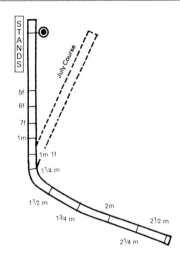

Course description on page 18.

After its summer sojourn with the arboreal charms of the July Course on the other side of the Devil's Dyke, Newmarket racing returns to the Rowley Mile for the October Meeting. Although this fixture is sometimes known as the Cambridgeshire Meeting, after the great nine-furlong handicap run on the final day, thoughts are turning to the Classics of next year, and the greatest interest centres on its big two-year-old races.

On the first day affairs are dominated by the CHEVELEY PARK STAKES (opposite), traditionally the top race of the season for two-year-old fillies, and the second day by the MIDDLE PARK STAKES (pages 115–16) for colts. Friday has the Listed TATTERSALL STAKES for two-year-olds over seven furlongs.

The Saturday of the Newmarket October Meeting is one of the very best days of Flat racing in the whole year, featuring the CAMBRIDGESHIRE HANDICAP (page 117) itself and two fascinating and very different Pattern races. The two-mile JOCKEY CLUB CUP (Group Three) for three-year-olds and upwards is the last Pattern race of the season for stayers in England, while the ten-furlong SUN CHARIOT STAKES (Group Two) for fillies and mares aged three and over perpetuates the memory of King George VI's brilliant filly who in 1942 won the One Thousand Guineas, Oaks and St Leger on the July Course at Newmarket, to which those races had been transferred on account of the war. Beaten only once in nine races, she was of a notoriously ungracious disposition. When the King and Queen went down to Fred Darling's yard at Beckhampton to watch her work before the Oaks, Gordon Richards could not persuade her to behave herself in front of her owner and start her gallop: Richards recalled how when the head lad gave her a tap with his hunting crop, 'she took me straight into the middle of a ploughed field, went down on her knees, and roared like a bull'. Nor did she comport herself much better in the Oaks itself, ruining the start three times and veering off to the left when the field was eventually sent on its way and letting her rivals get the best part of a furlong ahead of her before she consented to go after them: but once she had caught up her enthusiasm returned, and she won handily by a length. Recent winners of her race (first run 1966) include Oaks heroine Time Charter (1982), who went on to win the Champion Stakes over course and distance two weeks later – as did Swiss Maid (1978), Cormorant Wood (1983) and Indian Skimmer (1988).

Cheveley Park Stakes

Newmarket (Rowley Mile): 6 furlongs

Group One: two-year-old fillies

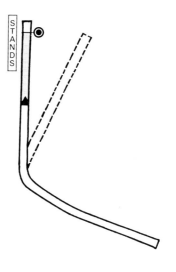

Before the Fillies' Mile at the Ascot September Meeting (pages 109–10) was upgraded to Group One status in 1990 the Cheveley Park Stakes was the only race in that category confined to two-year-old fillies. But the Ascot race is designed to attract staying fillies rather than those from whom great speed is expected, and its promotion is unlikely to affect the status of the Cheveley Park as the most significant two-year-old race of the year as far as pointers for the following season's One Thousand Guineas are concerned.

The race was first run in 1899, named after the Newmarket estate owned by Colonel Harry McCalmont (among whose horses was the 1893 Triple Crown winner Isinglass), and the first winner was Lutetia, ridden by the American jockey Tod Sloan whose 'monkey-on-a-stick' riding style revolutionized British jockeyship. Four years later the Cheveley Park Stakes went to probably the greatest horse ever to participate in it. Pretty Polly had run five times before she lined

The controversial running of the Tattersalls Cheveley Park Stakes, 1986: Forest Flower finishes well clear of Minstrella.

up against six other fillies on 14 October 1903, but had already achieved enough to prove herself an exceptional performer. She started at 100–8 on at Newmarket (with Flamma at 100–8 against and 50–1 bar two) and did not need to come out of a canter to win by three lengths, though she did for the first time show one of her little quirks when crossing her legs and nearly coming down just before the winning post – her personal sign of exuberant self-satisfaction. Two days later she won the Middle Park, and her daughter Molly Desmond won the Cheveley Park in 1916.

The early years of the Cheveley Park Stakes produced another notable winner in the form of Fifinella, who took the Newmarket race in 1915 and the following year was the last horse to win the Derby and the Oaks (and, indeed, the last filly to win the Derby). Between the wars came Selene (1921), dam of Hyperion; Scuttle (1927), who in 1928 won the One Thousand Guineas to become the only horse to win a Classic in the colours of King George V; Brown Betty (1932), who won the One Thousand Guineas as a three-year-old; and Light Brocade (1933), who went on to win the Oaks.

Since the Second World War the race's position as an indicator of One Thousand Guineas potential has been established by the victories of many fillies who have returned to the Rowley Mile the following spring to take the Classic: Belle Of All (1950), Zabara (1951), Night Off (1964), Fleet (1966), Humble Duty (1969), Waterloo (1971), Ma Biche (1982) and Ravinella (1987). The likes of Midget II (1955), Devon Ditty (1978), Mrs Penny (1979) and Marwell (1980) also maintained the class of the race, while fillies who were placed in the Cheveley Park went on to make big names for themselves subsequently: Rose Bowl, third in 1974, won the next two runnings of the Queen Elizabeth II Stakes (and the Champion Stakes in 1975); Fair Salinia, second in 1977, won the Oaks, the Irish Oaks and the Yorkshire Oaks; and in the 1980s two runners-up in the race won the One Thousand – On The House (1981) and Pebbles (1983), who in the Classic reversed two-year-old form with the Cheveley Park winner Desirable. But the most notorious running of the race in recent years was that of 1986 (run on the July Course while building work was carried out on the Rowley), when Forest Flower beat Minstrella by two and a half lengths. Forest Flower, ridden by Tony Ives, had given Minstrella a hefty bump as she moved out to make her challenge about a quarter of a mile from home, and Minstrella's jockey John Reid lodged an objection. The course stewards deemed the interference to be accidental and left the placings unaltered, but on Minstrella's connections lodging an appeal the opinion of the the the local stewards was overturned, Minstrella awarded the race and Forest Flower placed last, with the Disciplinary Committee of the Jockey Club handing Ives a hefty twelve-day suspension. The dreaded Rule 153 had struck again!

The Cheveley Park Stakes is in effect a junior version of the One Thousand Guineas, and a filly which has the speed, balance and resilience to do well in this race as a two-year-old should have every chance of being able to see out the extra two furlongs seven months later. It is no coincidence that the winner of the Cheveley Park often goes into winter quarters as ante-post favourite for the Classic.

Middle Park Stakes

Newmarket (Rowley Mile): 6 furlongs

Group One: two-year-old colts

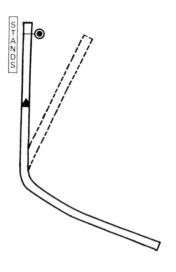

'Of all the two-year-old races in the Calendar there is none I would rather win than the Middle Park,' wrote John Hislop, owner-breeder of Brigadier Gerard; his great horse obligingly won the Middle Park Stakes (starting at 9–2) from Mummy's Pet and Swing Easy in 1970.

After that you have to move on nine years – to Known Fact in 1979 – to find a Middle Park Stakes winner who went on to take the Two Thousand Guineas, and Khalid Abdullah's colt won the Classic only on the disqualification of Nureyev. Known Fact was the fifth winner of the race since the Second World War to lift the Two Thousand, his predecessors being Nearula (1952), Our Babu (1954) and Right Tack (1968), as well as Brigadier Gerard. Nebbiolo, second to Tachypous in 1976, beat The Minstrel in the 1977 Two Thousand. Throw in Khaled (1945), Saravan (1946) and The Cobbler (1947), all second in the Two Thousand; Abernant (1948: second in the Two Thousand before becoming a very great sprinter); King's Bench (1951: second in the Two Thousand); Pipe Of Peace (1956: third in the Two Thousand Guineas and the Derby in 1957); Major Portion (1957: second in the Two Thousand); the brilliantly fast Skymaster (1960); Petingo (1967: second in the Two Thousand); Sharpen Up (1971); and Mattaboy (1980: beaten a neck by To-Agori-Mou in the 1981 Two Thousand) – and the position of the Middle Park Stakes as one of the year's best two-year-old races needs no special pleading.

But in the last decade the standard of winner and of field generally has gone sharply into decline. The proximity of the six-furlong Mill Reef Stakes at Newbury (first run in 1972) has weakened Middle Park fields, and the two-year-old campaigns of horses with Classic aims the following year have gradually taken on a different shape. Many of the top three-year-olds of recent times have had extremely light programmes as juveniles, and races such as the Dewhurst Stakes (pages 119–20) and the Racing Post Trophy (pages 125–6), coming later in the season than the Middle Park and run over a longer distance, are thus more suited to the sort of late-developing horse now thought to be the ideal Classic candidate. Accordingly the Middle Park is increasingly seen as a testing ground for future sprinters rather than true Classic horses.

Founded by William Blenkiron, who owned the Middle Park Stud at Eltham in Kent, the race was run as the Middle Park Plate until 1921. Blenkiron put up the £1,000 prize money for the inaugural running in October 1866, and had an instant success on his hands, with The Rake winning narrowly from Achievement, who would turn

> The town of Newmarket is in Suffolk. The runners on the Rowley Mile compete in Cambridgeshire, arriving in Suffolk as they pull up.

115

WINNERS SINCE 1970

1970 Brigadier Gerard
J. Mercer 9–2 (5 ran)

1971 Sharpen Up
W. Carson 5–6 (5 ran)

1972 Tudenham
J. Lindley 4–1 (7 ran)

1973 Habat
Pat Eddery 4–6 (7 ran)

1974 Steel Heart
L. Piggott 10–11 (8 ran)

1975 Hittite Glory
F. Durr 9–2 (8 ran)

1976 Tachypous
G. Lewis 5–1 (11 ran)

1977 Formidable
Pat Eddery 15–8 (7 ran)

1978 Junius
L. Piggott 7–1 (10 ran)

1979 Known Fact
W. Carson 10–1 (7 ran)

1980 Mattaboy
L. Piggott 7–1 (9 ran)

1981 Cajun
L. Piggott 20–1 (13 ran)

1982 Diesis
L. Piggott 10–11 (5 ran)

1983 Creag-An-Sgor
S. Cauthen 50–1 (9 ran)

1984 Bassenthwaite
Pat Eddery 7–2 (8 ran)

1985 Stalker
J. Mercer 9–2 (6 ran)

1986 Mister Majestic
R. Cochrane 33–1 (7 ran)

1987 Gallic League
S. Cauthen 6–4 (5 ran)

1988 Mon Tresor
M. Roberts 8–1 (6 ran)

1989 Balla Cove
S. Cauthen 20–1 (6 ran)

out to be one of the best fillies of the second half of the nineteenth century. Unplaced in the second running was Formosa, who the following year won three Classics outright and ran a dead heat in a fourth; two years after that another subsequently famous filly was beaten in the Middle Park: triple Classic winner Hannah. Later in the nineteenth century the race formed an important plank in the two-year-old careers of Triple Crown winners Isinglass (1892) and Galtee More (1896) as well as seven other Classic winners. Then Pretty Polly won in 1903, beating the 1904 Derby winner St Amant to write another footnote in history as the only horse ever to win both the Cheveley Park and the Middle Park; Bayardo, winner of the St Leger and one of the greatest horses of the century, in 1908; Derby winner Lemberg in 1909; and Craganour, to be disqualified after finishing first in the next year's Derby, in 1912. No wonder the race was known at the time as 'the two-year-old Derby' – though between the wars only 1926 winner Call Boy and Triple Crown winner Bahram (winner at Newmarket in 1934) won the Derby after scoring in the Middle Park. In the same period Tetratema (1919), Diophorn (1923) and Orwell (1931) used the Middle Park as a stepping stone to victory in the Two Thousand Guineas.

Just as the Cheveley Park is the juvenile version of the One Thousand Guineas, so – according to tradition – is the Middle Park (no longer open to fillies) in relation to the Two Thousand. Six furlongs hammering up the Rowley Mile is no joke for a young and probably very inexperienced horse, and though the quality of recent winners has been light years removed from that of Pretty Polly or Bahram or Brigadier Gerard, the race still has an important place in the racing calendar.

Pat Eddery on Bassenthwaite takes the Middle Park Stakes in 1984. The horse never won again.

Cambridgeshire Handicap

Newmarket (Rowley Mile): 1 mile 1 furlong

Handicap: three-year-olds and upwards

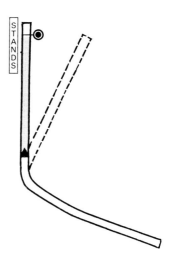

The Cambridgeshire was first run in 1839, and before long had become the biggest betting race of the latter part of the season. As there were few autumn opportunities for the best horses it often attracted Classic winners, a situation unheard-of today. Triple Crown winner Gladiateur was unplaced in the Cambridgeshire in 1865, and six years later Derby winner Favonius also ran unplaced (as did another Derby winner St Gatien in 1885). In 1892 the three-year-old La Fleche carried eight stone ten pounds to victory, having earlier won the One Thousand Guineas, Oaks and St Leger. (Hannah, winner of the same three Classics in 1871, was unplaced in 1872 and 1873.) Isonomy won the Cambridgeshire in 1878 and went on to win the Ascot Gold Cup twice. In the same period three horses achieved the now unthinkable double of the Cambridgeshire and the Cesarewitch, run over twice as far: Rosebery (1876), Foxhall (1881) and Plaisanterie (1885). Bendigo, first Eclipse Stakes winner in 1886, won that year and was three times second.

The Cambridgeshire remains one of the most exciting races of the season. And one of the most spectacular, for the sight of its huge field spread right out across the track and powering up the straight nine-furlong course, sweeping into the Dip and then forging up the hill to the winning post, is guaranteed to stir the blood, especially if you have partaken of one of the major gambles which keeps the race at the forefront of the year's betting events. It still attracts some very good horses – such as Teleprompter, beaten a head by Sagamore when favourite as a three-year-old in 1983, or Town and Country, a close-up fifth to Baronet under ten stone in 1978. Baronet was the greatest Cambridgeshire horse of recent memory: he first ran in the race as a five-year-old in 1977 (second to Sin Timon), won under nine stone in 1978, came sixth with nine stone eight in 1979, scored a second victory with nine stone three in 1980 and at the venerable age of nine was runner-up again (to Braughing) in 1981. Time and again Baronet showed the qualities required for a prominent display in the race: speed not to get left behind when the invariably fast pace is sustained into the closing stages, toughness not to shrink from the bustle of a big field, and courage to get home up the hill.

The nine-furlong trip of the Cambridgeshire is a highly unusual one, and the race tends to bring together milers stepping up in distance (such as – in his younger days – Teleprompter) and ten-furlong horses stepping down (such as Town and Country). Perhaps this is the key element in its fascination.

WINNERS SINCE 1980

1980 Baronet
   B. Rouse 22–1 (19 ran)

1981 Braughing
   S. Cauthen 50–1 (28 ran)

1982 Century City
   J. Mercer 20–1 (29 ran)

1983 Sagamore
   M. L. Thomas 35–1 (30 ran)

1984 Leysh
   J. Lowe 33–1 (34 ran)

1985 Tremblant
   Pat Eddery 16–1 (31 ran)

1986 Dallas
   R. Cochrane 10–1 (31 ran)

1987 Balthus
   D. McKeown 50–1 (31 ran)

1988 Quinlan Terry
   G. Duffield 11–1 (29 ran)

1989 Rambo's Hall
   D. McKeown 15–1 (34 ran)

NEWMARKET HOUGHTON MEETING

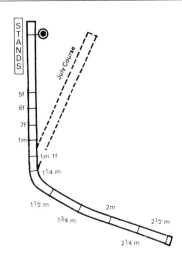

Course description on page 98.

Autumn is now well and truly here. Season of mists and mellow fruitfulness; and of the Dewhurst, the Cesarewitch and the Champion Stakes. The shadows are lengthening, and the sun – if it is to be seen – is low in the sky. The leaves have turned and are wafting down from the trees. The Arc has been run, and soon the Mackeson Gold Cup and winter will be upon us. If the sun is shining to combat the autumnal chill in the air, the Newmarket Houghton Meeting is a glorious experience, with the Heath at its very best and wonderful sport in prospect. If the rains have come, and the cold wind is gusting in unimpeded from the Urals, the Rowley Mile is the bleakest place imaginable, and only the hardiest racegoer will not tacitly crave to be snuggled up in front of the fire watching Channel Four Racing.

The first day of the meeting has the CHALLENGE STAKES, a Group Two seven-furlong race for three-year-olds and upwards which usually sees a top-class field: Boldboy won in 1973 as a three-year-old and again four years later; Kris took the race in 1979; and Moorestyle won in 1980 and 1981. On the Friday thoughts turn to two-year-olds, with the DEWHURST STAKES (opposite) and the Group Three ROCKFEL STAKES for two-year-old fillies over seven furlongs: Musical Bliss won this race in 1988 and went on to take the One Thousand Guineas.

The Saturday of the Houghton Meeting is one of the best days of the whole season on the Flat, offering both the CHAMPION STAKES (pages 121–3) and the CESAREWITCH (page 124). A huge gathering crowds into the stands to watch a feast of racing and undergo an experience unique in the racing year – the wait while the runners for the Cesarewitch make their way to the start. The race begins at a place so remote that it takes an age for the runners to get there, so having found your good position in the packed stand, you are confronted with the unusual situation of many minutes with nothing to do: it's too late to study the form one last time and change your mind and rush down to the bookies – you'll lose your place. So you gaze out across the Heath and take stock. You cast your mind back over the season, remembering the near misses, and the winners when you really should have doubled your usual stake; and – worst of all – those occasions when you were about to back a horse but then changed your mind, and suffered the exquisite pain of seeing your original selection stride home in front. For those few minutes time stands still. But then you hear the course commentator announcing that there's just one more to be loaded for the Cesarewitch, and you wonder whether you've had enough on . . .

Dewhurst Stakes

Newmarket (Rowley Mile): 7 furlongs

Group One: two-year-old colts and fillies

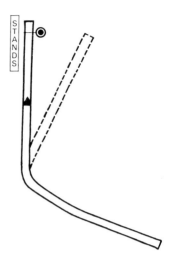

The first International Classification for two-year-olds was compiled in 1978, and of the eight horses top-rated (and in 1979 joint top-rated) between then and 1984 only two were not winners of the Dewhurst Stakes. The top-rated two-year-olds who had taken the race were Tromos (1978), Monteverdi (joint top-rated in 1979), Storm Bird (1980), Diesis (1982), El Gran Senor (1983) and Kala Dancer (1984). Of this sextet only El Gran Senor kept his form so well that the following year he was rated top three-year-old: the Dewhurst has an unfortunate habit of building reputations which do not stand the test of time.

The race was founded as the Dewhurst Plate in 1875 by Mr T. Gee, owner of the Dewhurst Stud in Sussex, who put up the money for the initial running in the hope of being able to create a race which would attract the sort of horse who might become a Classic candidate, and from its earliest years the Dewhurst had a remarkable record. The first winner was Kisber, who won the Derby; the second, Chamant, went on to win the Two Thousand Guineas; the third, Pilgrimage, won the One Thousand and the Two Thousand; and the fourth, Wheel Of Fortune, the One Thousand and Oaks. Before the First World War the Dewhurst was won by other future Classic winners, notably the Triple Crown heroes Ormonde (1885) and Rock Sand (1902), the St Leger winner Bayardo (1908) and the Derby winner Lemberg (1909), while Louvois (1912) and Kennymore (1913) both won the Two Thousand Guineas. The most famous winner of the inter-war period was Hyperion (1932), who took the Derby in 1933. His feat was matched in the 1950s by Sir Victor Sassoon's pair Pinza (1952) and Crepello (1956), also winner of the Two Thousand.

In the 1960s no Dewhurst winner went on to take an English Classic until the very end of the decade, but the 1969 winner was worth waiting for. Nijinsky had won his first four races in Ireland – all at The Curragh – and started at 3–1 on to beat five opponents in the Dewhurst, which he did without any fuss by three lengths. The following year another of the century's great horses, Mill Reef, cruised in from just two rivals, and the mid-1970s proved a glorious period for the race. Grundy (1974) went on to take the Derby, Irish Derby and King George; Wollow (1975) the Two Thousand Guineas, Eclipse Stakes, Sussex Stakes and Benson and Hedges Gold Cup; and The Minstrel (1976) the Derby, Irish Derby and King George. Of the eight runnings between 1969 and 1976, five had produced top-notch Classic winners, but Dewhurst victory was no guarantee of

No worries about the future reputation of the first two home in the 1983 William Hill Dewhurst Stakes: El Gran Senor beats Rainbow Quest.

WINNERS SINCE 1970

1970 Mill Reef
G. Lewis 4–7 (3 ran)

1971 Crowned Prince
L. Piggott 4–9 (11 ran)

1972 Lunchtime
Pat Eddery 11–8 (8 ran)

1973 Cellini
L. Piggott 40–85 (7 ran)

1974 Grundy
Pat Eddery 6–5 (8 ran)

1975 Wollow
G. Dettori 6–4 (7 ran)

1976 The Minstrel
L. Piggott 6–5 (11 ran)

1977 Try My Best
L. Piggott 4–6 (7 ran)

1978 Tromos
J. Lynch 11–4 (6 ran)

1979 Monteverdi
L. Piggott 15–8 (6 ran)

1980 Storm Bird
Pat Eddery 4–5 (5 ran)

1981 Wind And Wuthering
P. Waldron 11–1 (9 ran)

1982 Diesis
L. Piggott 2–1 (4 ran)

1983 El Gran Senor
Pat Eddery 7–4 (10 ran)

1984 Kala Dancer
G. Baxter 20–1 (11 ran)

1985 Huntingdale
M. Hills 12–1 (8 ran)

1986 Ajdal
W. R. Swinburn 4–9 (5 ran)

1987 abandoned – high winds

1988 dead heat:
Prince of Dance
W. Carson 6–4
Scenic
M. Hills 33–1 (6 ran)

1989 Dashing Blade
J. Matthias 8–1 (7 ran)

immortality, as the next few winners found out. Try My Best (1977) was praised to the skies after winning the race and started even-money favourite for the Two Thousand Guineas, only to trail in last of the nineteen runners. Worse was to follow. Tromos in 1978 put up a Dewhurst performance so devastating that he was hailed as one of the best two-year-olds since the war, but on his reappearance as a three-year-old in the Craven Stakes the next April he was sensationally beaten: he did not run in the Guineas and was exported to the USA. Then there was Monteverdi (1979), who failed to score in four attempts at three. Try My Best and Monteverdi were both trained by Vincent O'Brien, as were Nijinsky and The Minstrel, and when another O'Brien charge Storm Bird beat To-Agori-Mou half a length in 1980, out came the superlatives again. But Storm Bird's three-year-old career was a disaster: before the start of the season his box was broken into by an ex-stable lad who hacked chunks out of the horse's mane and tail, and then Storm Bird's solitary outing saw him unplaced at Longchamp in September (by which time he had been sold to a group of US breeders for $30 million; his second crop included Indian Skimmer).

It is reputation and its subsequent fate which makes each running of the Dewhurst such an intriguing race. And occasionally the race itself destroys rather than creates reputation. Gorytus in 1982 came to Newmarket having won his two earlier races in exceptional style. Yet he trailed in last of four behind Diesis (who became the latest of eight horses to have won both the Middle Park Stakes and the Dewhurst) after being virtually pulled up by Willie Carson. Rumours flew around that he had been got at, and attention centred on the large dropping that Gorytus had deposited on the way to the parade ring: had he been administered a laxative to prevent his winning – even, it was suggested, a purgative (known as croton oil) so strong that it was used on constipated elephants? The dope test proved negative, and there was no firm evidence of foul play. Gorytus's defeat remained a mystery, and he could not rebuild his reputation in three races as a three-year-old.

None of the Dewhurst winners between 1978 and 1982 managed to win again. But the reputation of the race was regained in 1983 when El Gran Senor, soon to be proved one of the best Two Thousand Guineas winners of the post-war period, beat the 1985 Arc winner Rainbow Quest by half a length. The 1987 running was controversially abandoned on account of the October 'hurricane' (it was felt in many quarters that the race should have been added to Saturday's card), and 1988 produced a memorable dead heat between Scenic and Prince Of Dance.

The Dewhurst is a furlong longer than the Middle Park, and that extra emphasis on stamina has much to do with the record of its winners in the Derby. If, like the Middle Park, it has suffered somewhat from the reluctance of the top trainers to expose their Derby hopes at the highest level as two-year-olds, it nevertheless remains the top juvenile race of the year.

Champion Stakes

Newmarket (Rowley Mile): 1¼ miles

Group One: three-year-olds and upwards

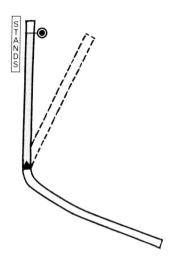

If the character of any long-established race is best expressed through the horses who have won it, then the Champion Stakes fully deserves its place as one of the most popular and prestigious races of the year. But there is more to its appeal than the famous names which grace its roll of honour. The great two-year-old races run at Newmarket in October look forward and anticipate feats to come; the Champion Stakes represents an ending, the last Group One race in Britain for older horses and a culmination of the very best middle-distance form. Here you should find Classic winners and some of the top horses from overseas. And then there is the course and the demands it puts upon the runners. This ten-furlong trip is unique in the world's major middle-distance races in being completely straight, demanding an unrelenting gallop up the yawning expanse of the Rowley Mile which only the toughest and freshest horses will be able to cope with at the end of a long season.

The Champion Stakes was first run in 1877, and before the end of the century had gone to five Classic winners. Oaks and St Leger heroine Jannette won the Champion on its second running; Robert The Devil, just touched off by Bend Or in the 1880 Derby (see page 51) and then triumphant in the St Leger, slammed Bend Or in the Champion (having previously taken the Cesarewitch); Bend Or himself won as a four-year-old in 1881; Triple Crown winner Ormonde won in 1886; and La Fleche, winner of the One Thousand Guineas, Oaks and St Leger in 1892, won the Champion Stakes as a five-year-old in 1894. Early in the twentieth century both Sceptre (1903) and Pretty Polly (1905) won, though Sceptre had only two opponents and Pretty Polly one. Bayardo won in 1909; Derby winner Lemberg won in 1910 and walked over in 1911; Triple Crown winner Gay Crusader won in 1917, and St Leger winner Fairway won twice – 1928 and 1929. (Brigadier Gerard and Triptych are among other dual winners.)

Since the war the best winners have included Bella Paola (1958), Petite Etoile (1959), Hula Dancer (1963), Rose Bowl (1975), Flying Water (1977), Time Charter (1982), Pebbles (1985), Triptych (1986 and 1987) and Indian Skimmer (1988) – all of whom have one very fundamental characteristic in common. They are fillies, and it is noticeable that fillies, whose physiology often brings about a marked improvement in form in the autumn, have a remarkable record in the Champion Stakes. Seventeen of the thirty-three runnings between 1957 and 1989 went to fillies; in the same period the Eclipse Stakes,

> The Champion Stakes has been sponsored since 1982 by the Maktoum family and run as the Dubai Champion Stakes.

the nearest equivalent to the Champion, was won by a filly just once, and the International Stakes, first run as the Benson and Hedges Gold Cup in 1972, to a filly four times in eighteen runnings.

Like all great races, the Champion Stakes produces great moments, whether it be the virtuoso displays of Time Charter in 1982 or Indian Skimmer in 1988 or the desperately exciting finishes delivered by Cormorant Wood, Tolomeo and Flame Of Tara (dam of Salsabil) in 1983 or Legal Case, Dolpour and Ile De Chypre in 1989. To taste something of the flavour of this great race, we can consider some of the memorable moments which the Champion Stakes has produced over the last two decades:

1970

One of the saddest moments in recent racing history, as Nijinsky, two weeks earlier beaten for the first time in his life in the Arc, came to Newmarket looking to end a glorious career on a winning note. But he was a shadow of his former self, became upset by the attentions of the adoring crowd, and ran a lifeless race to come second to Lorenzaccio.

1972

Another farewell to a great horse, but this time a joyful one. Brigadier Gerard had scrambled home in the Champion Stakes by a short head from Rarity in 1971, and now, amid scenes of wild enthusiasm, strode in from Riverman to record his seventeenth win from eighteen races.

1975

A typical Champion Stakes field included Star Appeal, fresh from winning the Arc, the famous French mare Allez France, two years earlier beaten in the race by 33–1 shot Hurry Harriet, and the three-year-old filly Rose Bowl, winner of the Queen Elizabeth II Stakes. Rose Bowl went clear on the hill to win stylishly, and in 1976 was back for a second go, only to be touched off by Vitiges.

1985

One of the most eagerly awaited Flat races of the 1980s, the Champion Stakes brought together Slip Anchor, who had won the Derby brilliantly; Commanche Run, winner of the 1984 St Leger and in 1985 of the Benson and Hedges Gold Cup and the Phoenix Champion Stakes and due for a million-dollar bonus if he could win the Champion; Pebbles, who had not run since becoming the first filly to win the Eclipse Stakes; Palace Music, who had beaten Pebbles a neck in the 1984 Champion; and Helen Street, winner of the Irish Oaks. It was a superb field, and Slip Anchor at 6–4 was marginally preferred in the betting to Commanche Run. Pebbles started at 9–2, but once Pat Eddery had asked her to improve her position up the rails the result was never in doubt. She came right away from her rivals before winning, easing down, by three lengths from Slip Anchor – a performance in the best traditions of the race.

Opposite (top): the Dubai Champion Stakes, 1985: Pebbles (Pat Eddery) is out on her own; *(bottom):* a desperate finish to the 1989 Champion: the winner Legal Case (no. 8) goes past Ile De Chypre (no. 2) as Dolpour scrambles through between them to claim second place.

WINNERS SINCE 1970

1970 Lorenzaccio
  G. Lewis 100–7 (8 ran)

1971 Brigadier Gerard
  J. Mercer 1–2 (10 ran)

1972 Brigadier Gerard
  J. Mercer 1–3 (9 ran)

1973 Hurry Harriet
  J. Cruguet 33–1 (16 ran)

1974 Giacometti
  L. Piggott 4–1 (14 ran)

1975 Rose Bowl
  W. Carson 11–2 (9 ran)

1976 Vitiges
  Pat Eddery 22–1 (19 ran)

1977 Flying Water
  Y. Saint-Martin 9–1 (8 ran)

1978 Swiss Maid
  G. Starkey 9–1 (10 ran)

1979 Northern Baby
  P. Paquet 9–1 (14 ran)

1980 Cairn Rouge
  A. Murray 6–1 (13 ran)

1981 Vayrann
  Y. Saint-Martin 15–2 (16 ran)

1982 Time Charter
  W. Newnes 9–2 (14 ran)

1983 Cormorant Wood
  S. Cauthen 18–1 (19 ran)

1984 Palace Music
  Y. Saint-Martin 18–1 (15 ran)

1985 Pebbles
  Pat Eddery 9–2 (10 ran)

1986 Triptych
  A. Cruz 4–1 (11 ran)

1987 Triptych
  A. Cruz 6–5 (11 ran)

1988 Indian Skimmer
  M. Roberts 8–15 (5 ran)

1989 Legal Case
  R. Cochrane 5–1 (11 ran)

Cesarewitch Handicap

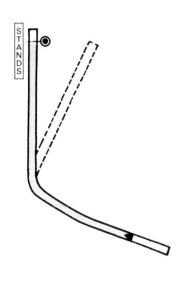

Newmarket (Rowley Mile): 2¼ miles
Handicap: three-year-olds and upwards

The Cesarewitch has an atmosphere all its own. Its major idiosyncrasy is that much of it is run completely out of sight of the spectators: the race starts near the furthest point of that stretch of the course which the Rowley Mile shares with the July Course, and the runners cover nearly a mile – mostly obscured from view by the Devil's Dyke – until making the turn into the straight before halfway. With the early stages effectively taking place *in camera*, it is a race with which it is difficult for the on-course spectator to become quickly involved, but once the field comes into the final half mile, the Cesarewitch often builds up to a gripping finish.

Like the Cambridgeshire, the race was first run in 1839, and owes its exotic name to a visit paid to Newmarket by the twenty-one-year-old Tsarevich, the future Emperor Alexander II of Russia. He donated £300 to the Jockey Club, who used the money as the purse for a recently devised long-distance handicap, anglicizing the donor's title in naming it. The Tsarevich continued to sponsor the race until 1849. Like so many of the big handicaps of the nineteenth century the Cesarewitch was a natural end-of-season target for Classic horses, who had little else of substance to compete for. Second in the 1840 running was the 1839 Derby winner Bloomsbury, and St Gatien won in 1884 after winning the Derby that year. Nor was Cesarewitch participation by a Classic winner just a Victorian value: third in 1935 was the Oaks winner Quashed, who beat Omaha in the famous 1936 Ascot Gold Cup.

Willonyx in 1911 heaved nine stone five pounds to victory, a record which stood until Grey Of Falloden carried one pound more when beating the Champion Hurdler Magic Court by three quarters of a length in 1964. John Cherry in 1976 set a new weight record with victory under nine stone thirteen, and an honourable mention must go to the game mare Double Dutch, who got home by a neck under nine stone ten pounds in 1989. But for an unforgettable modern Cesarewitch, how about the 1984 victory of Tom Sharp? Saddled with a mere seven stone five pounds and starting at 40–1, he was pushed into a very long lead by apprentice Steve Dawson in the early part of the race. The other jockeys were sure that Tom Sharp would come back to them, but the egg was all over their faces after Dawson kicked on half a mile out and kept him going to win unchallenged.

WINNERS SINCE 1980

1980 Popsi's Joy
L. Piggott 10–1 (27 ran)

1981 Halsbury
J. Mercer 14–1 (30 ran)

1982 Mountain Lodge
W. Carson 9–1 (28 ran)

1983 Bajan Sunshine
B. Rouse 7–1 (28 ran)

1984 Tom Sharp
S. Dawson 40–1 (26 ran)

1985 Kayudee
A. Murray 7–1 (21 ran)

1986 Orange Hill
R. Fox 20–1 (25 ran)

1987 Private Audition
G. Carter 50–1 (28 ran)

1988 Nomadic Way
W. Carson 6–1 (24 ran)

1989 Double Dutch
W. Newnes 15–2 (22 ran)

Racing Post Trophy

Doncaster: 1 mile

Group One: two-year-old colts and fillies

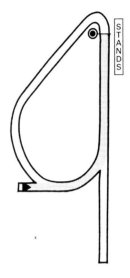

Phil Bull died in June 1989 at the age of seventy-nine. Probably the most influential Turf figure in Britain this century, his major legacy is the Timeform organization, which has transformed the quality of information available to the punter. Another example of Bull's revolutionary zeal lives on in the shape of what is now the Racing Post Trophy, the last Group One race of the season in Britain and the only one-mile Pattern race of the year open to two-year-old colts. Bull's conviction in the early 1960s that there was a crying need for a top juvenile race over a mile led, against sturdy opposition, to the first running of the Timeform Gold Cup in 1961. It became the Observer Gold Cup in 1965, the William Hill Futurity in 1976, and the Racing Post Trophy in 1989 – when it was run at Newcastle because the Doncaster course was still unfit after the subsidence problems which brought about the removal of the St Leger to Ayr.

Course description on page 98.

The race soon fulfilled its aim of giving future middle-distance Classic horses a high-level opportunity as youngsters. The winner of the inaugural race in 1961 was Miralgo, in whose wake ran Larkspur (the Derby winner in 1962) and Hethersett (a faller in Larkspur's Derby but later successful in the St Leger). In its second year the Timeform Gold Cup went to the brilliant Noblesse, trained in Ireland by Paddy Prendergast: she won by three lengths at Doncaster and proved exceptional at three, winning the Oaks by ten lengths at 11–4 on. A change of sponsorship in 1965 did not affect the standing of the race: winner Pretendre was narrowly beaten by Charlottown in the Derby. The 1966 winner Ribocco went on to win the St Leger, and though the 1967 victor had no Classic engagements he turned out to be possibly the best horse yet to have won the race: Vaguely Noble won the Observer Gold Cup by seven lengths and was then sold, to be trained subsequently in France by Etienne Pollet, in whose care he won the Prix de l'Arc de Triomphe in magnificent style from Sir Ivor. Phil Bull's brainchild had come of age.

In 1970 Linden Tree won and proceeded to finish runner-up to Mill Reef in the Derby. The 1971 race went to High Top (Two Thousand Guineas, 1972) from Steel Pulse (Irish Derby) and Pentland Firth (third to Roberto and Rheingold in the Derby). The less said about Apalachee (1973) the better: he was deemed a certainty in the Two Thousand Guineas but could finish only third, and did not race again. Green Dancer (1974) was the first French-trained winner: in 1975 he won the Poule d'Essai des Poulains and the Prix Lupin but was well beaten behind Grundy in the Derby. In 1977 it was the

┌─**WINNERS SINCE 1970**─────┐

1970 Linden Tree
    D. Keith 25–1 (9 ran)

1971 High Top
    W. Carson 11–2 (13 ran)

1972 Noble Decree
    L. Piggott 8–1 (10 ran)

1973 Apalachee
    L. Piggott evens (10 ran)

1974 Green Dancer
    F. Head 7–2 (10 ran)

1975 Take Your Place
    G. Dettori 4–1 (11 ran)

1976 Sporting Yankee
    Pat Eddery 9–2 (6 ran)

1977 Dactylographer
    Pat Eddery 100–30 (12 ran)

1978 Sandy Creek
    C. Roche 15–1 (11 ran)

1979 Hello Gorgeous
    J. Mercer 11–8 (7 ran)

1980 Beldale Flutter
    Pat Eddery 14–1 (7 ran)

1981 Count Pahlen
    G. Baxter 25–1 (13 ran)

1982 Dunbeath
    L. Piggott 4–7 (8 ran)

1983 Alphabatim
    G. Starkey 9–2 (9 ran)

1984 Lanfranco
    L. Piggott 100–30 (10 ran)

1985 Bakharoff
    G. Starkey 2–1 (9 ran)

1986 Reference Point
    Pat Eddery 4–1 (10 ran)

1987 Emmson
    W. Carson 7–1 (6 ran)

1988 Al Hareb
    W. Carson 100–30 (8 ran)

1989 Be My Chief
    S. Cauthen 4–7 (5 ran)

beaten horses who went on to better things: Julio Mariner (third) won the 1978 St Leger, while the unplaced Hawaiian Sound was beaten a head by Shirley Heights in the Derby and took the Benson and Hedges Gold Cup, and Ile De Bourbon won the King George. Another horse beaten in the race three years later rivals Vaguely Noble and Noblesse as the best to have taken part: an immature Shergar was second to Beldale Flutter in 1980 but still showed the promise which would bring him a glorious three-year-old campaign.

So by the mid-1980s the William Hill Futurity (as it then was) had an excellent record and had fully justified Bull's conviction. But still it lacked the crowning glory – a winner who would go on to lift the Derby itself. Enter, in 1986, Reference Point. He lined up at Doncaster on 25 October with just two races behind him – two outings at Sandown Park, the latter of which he had won. But Henry Cecil's jockey Steve Cauthen rated the stable's other runner Suhailie a better Futurity prospect, and the ride on Reference Point went to Pat Eddery. Suhailie started 2–1 favourite, with Reference Point third favourite at 4–1. Cauthen had chosen wrongly, and Reference Point led all the way to stride home by a long-looking five lengths, the widest winning margin in the history of the race apart from Vaguely Noble's. In 1987 Reference Point won the Derby, the King George and the St Leger.

In stark contrast to Reference Point, the 1988 winner Al Hareb was last of five in his only outing as a three-year-old and did not run again. A similar fate befell 1989 winner Be My Chief – likewise last in his only outing as a three-year-old, he was retired to the National Stud. But the overall record of the race is a vindication of Phil Bull's insistence that such an event was needed, and it now forms an important component of the two-year-old programme.

The 1987 William Hill Futurity:
Emmson *(left)* beats Sheriff's Star.

November Handicap

Doncaster: 1½ miles

Handicap: three-year-olds and upwards

Time was when the November Handicap was the last big betting race of the year on the Flat, the Getting-Out Stakes for the season. In the 1990s its hold on the public imagination – and pocket – has much diminished from the days of its glory.

Those days were when the race was held at Manchester, where it was first run in 1876. Notable among the Manchester winners early in the twentieth century was St Maclou, who at the other end of the season had caught Sceptre in the closing stages to win the Lincoln. Free Fare won the November Handicap in 1935 and went on to start favourite for the Champion Hurdle three times, winning at Cheltenham in 1937: twice he had thrown away his chance at Manchester by swerving near the finish, but he eventually won by five lengths in 1935, unfancied at 22–1. Las Vegas in 1946 gave Harry Wragg his last victory as a jockey, and the following year Regret won at 66–1 carrying just six stone three pounds. The quintessential November Handicap at Manchester was a huge field locking horns in a highly competitive handicap run in thick fog: in the 1958 running, for example, nothing could be seen until the final hundred yards, when Joe Mercer on Paul Jones emerged from the murk to win at 100–7. And one other post-war victory at the course on the banks of the River Irwell which deserves mention is that of Operatic Society in 1959. By the end of his ten-year career this durable white-faced gelding had won thirty of his seventy races, and his November Handicap victory was one of his most memorable. He carried eight stone nine pounds – a mammoth weight for a three-year-old – and faced forty-eight rivals in the second largest field ever seen in an English Flat race. First he charged the starting gate and dislodged Ken Gethin, then galloped off for a mile before he could be caught. When reunited with Gethin he cruised through a quarter of a mile out and won by a length.

The course at Manchester closed down in 1963 after Best Song had won the November Handicap from Damredub (both trained at Lewes by Towser Gosden), and the race was transferred across the Pennines to Doncaster, where the first running went to the four-year-old Osier: that was the first of three runnings sponsored by Ovaltine, an appropriate benefactor for a race held just before the lights are turned out on the season. Sponsored since 1976 by William Hill, the November Handicap remains a competitive event to stir the ante-post punter as the curtain is rung down, and can still make its bit of history: in 1985 20–1 chance Bold Rex provided the last riding winner for Joe Mercer.

Course description on page 98.

Course description on page 98.

WINNERS SINCE 1980

1980 Path of Peace
   J. Bleasdale 14–1 (22 ran)

1981 Lafontaine
   G. Duffield 16–1 (20 ran)

1982 dead heat:
      Double Shuffle
   G. Duffield 12–1
      Turkoman
   D. McKay 20–1 (17 ran)

1983 Asir
   G. Starkey 10–1 (25 ran)

1984 Abu Kadra
   W. R. Swinburn 25–1 (23 ran)

1985 Bold Rex
   J. Mercer 20–1 (24 ran)

1986 Beijing
   T. Quinn 16–1 (25 ran)

1987 Swingit Gunner
   M. Birch 9–1 (25 ran)

1988 Young Benz
   M. Birch 12–1 (22 ran)

1989 Firelight Fiesta
   B. Raymond 9–2 (19 ran)

Mackeson Gold Cup

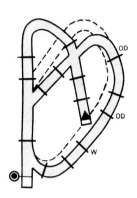

Course description on page 142.

WINNERS SINCE 1980

1980 Bright Highway
  G. Newman 5–1 (15 ran)

1981 Henry Kissinger
  P. Barton 5–1 (11 ran)

1982 Fifty Dollars More
  R. Linley 11–1 (11 ran)

1983 Pounentes
  N. Doughty 7–1 (9 ran)

1984 Half Free
  R. Linley 5–2 (10 ran)

1985 Half Free
  R. Linley 9–2 (10 ran)

1986 Very Promising
  R. Dunwoody 7–1 (11 ran)

1987 Beau Ranger
  M. Perrett 13–2 (14 ran)

1988 Pegwell Bay
  P. Scudamore 6–1 (13 ran)

1989 Joint Sovereignty
  G. McCourt 10–1 (15 ran)

Previous pages: John Francome on Burrough Hill Lad jumping clear of Colin Brown on Combs Ditch in the King George VI Chase at Kempton Park, December 1984.

Cheltenham: 2½ miles

Grade Three handicap steeplechase: five-year-olds and upwards

The Mackeson Gold Cup is the first big steeplechase of the National Hunt season, and although it takes place while the dying embers of the Flat season (at least on turf) are still feebly glowing, the Flat has effectively been shoved off the stage. With the Mackeson, jumping is well and truly back.

Towards the end of the 1950s the television appeal of National Hunt racing led to the establishing of the first two great sponsored chases – the Whitbread Gold Cup (pages 161–5) and the Hennessy Gold Cup (opposite). The Mackeson, first run in 1960, followed in their wake, and whereas the other two races were framed for the staying chaser, this new race was run over two miles: the distance was not increased to two and a half miles until 1970. Two of the first three runnings went to Fortria, who also took the Two Mile Champion Chase at Cheltenham's big March meeting in 1960 and again in 1961, yet had the stamina twice to run second in the Gold Cup over three and a quarter miles – to Mandarin in 1962 and Mill House in 1963. But perhaps the best winner in the race's first decade was Dunkirk, that dashing front-running chaser who the month after carrying twelve stone seven pounds up the Cheltenham hill to victory in 1965 was killed in the King George VI Chase at Kempton Park on Boxing Day when taking on Arkle. Another distinguished name from that period was Gay Trip, who won the Mackeson over two miles in 1969 and the Grand National over four and a half the following spring: there's versatility for you!

Since then the quality of the race has varied, but usually it attracts several of the best chasers around: Bula, carrying twelve stone one, was beaten only three quarters of a length by Cancello in 1976 (when the race was run at Haydock Park during development work at Cheltenham); Bachelor's Hall (1977) won the Hennessy and the King George VI Chase that season; Bright Highway (1980) went on to take the Hennessy; Half Free (1984 and 1985) became the first horse to win twice since Fortria; and Pegwell Bay (1988) won the A. F. Budge Gold Cup over course and distance a month later.

Whatever the composition of the field, the Mackeson invariably provides a great spectacle and a competitive betting market. Like all steeplechases at Cheltenham it requires, above all, jumping ability, the stamina to last every yard of the trip, and true grit.

Hennessy Cognac Gold Cup

Newbury: 3 miles 2 furlongs 82 yards

Grade Three handicap steeplechase: five-year-olds and upwards

You only need to glance down the list of past winners to see why the Hennessy Gold Cup is the highlight of the pre-Christmas period of the jumping season: Mandarin, Taxidermist, Mill House, Arkle, Diamond Edge, Bregawn, Burrough Hill Lad – the roll of honour includes most of the top staying chasers of the last thirty years. If the quality of the line-ups in the most recent runnings has declined somewhat, the spectacle of a large Hennessy field streaming over the water jump in front of the Newbury stands remains one to warm a winter afternoon.

In its early days, however, the Hennessy Gold Cup was run at Cheltenham. Mandarin beat eighteen opponents here in the the inaugural running in 1957, having the previous spring finished second in the first running of the other flagship sponsored steeplechase, the Whitbread Gold Cup (see page 164): in the Hennessy he received sixteen pounds from that year's Cheltenham Gold Cup winner Linwell and beat him three lengths. Mandarin was back the following year and started 11–10 on favourite, but could finish only fifth. The winner, Taxidermist, ridden by the 29-year-old amateur John Lawrence (better known in some quarters these days as The Noble Lord), was sixth at the final fence and in a seemingly hopeless position, but staged an extraordinary rally up the hill to pip Gold Cup winner Kerstin by – in the words of his partner – 'the length of a cigarette end'. In 1959 Kerstin had her consolation when beating twenty-five opponents, and the next year the race was moved to Newbury, where Mandarin had Taxidermist back in third place when winning it again in 1961.

By the early 1960s the Hennessy was to the autumn what the Whitbread was to the spring – a top-class and competitive handicap chase bringing together some of the best horses around – and the middle of that decade was a golden period in the race's fortunes. The 1963 running pitched Mill House, earlier that year the youngest winner of the Cheltenham Gold Cup since Golden Miller, against Arkle, who two days before Mill House's Gold Cup victory had scored a brilliant victory in Cheltenham's Broadway Chase. These were the two rising stars of steeplechasing, and their first clash was awaited with a tingling anticipation. Mill House had to concede Arkle five pounds and started 15–8 favourite, a market position which he justified by jumping with great panache and pulling easily away from his rivals in the straight to win from Happy Spring and Arkle. But

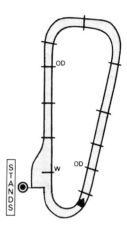

The steeplechase course at Newbury is one of the fairest in the country, flat and galloping with easy bends, but the fences are stiff.

John Francome rode the winner of the Hennessy twice: Brown Chamberlin for Fred Winter in 1983 and Burrough Hill Lad for Jenny Pitman in 1984.

Arkle had slipped on landing over the final open ditch – three out – when moving into a challenging position, and his band of fervent Irish supporters were convinced that Mill House would not beat him again. They were right, and when the two lined up for the following year's Hennessy the complexion of the race was very different. By then Arkle had slammed Mill House in the Gold Cup (see pages 150–1) and this time he was giving weight. Arkle started 5–4 favourite, with Mill House at 13–8, and there was no slip-up, Arkle winning effortlessly and Mill House finishing an exhausted fourth. In 1965 Mill House, slammed by the Irish champion in Sandown Park's Gallaher Gold Cup three weeks earlier when in receipt of sixteen pounds, was not asked to take on Arkle again, and though the Tom Dreaper-trained gelding, carrying twelve stone seven, scored a workmanlike victory from Freddie, he was not at his most impressive. A year later Arkle was back for his fourth Hennessy. Again he carried twelve stone seven pounds and again he was favourite (6–4 on), but he had not had a previous race that season and he was conceding lumps of weight to some very good horses. He led into the last fence but then failed by just half a length to withhold the late challenge of the grey Stalbridge Colonist, to whom he was giving two and a half stone, and on whom Stan Mellor rode a brilliant tactical race, kidding Pat Taaffe on Arkle that he was hard at work and delaying his challenge until Arkle's partner had taken a quick look back after leading over the last. Some measure of the merit of Arkle's performance – which, though a defeat, was surely one of his greatest efforts – is that Stalbridge Colonist was beaten a mere three quarters of a length when second in the 1967 Cheltenham Gold Cup and just over a length when third in 1968.

The last fence of the 1979 Hennessy Cognac Gold Cup: the winner Fighting Fit (*right*) comes to tackle Zongalero.

Welsh National

Chepstow: 3¾ miles

Grade Three handicap steeplechase: five-year-olds and upwards

The Welsh National dates back to the nineteenth century, though it has been run at Chepstow only since 1949. It was first held as the Welsh Grand National at Cardiff in 1895 (originally over two and a half miles): the fierce winter of 1946–7 prevented Cardiff staging the race again before the course went out of business, and it was run at Newport in 1948, moving to Chepstow the following year when Newport itself closed down. The move to Chepstow brought the distance of the race up to three and three quarter miles (it had been three and a half miles since 1920), and the long straights and marked undulations of its new home rendered it a real test of stamina. That first Chepstow running went to Fighting Line, ridden by Dick Francis, who in 1956 had his last big victory as a jockey when winning the Welsh Grand National on the remarkable ten-year-old Crudwell. Two years later Crudwell became the last horse in the country to win fifty races.

In the 1960s the Welsh Grand National was moved from its traditional Easter date to February, becoming a significant trial for the real thing at Liverpool a few weeks later: Rag Trade in 1976 went on from winning at Chepstow to beat Red Rum in the Grand National. The next Liverpool hero to have advertised his chances by winning at Chepstow was Corbiere, but by the the time he won the Welsh contest in 1982 it had been brought forward to the Christmas period, as the February weather was ruining the race, wiping it out in 1975, 1977, 1978 and 1979. It was in 1979, after the fourth abandonment in five years, that it was first run in December.

Its value greatly increased by sponsorship since the early 1970s, the race has become one of the high points of the first half of the season, and although proximity to the King George VI Chase on Boxing Day means that the very cream of chasers tend to be absent, it has in recent years attracted many top-notch horses. Burrough Hill Lad, ridden by John Francome, strolled home in 1983 and went on to win the Cheltenham Gold Cup; Run And Skip, winner in 1985, was fourth to Dawn Run in the Gold Cup later that season; Playschool (1987) had won the Hennessy the month before, and at Chepstow engaged in a stirring finish with Rhyme 'N' Reason, who won the Grand National the following spring. The 1988 and 1989 races belonged to the redoubtable Bonanza Boy, who had a-plenty the very qualities demanded of this famous race: courage, courage, and more courage.

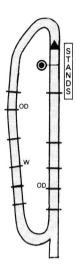

Twice round Chepstow's undulating circuit, with its stiff uphill climb from the home turn, puts a great demand on stamina.

WINNERS SINCE 1980

1980 Narvik
J. Francome 15–1 (18 ran)

1981 Peaty Sandy
Mr T. G. Dun 3–1 (23 ran)

1982 Corbiere
B. de Haan 12–1 (10 ran)

1983 Burrough Hill Lad
J. Francome 100–30 (18 ran)

1984 Righthand Man
G. Bradley 6–1 (18 ran)

1985 Run And Skip
P. Scudamore 13–1 (18 ran)

1986 Stearsby
G. Bradley 8–1 (17 ran)

1987 Playschool
P. Nicholls 5–1 (13 ran)

1988 Bonanza Boy
P. Scudamore 9–4 (12 ran)

1989 Bonanza Boy
P. Scudamore 15–8 (12 ran)

King George VI Chase

Three miles around Kempton is a very fair test for a jumper, with nineteen fences to be jumped – three in the straight – and speed more essential on this flat track than stamina.

Kempton Park: 3 miles

Grade One steeplechase: five-year-olds and upwards

Tidings of comfort and joy. The King George VI Chase on Boxing Day is, for chasing fans, an integral part of the celebration of Christmas, the centrepiece of a day's racing guaranteed to blow away the cobwebs left by seasonal excess and a race second in steeplechasing prestige only to the Cheltenham Gold Cup itself. But it is a race very different in character from the Cheltenham championship. Kempton Park, with its flat surface and tight turns, is a far cry from the long hills of Prestbury Park, and for some horses provides a much more congenial setting in which to display their abilities. The King George is best seen as a championship event in its own right, the mid-point peak of the steeplechasing season and a spectacle always to be savoured, for Kempton's track with three fences close together in the home straight is tailor-made for exciting finishes.

The 1989 King George VI Rank Chase was worth £40,986 to the winner. The first running of the race in 1937 was worth £392. That inaugural running, named to honour the king who had acceded to the throne on 11 December 1936, was run at the end of February, and was seen as a warm-up race for the Gold Cup (in itself, in those days, little more than a preparation for the Grand National, which still overshadowed everything else in the National Hunt season). From an original entry of twenty-four which included the likes of Golden Miller and Reynoldstown (winners between them of five Gold Cups and three Grand Nationals), just four horses went to post: the race was won by 5–4 joint favourite Southern Hero (who had twice won the Scottish Grand National and would win it again) from the other joint-favourite Royal Mail, who won the Grand National the following month. In 1938 a very different sort of horse gave an early illustration of the point that Kempton's three miles can suit speed merchants as well as stayers – if only we'd remembered with Desert Orchid in 1986! – when Airgead Sios, an ebullient front-runner who attacked his fences with breathtaking gusto, held off Macaulay and Morse Code.

When racing resumed at Kempton Park after the war in 1947 the King George was brought forward to Boxing Day to avoid the clash with the Gold Cup and Grand National, and its importance in the racing year was quickly established – as was its role as a traditional Christmas hangover cure for Londoners. Rowland Roy gave trainer Fulke Walwyn the first of his five King George successes when beating a field which included the Gold Cup winner Fortina, and the following year another Gold Cup winner was in the line-up – Cottage Rake, who beat Lord Bicester's Roimond for a first prize of £2,486

Five horses have won the King George VI Chase and the Cheltenham Gold Cup in the same season: Cottage Rake (1948–9), Limber Hill (1955–6), Saffron Tartan (1960–1), Arkle (1965–6) and Desert Orchid (1988–9).

(compared with £1,911 for his Gold Cup that year). Twelve months later Cottage Rake was back, having in the meantime won a second Gold Cup, but in the 1949 King George he went down after a desperate struggle to Lord Bicester's Finnure, ridden by Dick Francis: three months later Cottage Rake won a third Gold Cup, with Finnure ten lengths behind in second place (see page 150).

In 1950 Lord Bicester provided a leading candidate for the third year running when Silver Fame started 3–1 joint favourite, but had to settle for second behind Manicou. This was a highly popular victory, for Manicou (who, very unusually for a steeplechaser, was an entire horse, not a gelding) was owned by Queen Elizabeth, in honour of whose husband the race was named, and the King George was her most important victory to date. Silver Fame would win the Gold Cup (1951), as would another of the 1950 King George runners, Knock Hard (1953). The next phase of the race's history was dominated by two horses: Halloween won twice (1952 and 1954) and in 1953 came fourth to Galloway Braes, who was second to him in 1954 and second to Limber Hill (who won the Gold Cup on his next outing) in 1955.

Mandarin won in 1957 and 1959 and in the intervening year ran third behind Lochroe and Roddy Owen (another King George runner who would win the Gold Cup later in the season); Saffron Tartan won as 5–2 favourite in 1960. Then the weather took over, and the risk involved in running a top-class chase in the bleak midwinter loomed large with the abandonment of the 1961 and 1962 runnings due to frost. In 1963 Mill House, at 7–2 on, beat just two opponents without difficulty, but the next year 'the Big Horse', who had been dethroned by Arkle at Cheltenham (see pages 150–1) was withdrawn at the last minute on account of the state of the frost-bitten ground, and in his absence Frenchman's Cove beat a solitary rival by ten lengths. That rival, though, would have his own moment of glory before long: Jay Trump beat Freddie in a famous finish for the Grand National.

These were the Arkle years. The great horse ran in the King George twice, and both occasions were tinged with deep sadness. By December 1965 Arkle seemed invincible. He had already won two Cheltenham Gold Cups and several other big chases, and had been beaten only once – when conceding large amounts of weight to good horses in the Massey-Ferguson Gold Cup at Cheltenham in 1964 – in over two years. Among his three opponents in 1965 was Dunkirk, a spectacularly fast two-mile chaser but likely to be found short of stamina against opposition the quality of the Irish champion. In his own sphere Dunkirk was a great horse, but he had no real chance against Arkle (as the betting – 7–1 on Arkle, 7–1 against Dunkirk – suggested) and he had been entered by his owner Colonel Bill Whitbread in order to make a race of it. He did just that, charging off into the lead and opening up a huge gap by the time the field passed the winning post and swung right-handed for the second circuit. Dunkirk kept up his ferocious gallop, but as he belted down the far side the pace was beginning to tell, and Arkle was creeping inexorably and inevitably nearer. Dunkirk was slowing down, and Pat Taaffe on Arkle knew that the time had come to take control of the race. Approaching the final open ditch he brought Arkle alongside the front-runner and swept into the lead – as Dunkirk smashed through

WINNERS SINCE 1970

1970 abandoned – snow

1971 The Dikler
    B. Brogan 11–2 (10 ran)

1972 Pendil
    R. Pitman 4–5 (6 ran)

1973 Pendil
    R. Pitman 30–100 (4 ran)

1974 Captain Christy
    R. Coonan 5–1 (6 ran)

1975 Captain Christy
    G. Newman 11–10 (7 ran)

1976 Royal Marshal II
    G. Thorner 16–1 (10 ran)

1977 Bachelor's Hall
    M. O'Halloran 9–2 (9 ran)

1978 Gay Spartan
    T. Carmody 3–1 (16 ran)

1979 Silver Buck
    T. Carmody 3–1 (11 ran)

1980 Silver Buck
    T. Carmody 9–4 (8 ran)

1981 abandoned – frost

1982 Wayward Lad
    J. Francome 7–2 (6 ran)

1983 Wayward Lad
    R. Earnshaw 11–8 (5 ran)

1984 Burrough Hill Lad
    J. Francome 1–2 (3 ran)

1985 Wayward Lad
    G. Bradley 12–1 (5 ran)

1986 Desert Orchid
    S. Sherwood 16–1 (9 ran)

1987 Nupsala
    A. Pommier 25–1 (9 ran)

1988 Desert Orchid
    S. Sherwood 1–2 (5 ran)

1989 Desert Orchid
    R. Dunwoody 4–6 (6 ran)

the fence. Dunkirk was dead: he had had a congestion of blood in his lungs before he got to the fence, and the fall had broken his neck. As spectators rushed to drag jockey Bill Rees from under the smitten horse, Arkle swept on to win by a distance from Dormant.

Dormant was among Arkle's opponents in 1966, as were two other horses who were to make names for themselves the following spring: the Cheltenham Gold Cup winner Woodland Venture and Foinavon, whose achievement in the 1967 Grand National became part of racing legend. Since his 1965 King George victory Arkle had won a third Gold Cup and been beaten just once, in the Hennessy Gold Cup by Stalbridge Colonist (see page 132), and defeat at Kempton seemed out of the question. But on the second circuit of the race Arkle was clearly uneasy, and coming round the final bend he could not shake off Woodland Venture. When that horse crashed to the ground at the second last, however, it seemed that another Arkle victory was a formality. He was well clear of Dormant, and though he fiddled the last fence he surely could not be caught. But Arkle's stride got ever shorter, and Dormant got ever closer. The unthinkable was about to happen, and a few yards before the post it did. Dormant, under strong driving from Jeff King, snatched the race by a length. It did not take long for Arkle's sensational defeat to be explained: he limped back to unsaddle, and it transpired that he had broken a pedal bone in his off-fore hoof – possibly when striking the guard rail of a fence early on the second circuit. He had run his last race.

JOHN McCRIRICK'S DAY OF THE YEAR

Being the original little boy that Santa forgot, I've found Christmas progressively more intolerable save for exultant relief at Kempton Park on Boxing Day.

Yuletide is just a hyped-up, commercially inspired junket, fine for anyone wishing to fantasize away in their own manger. Being a dog in one doesn't mean that I'm a killjoy: kids revel in the wonder and greed of it all, and good luck to them – though my empathy with tots (the in-word for these horrors) is minimal. The Booby has yet to receive a Christmas gift from her boy after more than twenty years of marriage, but don't label me a Scrooge: she can – and unfortunately does – buy whatever she likes. Her greatest holiday joy is driving her wonderful hunk to Kempton for the sole reason any sensible individual has for festive rejoicing – splendid Boxing Day jumping. Memories of those King George VI Chase legends of Christmas Past, mellowed by constant recalling, are better than any lukewarm rum punch. Manicou, Lochroe, Galloway Braes, Halloween and Mandarin; then the giant Mill House, Arkle's triumph and final tragedy; The Dikler, Pendil and Captain Christy; and more recently Silver Buck, Wayward Lad, Burrough Hill Lad and Desert Orchid – each one of their Kempton exploits is worth a hundred times any victory by an ephemeral, pampered 'star' of the Flat.

At Kempton Park on Boxing Day the sheer joy of being alive and of escaping from the enforced jollity and japes of loathsome Christmas transforms the horror of the holiday into a corking cracker of the true sportsman's outing of the year. Come racing!

The next two runnings were abandoned – on account of the foot-and-mouth epidemic in 1967 and a waterlogged course in 1968. But if the King George produces gloom and disappointment, it also produces brilliance. Pendil, so unfortunate in the Gold Cup (see page 151), was in his element around Kempton, as spring-heeled victories in the King George over The Dikler and Shawnigan in 1972 and Inkslinger and The Dikler in 1973 attested. But the Fred Winter-trained gelding found one too good when 7–4 on favourite in 1974 to become the first horse ever to win the race three times. His conqueror was Captain Christy, who had beaten The Dikler in the Gold Cup after Pendil had been brought down at the third last. Scorching round Kempton, Captain Christy won by eight lengths. He returned a year later to put up what John Oaksey described as 'the finest performance seen in a three-mile chase since Arkle retired' as he attacked his fences like a greyhound and drew further and further clear to crush Bula by thirty lengths in course record time.

Wayward Lad ran in the King George five times. In 1982 John Francome had to push him along as Night Nurse and Little Owl made the pace, but he was prominent coming into the straight and at the last fence was upsides another Michael Dickinson runner Silver Buck (winner of that year's Gold Cup) and Fifty Dollars More, then showed his famed turn of foot on the run-in to win at 7–2. The following year he started 11–8 favourite, and with his regular pilot Robert Earnshaw (who had partnered Silver Buck in 1982) back in the saddle unleashed that finishing burst after the second last to beat Brown Chamberlin and The Mighty Mac (also trained by Dickinson). In 1984 – now trained by Dickinson's mother Monica – he was a remote last of three as Burrough Hill Lad and Combs Ditch fought out a pulsating climax, but a year later, starting at 12–1 and ridden by Graham Bradley, held off the luckless Combs Ditch in a memorable run from the last fence to become the first horse to win the race on three occasions.

Wayward Lad was again in the line-up in 1986, when Desert Orchid – allowed to start at 16–1 because few took seriously trainer David Elsworth's assurance that this spectacularly fast two-mile chaser could stay three miles in top company – led from the start and simply kept going in the final stages as the riders of the more fancied staying chasers (including stable jockey Colin Brown, who had deserted the grey in favour of Combs Ditch) vainly tried to get to him. You could almost see Desert Orchid laughing as he skipped over the last fence to win easily from Door Latch and Boland's Cross. The following year he had no breath for laughing, as after having set a breakneck pace with Beau Ranger and Cybrandian he was left flat-footed by the French-trained Nupsala, who strolled in at 25–1 after Forgive 'N Forget had taken a crashing fall at the last and became the first horse trained in France to win a chase in England since 1963. But Desert Orchid, as much a true Kempton horse as Pendil, was back in the winner's enclosure after easy victories in 1988 and 1989 to emulate Wayward Lad's three wins.

A small but top-class field of chasers hammering around Kempton in front of a huge and excited crowd makes the King George a very special moment in the racing year and Kempton on Boxing Day an occasion to be relished. Oh come, all ye faithful . . .

> The King George first received commercial sponsorship in 1986, since when it has been run as the King George VI Rank Chase. The Rank Organisation's support now covers the entire two-day Christmas meeting – the Rank Holiday Festival.

The 1986 King George VI Rank Chase: Desert Orchid at the climax of a breathtaking performance.

Christmas Hurdle

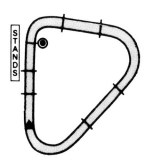

The two-mile hurdle circuit at Kempton Park is flat and sharp, with a straight of three and a half furlongs.

Kempton Park: 2 miles

Grade One hurdle: four-year-olds and upwards

The implementation of the new jumping Pattern system for the 1990–1 season formally established the two-day Rank Holiday Festival as the first peak of the jumping year, and the Christmas Hurdle (run on the second day) became the mid-term hurdling championship, the only two-mile all-aged hurdle race other than the Champion Hurdle itself to be accorded Grade One status and thus a parallel to the King George VI Chase's relationship with the Gold Cup.

The race has long enjoyed a lofty status. Its first running in 1969 went to Terry Biddlecombe on Fred Rimell's Coral Diver, who repeated the feat in the second running in 1971 (the 1970 race having been lost to the snow). In 1973 Lanzarote started at 6–1 on and became the first of three horses to win the Christmas Hurdle and go on to lift the hurdling crown at Cheltenham less than three months later. Lanzarote won the Christmas Hurdle again in 1975, ridden by 23-year-old John Francome on his way to his first jockey's championship. This fine horse, killed in the 1977 Cheltenham Gold Cup, was unbeaten in eight hurdle races at Kempton, where a valuable handicap hurdle in January perpetuates his memory.

The field for the Christmas Hurdle is usually small (the largest yet consisted of just nine runners) but always select, and like so many hurdles around Kempton's tight and flat circuit, the race has often produced memorable finishes. In 1976 Dramatist faced the first two in that year's Champion Hurdle, Night Nurse and Bird's Nest: the three were practically level at the final flight and a magnificent finish ensued, with Dramatist – receiving three pounds from the other two – beating Night Nurse by a neck, with Bird's Nest a head further back. There were only three runners a year later but they were inseparable at the last – Dramatist and Night Nurse again, this time with Jim Joel's Beacon Light; but Night Nurse took a crashing fall which brought about the end of jockey Paddy Broderick's career and Beacon Light strode home. Dawn Run in 1983 beat Gaye Brief (the reigning Champion Hurdler) by a neck after a thrilling duel up the straight and went on to win the 1984 Champion, a feat repeated by Kribensis in the 1989–90 season. Kribensis – who had also won the race in 1988 – had been a high-class performer on the Flat and possessed in abundance the two qualities required for the race: speed and fluent, accurate jumping.

WINNERS SINCE 1980

1980 Celtic Ryde
   J. Francome 2–1 (7 ran)

1981 abandoned – frost

1982 Ekbalco
   J. J. O'Neill 1–2 (4 ran)

1983 Dawn Run
   J. J. O'Neill 9–4 (4 ran)

1984 Browne's Gazette
   D. Browne 11–8 (7 ran)

1985 Aonoch
   J. Duggan 14–1 (9 ran)

1986 Nohalmdun
   P. Scudamore 15–8 (7 ran)

1987 Osric
   G. McCourt 12–1 (8 ran)

1988 Kribensis
   R. Dunwoody 4–9 (7 ran)

1989 Kribensis
   R. Dunwoody 4–6 (8 ran)

Anthony Mildmay, Peter Cazalet Memorial Handicap Chase

Sandown Park: 3 miles 5 furlongs 18 yards

Handicap steeplechase: five-year-olds and upwards

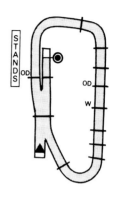

Course description on page 161.

Anthony Mildmay's death at the age of forty-one in 1950 robbed National Hunt racing of one its greatest figures. Immediately after the war he was leading amateur rider five times running, though it was two losing rides that ensured him a place in the history of the Grand National. In 1936, riding 100–1 outsider Davy Jones, he came to the second last going easily and with a good lead over Reynoldstown, but Davy Jones pecked on landing over the fence: Mildmay let the reins slide through his hands to the buckle – but the buckle slipped, the reins parted and fell uselessly under Davy Jones's neck, and the jockey had no control: Davy Jones ran out at the final fence. 'For the rest of his life he loved to watch the film of the race,' wrote Roger Mortimer, 'but its conclusion was always too much for him; after the second last fence it was his invariable custom to emit a dreadful groan and to leave the room.' In 1948 – by which time he had succeeded to his father's title Lord Mildmay of Flete – Mildmay was cruising along on Cromwell with half a mile to go when an attack of cramp in his neck muscles forced his head down on to his chest, rendering him a passenger on his horse, who still managed to finish third behind Sheila's Cottage. Mildmay was an immensely popular rider and was influential in involving Queen Elizabeth in the sport. On the morning of 12 May 1950 he went for a swim in the sea near his home in Devon and was never seen alive again: it is assumed that he suffered another attack of cramp and was drowned.

The race founded to commemorate him was first run in 1952, when Cromwell – on whom Mildmay had scored a famous victory by a neck over Freebooter at Sandown two years previously and who had been left in his will to Mildmay's sister Helen – pulled off an emotional triumph. Cromwell was trained by Peter Cazalet, whose association with Mildmay went back to Davy Jones and beyond and who trained the Queen Mother's horses (including the most sensational National loser of all, Devon Loch) until his death in 1973, and it was entirely appropriate that Cazalet's name should join Mildmay's from 1974.

Several winners have gone on to take the Grand National which so cruelly eluded both men. Team Spirit (1960) won at Liverpool in 1964, West Tip (1985) in 1986 and Mr Frisk (1989) in 1990; Rhyme 'N' Reason (1988) won the National in the same year. The race has also gone to Gold Cup winners Linwell (1956), What A Myth (1966) and Burrough Hill Lad (1984).

---WINNERS SINCE 1980---

1980 Modesty Forbids
   R. Rowe 9–1 (13 ran)

1981 Peter Scot
   P. Barton 6–1 (9 ran)

1982 abandoned – frost and snow

1983 Fifty Dollars More
   R. Linley 4–6 (5 ran)

1984 Burrough Hill Lad
   J. Francome 11–8 (9 ran)

1985 West Tip
   R. Dunwoody 11–4 (5 ran)

1986 Run And Skip
   P. Scudamore 7–2 (8 ran)

1987 Stearsby
   G. McCourt 11–8 (7 ran)

1988 Rhyme 'N' Reason
   C. Brown 11–8 (6 ran)

1989 Mr Frisk
   R. Dunwoody 3–1 (7 ran)

1990 Cool Ground
   A. Tory 6–1 (12 ran)

Tote Gold Trophy

Newbury: 2 miles 100 yards

Grade Three handicap hurdle: four-year-olds and upwards

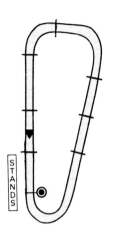

The Newbury hurdle course is ideal for the galloping, long-striding horse: it is wide and flat.

The Tote Gold Trophy began life as the Schweppes Gold Trophy (as some forgetful types persist in calling it) at Liverpool in 1963: forty-two went to post and the race fell to Rosyth, ridden by Josh Gifford and trained by Ryan Price. The tight Liverpool circuit clearly did not suit the race, and in 1964 it was transferred to the much more appropriate track at Newbury, where it again went to Rosyth. But hardly had Gifford dismounted after beating Salmon Spray than the controversy started: Salmon Spray had finished well ahead of Rosyth at Sandown Park in January, and just over a month later Rosyth had reversed the form to the tune of eleven lengths on only four pounds better terms. Abnormal improvement! The National Hunt Committee removed Price's licence until the end of the season, and Gifford was suspended for six weeks. Price's horses were sent to other trainers, and Rosyth – trained by Tom Masson – ran second to Elan in 1965.

Licence restored for the 1965–6 season, Price won his third Schweppes with Le Vermontois in 1966 and his fourth with Hill House in 1967. Hill House's form throughout the season had been indifferent, but rumours abounded that he was being laid out for the Schweppes, and it was even reported that a member of the National Hunt Committee had warned Price that if Hill House were to win the trainer would again be in serious trouble. Win Hill House did, but with many punters sniffing something of a disagreeable odour the booing broke out even before he reached the final flight. Ugly scenes followed at the winner's enclosure, and again Price and Gifford were up before the National Hunt Committee. Then the affair took an even more sensational turn: Hill House's dope test had proved positive to the steroid cortisol. The case dragged on for months: finally Price, Gifford and owner Len Coville were cleared when Hill House was shown to produce his own cortisol to an abnormal level. He became famous as the horse who made his own dope.

The life of the race since then is dull by comparison, though the performance of Persian War when carrying eleven stone thirteen to victory as a five-year-old in 1968 deserves a special mention: no horse before or since has won carrying as much, and the month after the Schweppes, Persian War won the first of his three Champion Hurdles. The weather put paid to eight of the next eighteen runnings, and in 1987 Schweppes transferred their largesse to a valuable handicap at the more temperate Goodwood July Meeting. The Tote stepped into the breach, and the race has remained the big betting event of the period between Christmas and Cheltenham.

WINNERS SINCE 1980

1980 Bootlaces
   P. Leach 20–1 (21 ran)

1981 abandoned – frost

1982 Donegal Prince
   J. Francome 13–1 (27 ran)

1983 abandoned – snow and frost

1984 Ra Nova
   P. A. Farrell 16–1 (26 ran)

1985 abandoned – snow

1986 abandoned – snow

1987 Neblin
   S. Moore 10–1 (21 ran)

1988 Jamesmead
   B. Powell 11–1 (19 ran)

1989 Grey Salute
   R. Dunwoody 8–1 (10 ran)

1990 Deep Sensation
   R. Rowe 7–1 (17 ran)

Racing Post Chase

Kempton Park: 3 miles

Grade Three handicap steeplechase: five-year-olds and upwards

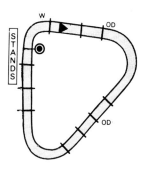

Course description on page 134.

The *Racing Post* had full value from the first three runnings of the event which, having started life as the Coventry Chase before the war (Easter Hero won it in 1928) and then benefited from a variety of sponsors, now bears its name. The 1988 winner Rhyme 'N' Reason went on to win the Grand National. In 1989 Bonanza Boy put up one of the most remarkable performances seen that season. Having failed to keep up in the early stages of a race run on very heavy going, Martin Pipe's game little chaser was getting further and further behind, and at halfway was being scrubbed along by Peter Scudamore. But he plugged on and manoeuvred himself into a challenging position in the straight. At the last fence he was third behind Gainsay and Ballyhane, but on the run-in forged his way to the front to snatch victory from what half a minute earlier had looked certain defeat. There were no such shifts in the complexion of the 1989 race, when Desert Orchid, conceding two stone or more to his seven rivals, led for the first circuit, had a breather while Solidasarock took up the running, and then regained the lead in the home straight, going on to record what for many was his finest victory to date.

So Desert Orchid's name was added to a list of winners which already contained some of the best post-war chasers. The novice Mont Tremblant had won in 1952 before going on to take the Cheltenham Gold Cup, and other winners in the 1950s were Halloween (1955), Pointsman (1957) and Lochroe (1958). In the sixties came Frenchman's Cove (1962), the Queen Mother's dashing chaser The Rip (1965), Kapeno (1966) and Different Class (1968). In the early 1970s the status of the race was raised a notch, with winners as good as Titus Oates (1970), The Laird (1971) and Crisp (1972), and the following two runnings going to that great Kempton specialist Pendil. In 1973 he faced just two opponents in what was then the Yellow Pages Pattern Chase and, starting at 7–1 on, coasted in to set him up for his unfortunate first attempt at the Gold Cup. A year later Pendil was back: again he had just two opponents, again he started at prohibitive odds (6–1 on), and again he won easily. He ran in the Yellow Pages in 1975 but finished lame, third behind Cuckolder. Nearly two years later he returned to action, and after winning his first three races in the 1976–7 term found the concession of thirty-three pounds to Don't Hesitate in the Yellow Pages too much, going down by four lengths. He ran only once more, pulling up lame at Kempton in December 1977: his thirteen races there had brought nine victories.

WINNERS SINCE 1980

1980 Father Delaney
A. Brown 9–1 (10 ran)

1981 Sugarally
P. Scudamore 9–2 (8 ran)

1982 Two Swallows
A. Webber 6–1 (7 ran)

1983 Manton Castle
H. Davies 15–2 (10 ran)

1984 Tom's Little Al
C. Brown 6–1 (10 ran)

1985 abandoned – frost

1986 abandoned – frost

1987 Combs Ditch
C. Brown 11–10 (4 ran)

1988 Rhyme 'N' Reason
B. Powell 7–2 (12 ran)

1989 Bonanza Boy
P. Scudamore 5–1 (11 ran)

1990 Desert Orchid
R. Dunwoody 8–11 (8 ran)

CHELTENHAM NATIONAL HUNT FESTIVAL

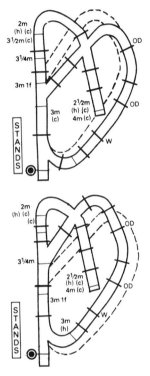

Breathes there a man with soul so dead who never to himself hath said: 'It's Cheltenham week!'? Sadly there breathe quite a few, for in recent years it has become fashionable to carp at the Cheltenham National Hunt Festival: the crush is so oppressive that it's impossible to get to any bar for a drink, the spreading bindweed of the tented hospitality village chokes the enjoyment of real racegoers, the place is overrun by lager louts, yuppies and Dessiemaniacs, blah blah blah. But the discomforts of the Festival are grossly exaggerated, and if the crabbed spirits stay away that simply makes the week the more enjoyable for the tens of thousands – over 50,000 on Gold Cup day alone – who flock to this most spectacularly situated of racecourses to create the inimitable atmosphere of the three-day Festival meeting. Despite the flow of Irish winners having dwindled in recent years to a trickle, the Festival is still a magnet to a huge contingent of enthusiasts from across the Irish Sea, who play their part in making the Cheltenham betting ring the strongest in the world. If Derby Day is popular celebration, Cheltenham is celebration of the sport itself – three days of the very best that National Hunt racing can provide, in a wonderful setting and in front of a crowd who are drawn there by their love of the game.

The traditional curtain-raiser on the Tuesday is the SUPREME NOVICES' HURDLE over two miles, after which follows a succession of major races: the ARKLE CHALLENGE TROPHY (two miles) for novice chasers, the CHAMPION HURDLE (see opposite) and the STAYERS' HURDLE (three miles one furlong). Wednesday features the SUN ALLIANCE NOVICES' HURDLE (two and a half miles) and the SUN ALLIANCE CHASE (three miles) as well as the QUEEN MOTHER CHAMPION CHASE (page 146), the CORAL GOLDEN HURDLE FINAL (a three-mile handicap hurdle which attracts a large volume of betting) and the NATIONAL HUNT CHASE over four miles for amateur riders. Thursday starts off with the TRIUMPH HURDLE (page 147) and moves on to the FOXHUNTER CHALLENGE CUP, the top race of the season for hunter-chasers – and the GOLD CUP (pages 148–51) itself.

But Cheltenham is more than the sum of its parts. It is an occasion unparalleled in the racing year for excitement, quality of sport and the sheer enjoyment of National Hunt racing at its very best.

There are two intertwined courses at Cheltenham, sharing the same characteristics. The lowest point of the course is at the entrance to the straight, from where the runners face a gradual climb through left-hand turns to the top of the hill, about a mile out. They then negotiate a sharp descent (on which the fences are particularly trappy) before turning into the straight to face the last fence or hurdle (two fences in the straight on the New Course) and then haul themselves up the very steep hill to the winning post. Races over 2½ miles and 4 miles start on a spur in the middle of the course and take the runners way out to the left of the stands before a long sweeping turn round towards the straight. (Indicated above are the positions of the steeplechase fences: hurdle positions are shown in the appropriate race entry.)

Champion Hurdle Challenge Trophy

Cheltenham: 2 miles

Grade One hurdle: four-year-olds and upwards

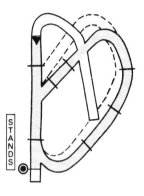

The Champion Hurdle might hardly have seemed worthy of the name when four horses went out for its first running on Wednesday 9 March 1927. With a prize to the winner of just £365 it was the least valuable of the four hurdle races run at the meeting, but the race was none the less recognized to be an important breakthrough in the history of National Hunt racing: the most valuable hurdles at that time were all handicaps, and here was a new contest at the season's principal meeting being run on weight-for-age terms, following the example of its steeplechasing equivalent the Gold Cup, first run three years earlier. Despite its paltry prize, that first Champion Hurdle did attract one of the best hurdlers around in Blaris (who had won seven hurdle races and had warmed up for Cheltenham with the unorthodox preparation of a two-mile steeplechase), ridden by the famous hurdle-race specialist George Duller. Favourite at 11–10, Blaris won by eight lengths (a winning distance not equalled until Bula in 1972).

Six months after Blaris's victory a four-year-old gelding named Brown Jack finished third on his hurdling debut at Bournemouth. Third favourite for the 1928 Champion at 4–1 (Blaris was favourite at 6–4), he took up the running after the final flight of hurdles to win by one and a half lengths. Brown Jack did not race over hurdles again: he won eighteen races on the Flat, including the Queen Alexandra Stakes at Royal Ascot six years running from 1929 to 1934.

The other great hero of the Champion Hurdle in the pre-war period was Dorothy Paget's Insurance, who beat just two opponents in 1932 when 5–4 on favourite. Second that year was his great rival Song of Essex, who took on Insurance again in 1933 and tried to gain an advantage before the start by the crude means of clamping his teeth round the arm of Insurance's jockey Billy Stott. Such behaviour got the answer it merited as Stott, having bound his wound with a handkerchief, rode Insurance to a three-quarter length victory over Windermere Laddie. Song Of Essex fell when challenging at the last: serves him right. Dorothy Paget won the race again when Sean Magee brought Solford home in 1940 from African Sister, who the previous year had become the first (and until Dawn Run the only) mare to win the race. Solford, who had fallen at the last in 1939, was 7–4 on to win for a second time in 1941, but finished unplaced. Miss Paget's fourth Champion came with Distel in 1946.

Like many famous races, the Champion Hurdle has had its purple

> The longest-priced Champion Hurdle winners were Kirriemuir (1965) and Beech Road (1989) at 50–1. The shortest-priced was Sir Ken (1953) at 5–2 on.

WINNERS SINCE 1970

1970 Persian War
J. Uttley 5–4 (14 ran)

1971 Bula
P. Kelleway 15–8 (9 ran)

1972 Bula
P. Kelleway 8–11 (12 ran)

1973 Comedy Of Errors
W. Smith 8–1 (8 ran)

1974 Lanzarote
R. Pitman 7–4 (7 ran)

1975 Comedy Of Errors
K. White 11–8 (13 ran)

1976 Night Nurse
P. Broderick 2–1 (8 ran)

1977 Night Nurse
P. Broderick 15–2 (10 ran)

1978 Monksfield
T. Kinane 11–2 (13 ran)

1979 Monksfield
D. T. Hughes 9–4 (10 ran)

1980 Sea Pigeon
J. J. O'Neill 13–2 (9 ran)

1981 Sea Pigeon
J. Francome 7–4 (14 ran)

1982 For Auction
Mr C. Magnier 40–1 (14 ran)

1983 Gaye Brief
R. Linley 7–1 (17 ran)

1984 Dawn Run
J. J. O'Neill 4–5 (14 ran)

1985 See You Then
S. Smith Eccles 16–1 (14 ran)

1986 See You Then
S. Smith Eccles 5–6 (23 ran)

1987 See You Then
S. Smith Eccles 11–10 (18 ran)

1988 Celtic Shot
P. Scudamore 7–1 (21 ran)

1989 Beech Road
R. Guest 50–1 (15 ran)

1990 Kribensis
R. Dunwoody 95–40 (19 ran)

patches of interest, excellence and excitement, and the first of these was certainly the ten years after the war. This was a period dominated by three great hurdlers, whose achievements in the race did much to raise the profile of hurdle racing. In 1947 (when the race was run in April after the hard winter had caused cancellation of the March fixture) the favourite was the French horse Le Paillon, ridden by Alec Head, but Head steered an unusual course round the outside, forfeiting many lengths; in the straight he still had a chance but National Spirit on the inside had more in hand and won by a length. (Later that year Le Paillon booked himself into racing trivia quizzes by becoming the only horse to be placed in a Champion Hurdle and win the Prix de l'Arc de Triomphe.) National Spirit, trained at Epsom by Vic Smyth, was back a year later and started 6–4 favourite: he won comfortably by two lengths, but among the also-rans was a horse of whom National Spirit would be seeing a great deal – Hatton's Grace. By the time of the 1950 Champion Hurdle, Hatton's Grace was trained by Vincent O'Brien, who had already made his mark on Cheltenham by sending out Cottage Rake to win the Gold Cup in 1948 and 1949 (with the 1950 title to come). A singularly unprepossessing animal, Hatton's Grace had originally been sold for just eighteen guineas, but his performances in three Champion Hurdles endeared him to the racing public, and he turned out to be a horse of extreme versatility, winning the Irish Lincoln and the Irish Cesarewitch on the Flat and one of his four steeplechases. His first Champion Hurdle victory came at the age of nine – old for a hurdler – when he beat Vatelys by six lengths in 1949, with National Spirit fourth. The following year he started 5–2 favourite and beat Harlech, with National Spirit, who had blundered badly when leading at the final flight, again fourth. In 1951 the favourite had the uninspiring name of Average, but it was the eleven-year-old Hatton's Grace and the ten-year-old National Spirit who again came to the last together: National Spirit was just in the lead and attempted a prodigious leap but slipped on landing, hurling jockey Dennis Dillon off as Hatton's Grace charged up the hill for a third victory.

The two were back the following year, but now a new star emerged: Sir Ken. A five-year-old, he arrived at Cheltenham unbeaten in eight hurdle races, and started the 3–1 favourite: he won by two lengths from Noholme. In 1953 he won at 5–2 on, and was not beaten in a hurdle race until October that year, when third (at 7–1 on) at Uttoxeter to Impney. In the 1954 Champion Hurdle it was Impney who for a while looked like denying Sir Ken his third title, going well clear before the last; but Tim Molony on Sir Ken collared Impney on the run-in to win by a length.

The second golden period in the race's life begins with another triple winner. Persian War's first victory came in 1968 as a five-year-old, a few weeks after he had won the Schweppes Gold Trophy carrying eleven stone thirteen: he started second favourite and beat the more fancied Chorus II by four lengths. That was on firm going, but heavy ground in 1969 made no difference: another four-length victory. And in 1970 he beat Major Rose by one and a half lengths. Like Sir Ken, Persian War came back to try for a unique fourth title, but in 1971 he found one too good – Bula. And so the glorious roll of honour through the 1970s continued. Bula won again in 1972 and in 1973 was 6–5 on to join Sir Ken and Persian War as triple winners, only to be well and truly turned over by yet another new hurdling star, Comedy Of Errors. (Third in that race was Captain Christy, who a year later would win the Gold Cup.) But Comedy Of Errors went down three lengths in 1974 to Lanzarote, then regained the title in 1975 when beating Flash Imp and Tree Tangle, with Lanzarote unplaced. Both Comedy Of Errors and Lanzarote were back in 1976, but by now a younger generation of crack hurdlers was ready to dominate the race – and what contests ensued! Consider the placed horses in the next six runnings:

1976 Night Nurse, Bird's Nest, Flash Imp
1977 Night Nurse, Monksfield, Dramatist
1978 Monksfield, Sea Pigeon, Night Nurse
1979 Monksfield, Sea Pigeon, Beacon Light
1980 Sea Pigeon, Monksfield, Bird's Nest
1981 Sea Pigeon, Pollardstown, Daring Run.

Of those six memorable contests special mention must be made of the three races in 1978, 1979 and 1980 when Monksfield and Sea Pigeon came to the last flight together. In 1978 the diminutive Irish-trained entire Monksfield sprinted up the hill to a two-length victory, but 1979 produced perhaps the greatest Champion Hurdle of the lot. Monksfield led at every flight until, coming to the last, Jonjo O'Neill on Sea Pigeon cruised up on his inside and edged ahead, apparently going much the better. Monksfield, flat to the boards, responded with a huge jump which brought him back alongside as the two landed, but Sea Pigeon sneaked into the lead again and looked set for victory. The next few seconds saw Monksfield at his very best, as he stuck his head down and inched back towards his rival. Halfway up the run-in Sea Pigeon still looked to have the race sewn up, but Monksfield – as game a horse as ever ran – would not be denied, and scrambled back to win by three quarters of a length. A year later the distance of the race had been shortened by nearly a furlong to two miles, no longer requiring the runners to negotiate the sharp bend beyond the winning post, and the Champion Hurdle was now run on the first day of the meeting, thus ensuring better ground. Possibly benefiting from these changes, Sea Pigeon (again ridden by O'Neill) this time delayed the full force of his challenge until after the last, passing Monksfield on the run-in to win by seven lengths. By the time of the 1981 race Monksfield had been retired, and John Francome displayed his riding skills at their very peak to bring Sea Pigeon up the hill with nonchalant ease to beat Pollardstown and Daring Run.

Between Saucy Kit in 1967 and For Auction in 1982 only Lanzarote had won the Champion Hurdle without repeating the feat, and the way the race year after year brought the same great hurdlers into opposition added lustre to the whole season: the Champion Hurdle was sometimes a more keenly awaited and contested race than the Gold Cup itself. And in the 1980s we had Dawn Run, and another triple winner in the curmudgeonly See You Then. No wonder the Champion Hurdle is one of those special events in the racing year, a watershed: the complexion of the sport changes with its every running.

> The 1963 victor Winning Fair had only one eye. He was ridden by Alan Lillingston, the second amateur to win the race.

Monksfield (*left*) and Sea Pigeon inseparable at the final flight in the 1979 Waterford Crystal Champion Hurdle.

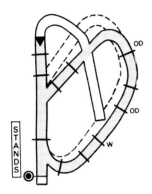

Queen Mother Champion Chase

Cheltenham: 2 miles

Grade One steeplechase: five-year-olds and upwards

Queen Elizabeth had her first winner as an owner when Monaveen (owned in partnership with her daughter the present Queen) won at Fontwell Park on 10 October 1949. Thereafter her enthusiasm for National Hunt racing blossomed, and a succession of famous horses ran in the colours – blue, buff stripes, blue sleeves, black cap and gold tassel – which she registered in the autumn of 1950. There was Manicou, who won the King George at Kempton Park; that bold chaser The Rip; Game Spirit, who won twenty-one races; Tammuz, who won the 1975 Schweppes Gold Trophy; Sunyboy, who gave the Queen Mother her 300th victory when winning at Ascot in February 1976; Devon Loch, whose experience in the 1956 Grand National is so painful to recall; and many others, including Makaldar, Laffy, Gay Record, Inch Arran and Double Star. Two of her old warriors joined Desert Orchid to salute her in the parade held in London in June 1990 as part of the celebrations to mark her ninetieth birthday: Special Cargo, who delivered her greatest victory in that heart-stopping race for the 1984 Whitbread Gold Cup, and The Argonaut.

The Queen Mother's involvement with National Hunt racing has been its greatest blessing, and it was fitting that in 1980 – the year of her eightieth birthday – her name should first grace the title of one of the three most important events at jump racing's most important meeting. The National Hunt Two Mile Champion Chase Trophy, as it had been called, was first run in 1959, when it was won by Quita Que (runner-up in the Champion Hurdle in 1956 and 1957). The next two runnings went to Tom Dreaper's Fortria, a brilliant two-miler who finished second in the 1962 and 1963 Gold Cups. So the race quickly filled the bill of a championship contest for chasers over the shortest distance: it was *the* race for a two-mile chaser to be aimed at, and is always a thrilling sight. Dunkirk charged round to win in 1965 under Dave Dick (whose post-race comment to owner Bill Whitbread after another victory on this flying horse was eloquent in its simplicity – 'Blimey!'). Flyingbolt, the Dreaper stalwart who at one stage was handicapped within two pounds of Arkle, won at 5–1 on in 1966 and the next day was a close-up third in the Champion Hurdle. Crisp won in 1971, Royal Relief in 1972 and 1974 (one of several dual winners, the most recent of which were Pearlyman in 1987 and 1988 and Barnbrook Again in 1989 and then after a stirring duel with Waterloo Boy in 1990), and the Dickinson horse Badsworth Boy took the race three times in 1983–5. Champions all.

Triumph Hurdle

Cheltenham: 2 miles

Grade One hurdle: four-year-olds only

For months before the race interest in the Triumph Hurdle runs high, and every promising run by a juvenile hurdler has the lively ante-post betting market re-forming. It is baffling why this should be so, for the Triumph is a notoriously difficult contest to predict on the day, let alone months in advance, and has rarely produced the sort of result which has punters rushing round to the bookies with their ante-post vouchers. It could hardly be otherwise, for the form of the youngest age-group of the National Hunt game is woefully difficult to unravel, and many of the runners have never been subjected to the huge field, breakneck pace and highly demanding terrain which form the essence of this event. Nor does it have a good record in pointing out future Champion Hurdlers: since the race was moved to Cheltenham only Persian War (1967) and Kribensis (1988) have gone on from winning the Triumph to take the Champion, though Monksfield (1976) and See You Then (1984) were second.

The Triumph Hurdle was first run in 1939 at the now defunct course of Hurst Park. Clair Soleil, Champion Hurdler in 1955, won in 1953, and the following year the race went to 11–4 favourite Prince Charlemagne, unplaced in Pinza's Derby and at Hurst Park giving Lester Piggott one of his twenty wins over hurdles. The last Triumph at Hurst Park was in 1962, when Beaver II at 100–6 beat his more fancied stable-companion Catapult II (7–4 favourite). The race was revived – and first attracted the sponsorship from the *Daily Express* which has lasted to the present – at the Cheltenham April meeting in 1965, transferring to the Festival fixture in 1968.

Since then the Daily Express Triumph Hurdle has produced many memorable occasions: Peter O'Sullevan's wonderful little Attivo demolished the last flight in 1974 before scampering up the hill to beat twenty rivals; Baron Blakeney scored at 66–1 in 1981 to provide a first big-race victory for a little-known West Country trainer named Martin Pipe; and in 1986 Solar Cloud – another outsider at 40–1 – gave trainer David Nicholson and jockey Peter Scudamore the first Festival winner which had eluded each of them for so long.

Even fresher in the memory are the victories of 66–1 shot Ikdam in 1989 and Rare Holiday at 25–1 in 1990. Indeed, six of the last eleven winners have started at 25–1 or longer. Clearly this is not a race to bet on seriously. But wasn't that a nice performance for a raw juvenile hurdler? Pass me an ante-post slip, please ...

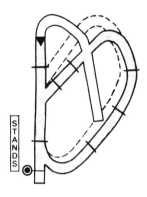

WINNERS SINCE 1980

1980 Heighlin
   S. Jobar 40–1 (26 ran)

1981 Baron Blakeney
   P. Leach 66–1 (29 ran)

1982 Shiny Copper
   A. Webb 66–1 (29 ran)

1983 Saxon Farm
   M. Perrett 12–1 (30 ran)

1984 Northern Game
   T. J. Ryan 20–1 (30 ran)

1985 First Bout
   S. Smith Eccles 5–1 (27 ran)

1986 Solar Cloud
   P. Scudamore 40–1 (28 ran)

1987 Alone Success
   S. Smith Eccles 11 1 (29 ran)

1988 Kribensis
   R. Dunwoody 6–1 (26 ran)

1989 Ikdam
   N. Coleman 66–1 (27 ran)

1990 Rare Holiday
   B. Sheridan 25–1 (30 ran)

Cheltenham Gold Cup

Cheltenham: 3¼ miles

Grade One steeplechase: five-year-olds and upwards

Between the victory of Red Splash in the first Cheltenham Gold Cup on 12 March 1924 and that of Norton's Coin on 15 March 1990 the history of the race unfolds like a rich tapestry illustrating all that is the very best in steeplechasing. To sample its flavour we can remember one contest from each of the eight decades in which it has been run.

1929: Easter Hero

The Gold Cup did not immediately become the acknowledged championship of chasing. At the time of its foundation the National Hunt season was still completely dominated by the Grand National, which was the only worthwhile target for top chasers. But the executive at Cheltenham racecourse decided to add the comparative novelty of a weight-for-age steeplechase to the important National Hunt Meeting in March in order to offer the best long-distance chasers the chance to race against each other on level terms, and the Gold Cup was the result. In the season of its first running there was little hint of the pre-eminent place it was to occupy in the racing year: it was not even the most valuable steeplechase of the meeting, that distinction going to the National Hunt Steeplechase, worth £1,285 to the winner. The Gold Cup was worth just over half that at £685 (compared with the Grand National at £8,240). But by the end of the 1920s the race had gained something in prestige, if not much in value: the sum of just £776 which went to Jock Whitney, owner of the 1929 winner Easter Hero, was still less than the prize for the National Hunt Chase.

    Easter Hero had already made his mark in sensational fashion. A horse of exceptional physical quality by the standards of 1920s chasers, he had started a well-backed 100–7 chance for the 1928 Grand National in the colours of the Belgian financier Captain Lowenstein. At the Canal Turn (then an open ditch) on the first circuit he was well clear of his rivals but misjudged his take-off, landed smack on top of the fence, and was stuck; as he tried to wriggle his way off he slid back into the ditch, where he regained his feet but could not clamber out. All but nine of the pursuing pack were brought to a complete halt by this display, and pandemonium reigned: the ditch was subsequently filled in. By the beginning of 1929 Easter Hero had been sold to the American multi-millionaire Jock Whitney after Lowenstein's plane had disappeared over the North Sea.

    Four victories in hurdle races were the unusual preface to Easter Hero's first attempt on the Gold Cup, and in the race itself he started

> The shortest-priced winner of the Cheltenham Gold Cup was Arkle at 10–1 on in 1966, the longest Norton's Coin at 100–1 in 1990.

Norton's Coin returns in triumph after his sensational 1990 victory.

7–4 favourite against nine rivals, the largest field the event had yet attracted and a line-up of great class: Koko had won the race in 1926, Grakle had been second in 1927 (and was to win the National in 1931), and Bright's Boy had twice come third in the Liverpool race. For Easter Hero, as for all Gold Cup aspirants in those days, the Cheltenham race was a preparation for more serious business to come in the National, but he none the less faced a stiff task against such opposition. He took the lead soon after the start and went further and further ahead, so that by the time the field passed the stands after one circuit he was thirty lengths in front. Grakle and Bright's Boy came closer when jockey Fred Rees eased Easter Hero going out on the second circuit, but when Whitney's horse was sent about his business again he cruised down the hill and swung into the straight unchallenged to win by twenty lengths from Lloydie and Grakle. It was a brilliant performance, but it did more than just proclaim Easter Hero's class: it helped to raise the status of the Gold Cup, for the winner was a horse who proclaimed the arrival of a new mould of chaser, altogether finer physically than his predecessors. That prestige was further enhanced when Easter Hero won again in 1930 – again by twenty lengths – from Gib.

1935: Golden Miller and Thomond II

This was possibly the greatest Gold Cup ever run. Dorothy Paget's Golden Miller was already the best chaser yet, winner of three Cheltenham Gold Cups and in 1934 becoming the only horse to win the Gold Cup and the Grand National in the same year. The 1935 race was expected to be a simple warm-up for Golden Miller's Liverpool bid, for his great rival Thomond II (owned, like Easter Hero, by Jock Whitney) was to miss the race. Consequently Golden Miller was not brought to peak fitness for Cheltenham, and his trainer Basil Briscoe was aggrieved to learn just two days before the race that Whitney had changed his mind: Thomond would run. Kellsboro' Jack (Grand National winner in 1933), Southern Hero (who had beaten Golden Miller in a handicap in 1934) and Avenger made up the field, but it was Thomond and Golden Miller who produced a scintillating race. At the third last the two were disputing affairs at a ferocious pace, with Kellsboro' Jack trying to get on terms. But the upstart was beaten off and at the second last Thomond and the Miller were upsides. Then Golden Miller's giant stride started to tell, and he went half a length up as they hurtled towards the last. Billy Speck on Thomond, hugging the inside, went for his whip and threw his mount at the fence, so that the two landed dead level and set off up the hill amid scenes of delirious excitement. Neither would succumb, but ever so slowly Golden Miller forced his head in front and won by three quarters of a length. He would take the race for an extraordinary fifth time in 1936 and finish second to Morse Code in 1938 (the 1937 race was abandoned). No horse has a Cheltenham Gold Cup record remotely to match his.

1946: Prince Regent

It is a tribute to the stature of Prince Regent – in some ways the forgotten idol in the pantheon of great chasers – that his trainer Tom

┌─ **WINNERS SINCE 1970** ─┐

1970 L'Escargot
   T. Carberry 33–1 (12 ran)

1971 L'Escargot
   T. Carberry 7–2 (8 ran)

1972 Glencaraig Lady
   F. Berry 6–1 (12 ran)

1973 The Dikler
   R. Barry 9–1 (8 ran)

1974 Captain Christy
   H. Beasley 7–1 (7 ran)

1975 Ten Up
   T. Carberry 2–1 (8 ran)

1976 Royal Frolic
   J. Burke 14–1 (11 ran)

1977 Davy Lad
   D. T. Hughes 14–1 (13 ran)

1978 Midnight Court
   J. Francome 5–2 (10 ran)

1979 Alverton
   J. J. O'Neill 5–1 (14 ran)

1980 Master Smudge
   R. Hoare 14–1 (15 ran)

1981 Little Owl
   Mr A. J. Wilson 6–1 (15 ran)

1982 Silver Buck
   R. Earnshaw 8–1 (22 ran)

1983 Bregawn
   G. Bradley 100–30 (11 ran)

1984 Burrough Hill Lad
   P. Tuck 7–2 (12 ran)

1985 Forgive 'N Forget
   M. Dwyer 7–1 (15 ran)

1986 Dawn Run
   J. J. O'Neill 15–8 (11 ran)

1987 The Thinker
   R. Lamb 13–2 (12 ran)

1988 Charter Party
   R. Dunwoody 10–1 (15 ran)

1989 Desert Orchid
   S. Sherwood 5–2 (13 ran)

1990 Norton's Coin
   G. McCourt 100–1 (12 ran)

MICHAEL DICKINSON, 1983

Michael Dickinson's first five home in the 1983 Cheltenham Gold represented the most extraordinary training feat of the modern era. The first two in the 1982 running, Silver Buck and Bregawn, had both been sent out from the Harewood yard where Dickinson had taken over the licence from his father Tony, and these two horses were joined in the 1983 line-up by three stable-companions: Captain John, Wayward Lad and Ashley House. Six horses opposed the quintet, but at the last fence only Combs Ditch was still threatening to spoil a clean sweep as Bregawn charged away from Captain John, with Wayward Lad and Silver Buck third and fourth. Then Ashley House stayed on up the final incline to pass Combs Ditch and reach fifth place. The Stewards gave Ashley House the unique privilege of being unsaddled with the placed horses in the winner's enclosure, an appropriate gesture to mark Dickinson's surely unrepeatable achievement.

Arkle (Pat Taaffe) on his way to his third Gold Cup in 1966.

Dreaper would not acknowledge his other great charge Arkle to be the better horse until after Arkle had won two Gold Cups. But for the war, and the disruption it caused to National Hunt racing, Prince Regent may well have achieved enough to join Golden Miller and Arkle in discussions about who was the greatest. Prince Regent was eleven before he had his chance in the Gold Cup, but he was worshipped in Ireland (where he had won fifteen races, in addition to one on his only previous visit to England) and he came with such a mammoth reputation that he started at 7–4 on to take a first prize of £1,130. He won by seven lengths from Poor Flame (ridden by Fred Rimell) in majestic style, but at his moment of greatest glory he was past his best. 'It took me a minute or two to beat that fellow today, Tom,' jockey Tim Hyde reported to Dreaper on dismounting. Three weeks later Prince Regent was third in the Grand National under twelve stone five pounds, but he did not run again in the Gold Cup. Who knows just how good he was?

1950: Cottage Rake

Cottage Rake, trained by Vincent O'Brien and ridden by Aubrey Brabazon, won the Gold Cup three times, beating Happy Home by one and a half lengths when 10–1 in 1948, Cool Customer by two lengths when 6–4 on favourite the following year, and Finnure by ten when 6–5 on (5–4 Finnure, 28–1 bar in a field of six) in 1950. By March 1950 Cottage Rake was eleven and Finnure nine, and they had last met in a memorable finish for the King George VI Chase at Kempton, when Finnure had just prevailed. But 'the Rake' was in his true domain at Cheltenham, and after Martin Molony on Finnure had set a funereal early pace in the hope of being able to beat the Irish horse with a late burst of speed, Brabazon kicked on for all he was worth at the top of the hill and Cottage Rake rocketed down towards the straight to go further and further clear. Finnure was beaten ten lengths.

1964: Arkle and Mill House

After notable victories by Kerstin (1958, only the second mare to win), Pas Seul (1960) and Mandarin (1962), we come to possibly the most keenly anticipated steeplechase of modern times. Trained by Fulke Walwyn, Mill House was a brilliant young chaser who had won the Gold Cup at the tender age of six in 1963; Arkle, trained by Tom Dreaper, was the same age as his giant rival and had only once been beaten in a chase, by Mill House himself in the Hennessy Gold Cup the previous November – but he had slipped on landing over the last open ditch at Newbury and his supporters were convinced that he was the better horse. The English were equally sure that Mill House was the best chaser since Golden Miller. The Gold Cup would sort the matter out. The two horses who opposed them – Pas Seul and King's Nephew – were never seen with a chance once Mill House turned on the style for the second circuit, and by the top of the hill Willie Robinson on Mill House was trying to settle the issue through a succession of huge jumps. But the hard-pulling Arkle kept on in his wake with nonchalant ease, and as they turned down the hill for the last time the writing was on the wall. Mill House still had an advantage jumping the third from home, when Pat Taaffe on the Irish-trained horse rousted Arkle for a decisive effort. The response was instant, and Arkle swung into the straight and headed for the last with the race in his grasp: he sailed over the fence, and though Mill House made one last-gasp effort on the run-in there was no doubt who was the real champion. Arkle scampered up to the post to win by five lengths.

Arkle won the Gold Cup twice more, beating Mill House again in 1965 and coasting round to win (despite his famous bloomer at the fence in front of the stands) in 1966.

1973: The Dikler and Pendil
The Dikler was the last of Fulke Walwyn's four Gold Cup winners, but the 1973 race is mainly remembered as the race which Pendil did not win. Favourite at 6–4 on, Fred Winter-trained Pendil had been hailed by some as the best chaser since Arkle after remaining unbeaten in eleven chases (including the 1972 King George), and at the last fence in the Gold Cup jockey Richard Pitman had shot him clear and seemed to have the race at his mercy. He skipped over and made his way up the hill to certain victory, but halfway up the run-in faltered, pricked his ears momentarily at the wall of noise greeting him, and lost his action, allowing the gigantic form of The Dikler, roused to full power by Ron Barry, to get to him; Pendil revived, but too late, and was beaten a short head. In 1974 Pendil was back – an even shorter-priced favourite – but was brought down when moving up to challenge at the third last.

1989: Desert Orchid
Everything seemed to be against Desert Orchid – not least the weather (snow had fallen heavily that morning) which had turned the course into a sodden morass which would plumb the depths of his stamina and make his task even more difficult on a course which many thought did not bring out his best. But he plugged on stoically in conditions he was clearly loathing, and with leader Ten Plus suffering a fatal fall at the third last only soft-ground specialist Yahoo stood between the beloved Dessie and his finest hour. Though looking beaten between the last two fences, Desert Orchid was only just behind Yahoo at the last, and with a finishing burst which is etched on the memory of all who witnessed it shoved his way back to seize as glorious a moment as any in Cheltenham history.

1990: Norton's Coin
Desert Orchid was back, and odds-on favourite to win again in much more congenial conditions. But he could finish only third as 100–1 chance Norton's Coin – whose stable was in a converted milking shed on the dairy farm in Carmarthen run by Sirrell Griffiths, trainer of just three horses – fought out a duel with Toby Tobias on the run-in to pull off one of the Gold Cup's most glorious results.

So Norton's Coin joined the most distinguished roll of honour in steeplechasing. The ghosts of Easter Hero, Golden Miller, Prince Regent and Arkle would have nodded approval of their unlikely companion.

DAWN RUN, 1986

Dawn Run was the first horse ever to win the Champion Hurdle and the Cheltenham Gold Cup. She notched up a hard-fought Champion Hurdle success when beating Cima by three quarters of a length in 1984, and the following season turned to chasing. Having won her first steeplechase in November 1984, she was then injured, and did not reappear until over a year later. By the time of the 1986 Gold Cup she had run in just four chases, and at Cheltenham was opposed by such seasoned performers as Forgive 'N Forget, Combs Ditch, Run And Skip and Wayward Lad. None the less she started the 15–8 favourite, though the confidence of her supporters was dwindling as between the last two fences she struggled to keep with Forgive 'N Forget and Wayward Lad. Third over the last and apparently going nowhere as Wayward Lad went two lengths up, she rallied in the closing stages and fought back, getting up a few yards from the post to win by a length. Then complete bedlam broke out, and she was mobbed by her supporters all the way back to the unsaddling enclosure – and inside it, where the scenes of celebration have never been paralleled at Cheltenham. Less than four months later she was killed in a fall at Auteuil.

The prize money for the Cheltenham Gold Cup was first boosted by commercial sponsorship in 1972, when it was supported by the champagne company Piper Heidsieck. It has been sponsored by the Tote since 1980.

Grand National

Red Rum (Tommy Stack) at the start before the 1977 News Of The World Grand National: ten minutes later he had recorded a unique third victory.

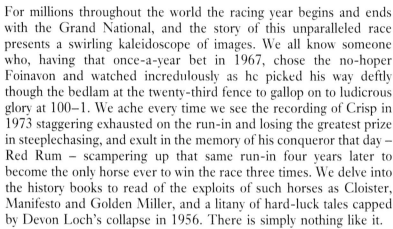

Liverpool: 4½ miles

Grade Three handicap steeplechase: six-year-olds and upwards

For millions throughout the world the racing year begins and ends with the Grand National, and the story of this unparalleled race presents a swirling kaleidoscope of images. We all know someone who, having that once-a-year bet in 1967, chose the no-hoper Foinavon and watched incredulously as he picked his way deftly though the bedlam at the twenty-third fence to gallop on to ludicrous glory at 100–1. We ache every time we see the recording of Crisp in 1973 staggering exhausted on the run-in and losing the greatest prize in steeplechasing, and exult in the memory of his conqueror that day – Red Rum – scampering up that same run-in four years later to become the only horse ever to win the race three times. We delve into the history books to read of the exploits of such horses as Cloister, Manifesto and Golden Miller, and a litany of hard-luck tales capped by Devon Loch's collapse in 1956. There is simply nothing like it.

The Grand National is the people's race. There were over ten million television viewers in the United Kingdom watching Mr Frisk's victory in 1990, and over £50 million was placed in bets. (The worldwide television audience is estimated to be over 800 million.) The essence of its hold on the public imagination is not hard to find. Demanding an extraordinary blend of courage, skill and dogged determination from both horse and rider, it is the race in which absolutely anything not only can happen, but does.

The root of its appeal lies in the very nature of the course (see page 155). The Grand National requires stamina rarely tested elsewhere, and its thirty obstacles are unlike any other steeplechase fences: whereas normal fences are constructed of birch packed into a wooden frame, the National jumps consist of hawthorn dressed with spruce, fir or gorse. The dressing flies out as the runners crash through the top, but the thorn base beneath is of uncompromising solidity, and Liverpool is no place to take liberties with the fences. More tricky to a horse than the actual construction of the fences are the drops which many of them have on the landing side – so that the horse lands lower than he took off. As off-putting is the fact that just as the horse has become accustomed to this curious experience over the first five fences and then negotiated the worst of all – Becher's Brook – the seventh fence has no drop.

A horse has to be able to jump well in order to get round in the National, but the athletic quality most required for success is not spectacular leaping but nimbleness and agility – as Red Rum was to

In 1929 no fewer than sixty-six horses lined up for the Grand National, the largest field ever for a race in Britain. They had to start in two rows.

show so often. For the Grand National, more than any other race, is a rapidly moving scrum, and the ability to sidestep fallen horses and adjust to the changing conditions at each fence is vital. Some very good horses have won it; some equally good horses have failed; some less good horses have won it – but there is no such thing as a 'bad' Grand National winner. Don't knock Foinavon: he jumped all thirty fences at the first time of asking and his rivals did not.

The race which became the Grand National was first run in 1837 (possibly not at Aintree but at nearby Maghull) and was won by The Duke. Or it was first run in 1839 as the Grand Liverpool Steeplechase (certainly at Aintree) and won by Lottery. Take your pick: the official 150th anniversary celebration split the difference and took place in 1988. Whatever the niceties of the historical record, the 1839 running was a race of great significance, and the conditions make interesting reading:

> A sweepstake of 20 sovereigns each, 5 forfeit, with 100 added; 12 stone each, gentlemen riders; four miles across country; the second to save his stake and the winner to pay 10 sovereigns towards expenses; no rider to open a gate or ride through a gateway, or more than 100 yards along any road, footpath or driftway.

Despite no jockey nipping through a gate, the race billed as 'four miles across country' took nearly fifteen minutes to run, over a course nothing like today's well maintained track and superbly constructed fences. The majority of the twenty-nine obstacles consisted of banks topped with gorse and faced with small ditches, and the last two were upright sheep hurdles (not dissimilar to modern hurdles). There were some especially difficult jumps, one of which was a five-foot stone wall in front of the stands and another, according to a contemporary description, 'a strong paling, next a rough, high jagged hedge, and lastly a brook about six feet wide', approached across a ploughed field. By the time Jem Mason on Lottery had won the race that latter jump was already entering racing lore, for on the first circuit Conrad hit the top of the rails hard and dumped his rider Captain Martin Becher into the brook. Becher's Brook, the most famous steeplechase fence in the world, was born. The intrepid jockey remounted, only to find himself deposited in water again at the second brook, now known as Valentine's. (Away from the racecourse Captain Becher's party trick was to run round a room on the wainscoting without touching the floor, and then kick the ceiling. Lottery's was even better: he would canter up to a fully stocked lunch table and jump it without disturbing so much as a wine glass.)

Lottery ran four more times in the race, falling at the vicious stone wall in 1840, being pulled up in 1841 and 1842 and finishing unplaced in 1843. This remarkable horse foreshadowed Arkle in causing the conditions of races to be changed to accommodate his superiority: a race at Horncastle in 1840 was 'open to all horses – except Mr Elmore's Lottery', and the conditions for one event at Finchley in October 1842 included 'Lottery's entry fee £40, others £10'.

Red Rum ran in the Grand National five times:

1973 (aged 8, carried 10 stone 5 pounds): won by three quarters of a length from Crisp
1974 (aged 9, carried 12 stone): won by seven lengths from L'Escargot
1975 (aged 10, carried 12 stone): second, beaten fifteen lengths, to L'Escargot
1976 (aged 11, carried 11 stone 10 pounds): second, beaten two lengths, to Rag Trade
1977 (aged 12, carried 11 stone 8 pounds): won by twenty-five lengths from Churchtown Boy

---

The fatal falls of Brown Trix and Seeandem at Becher's Brook in the 1989 Grand National raised once again the spectre of death which has haunted the race throughout its history and which has particularly centred on its most famous obstacle: in recent memory the Gold Cup winner Alverton was killed at Becher's in 1979, following Beau Bob in 1975 and Winter Rain in 1977, and the second favourite Dark Ivy met his end at the fence in 1987. After a fresh outbreak of public concern over the price which the Grand National exacts, the format of Becher's was altered: the fierce drop remains, but for the 1990 running the ground on the inner side was levelled out so that the horses no longer land there on steeply rising ground, the depth of the brook itself was greatly reduced, and the rails after the fence were realigned to avoid horses having to be steered to the left as they take the obstacle.

Manifesto ran in the Grand National eight times:

1895 (aged 7, carried 11 stone 2 pounds): fourth behind Wild Man From Borneo

1896 (aged 8, carried 11 stone 4 pounds): brought down at the first fence

1897 (aged 9, carried 11 stone 3 pounds): won by twenty lengths from Filbert

1899 (aged 11, carried 12 stone 7 pounds): won by five lengths from Ford Of Fyne

1900 (aged 12, carried 12 stone 13 pounds): third, beaten four lengths and a neck, to Ambush II and Barsac

1902 (aged 14, carried 12 stone 8 pounds): third, beaten three lengths and the same, to Shannon Lass and Matthew

1903 (aged 15, carried 12 stone 3 pounds): third, beaten three lengths and twenty lengths, to Drumcree and Detail

1904 (aged 16, carried 12 stone 1 pound): eighth behind Moifaa

---

The 1960 Grand National won by Merryman II was historic for two reasons. It was the last running of the race over the old-style jumps, sheer on the take-off side: from 1961 the fences incorporated the sloping apron common to steeplechase fences on other courses.

It was also the first Grand National televised by the BBC, whose superb coverage has done so much to widen the appeal of the race: nothing in the racing year on television can quite match those pictures – shot from a camera on top of a car on the old Aintree motor-racing circuit – of the fences on the run up to Becher's.

The stone wall, included in the course to encourage entries from Ireland, was lowered to four feet six inches in 1840 and dispensed with altogether the following year. The race has been run as a handicap since 1843, and first carried the name 'Grand National' in 1847, the last occasion on which riders were instructed not to open gates.

By the end of the nineteenth century the Grand National had settled comfortably into its unrivalled place in public affection, completely dominating the National Hunt scene and creating its own special brand of hero. Cloister carried twelve stone seven to victory in 1893 after running second the previous two years. Manifesto, until Red Rum the greatest National horse of all (see panel), won in 1897 and 1899. Ambush II in 1900 provided the only royal winner: he was owned by the Prince of Wales, who later that year would land the Derby with Diamond Jubilee. The National was moved to Gatwick from 1916 until 1918 on account of the war, and 1918 winner Poethlyn won at Liverpool when the race returned there in 1919.

The National has always been a fiercely demanding race, and in these years it was common for only a handful of horses to get round: five in 1920, four in 1921 (when only the winner Shaun Spadah did not fall: the other three finishers had been remounted, including runner-up The Bore, whose jockey Harry Brown had broken a collar bone when falling at the twenty-ninth fence), five in 1922. In 1923 Sergeant Murphy at thirteen became the oldest horse ever to win. In 1928 only two finished – 100–1 outsider Tipperary Tim and the remounted Billy Barton, who had fallen at the last: this was the year when Easter Hero caused chaos by landing astride the Canal Turn and slipping back into the ditch, causing most of the field to seize up. Easter Hero was second under twelve stone seven in 1929, having spread a plate with a mile to run and being unable to resist Gregalach from two fences out.

Golden Miller first ran in the race in 1933, unshipping Ted Leader at the Canal Turn on the second circuit. In 1934 he beat Delaneige and Thomond II to become the only horse ever to win the National and the Cheltenham Gold Cup in the same year. In 1935 – two weeks after his famous Gold Cup battle with Thomond (see page 000) – he parted company with Gerry Wilson in a controversial incident at the tenth fence after, according to some accounts, trying to refuse. (The following day he ran in the Champion Chase, unseating his rider at the first.) In 1936 he was brought down at the first, and in 1937 again refused at the tenth. Despite that victory in 1934, he hated the race. Not so the minute Battleship, hero of 1938, who at 15.2 hands was the smallest winner this century, and the last entire horse to win: he was ridden by seventeen-year-old Bruce Hobbs, later a notable trainer, to beat Royal Danieli by a head.

The race was not run between 1941 and 1945, and the post-war memories come pouring down like a National field at first Becher's. Caughoo at 100–1 won so easily in 1947 that his rider Eddie Dempsey was accused of taking a short cut in the fog! In 1948 Zahia looked like providing another 100–1 shock, but jockey Eddie Reavey took the wrong course after the second last and the race was lost. Vincent O'Brien trained three successive winners in the 1950s: Early

THE COURSE

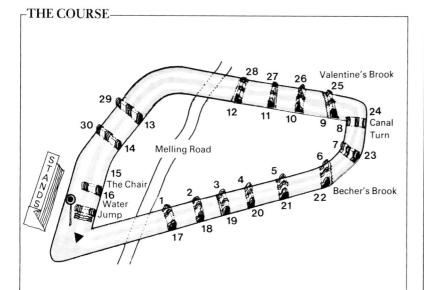

There is a run of over two furlongs to the first fence, where some pay an early price for impetuosity: twelve runners – a third of the field – went at the first in 1951 after a ragged start. The second is another plain fence, and then comes a five-foot high fence preceded by a ditch six feet wide. Then two more plain fences lead up to Becher's Brook with its huge drop – 'like jumping off the end of the earth', riders have described it – before making a left-hand turn towards the supposedly innocuous seventh (though after Becher's a horse will not know what to expect) and then on to the Canal Turn. This fence must be jumped at a sharp angle, for it marks a ninety-degree turn in the course, which very soon produces Valentine's Brook (named after Valentine, who was a furlong ahead at this fence in 1840, reared and tried to refuse, then corkscrewed to the other side). Then one plain fence, an open ditch and another plain fence (with a ditch on the landing side) before they swing left-handed towards two plain fences, and then on to the Chair – five feet two inches high, preceded by a gaping six-foot ditch and significantly narrower than other fences on the circuit. (Its name derives from the distance judge's chair which in bygone days was situated 240 yards from the winning post: the pedestal which held the judge's chair is still in its original position.) Then the water jump, and those who have survived the first circuit sweep left and head off on the sequence of six fences culminating in Becher's, by which time the winner is likely to be in a prominent position. Not always, though, for the next fence had its moment of National notoriety when hosting the infamous pile-up in 1967 which allowed Foinavon to steal past his felled rivals Then over the Canal Turn and the three fences which bring the runners back towards the racecourse proper and the last two jumps. But Liverpool saves its cruellest trick for the end of the race, for the run from the final fence to the winning post is an abnormally long 494 yards, and includes the 'elbow' halfway along where the runners swerve off to the right in order to bypass the Chair and the water jump. From the elbow to the winning post is over a furlong, and so often the complexion of the race can change in those final few heartbreaking yards. Just ask Lord Oaksey.

WINNERS SINCE 1970

1970 Gay Trip
  P. Taaffe 15–1 (28 ran)

1971 Specify
  J. Cook 28–1 (38 ran)

1972 Well To Do
  G. Thorner 14–1 (42 ran)

1973 Red Rum
  B. Fletcher 9–1 (38 ran)

1974 Red Rum
  B. Fletcher 11–1 (42 ran)

1975 L'Escargot
  T. Carberry 13–2 (31 ran)

1976 Rag Trade
  J. Burke 14–1 (32 ran)

1977 Red Rum
  T. Stack 9–1 (42 ran)

1978 Lucius
  B. Davies 14–1 (37 ran)

1979 Rubstic
  M. Barnes 25–1 (34 ran)

1980 Ben Nevis
  Mr C. Fenwick 40–1 (30 ran)

1981 Aldaniti
  R. Champion 10–1 (39 ran)

1982 Grittar
  Mr C. Saunders 7–1 (39 ran)

1983 Corbiere
  B. de Haan 13–1 (41 ran)

1984 Hallo Dandy
  N. Doughty 13–1 (40 ran)

1985 Last Suspect
  H. Davies 50–1 (40 ran)

1986 West Tip
  R. Dunwoody 15–2 (40 ran)

1987 Maori Venture
  S. C. Knight 28–1 (10 ran)

1988 Rhyme 'N' Reason
  B. Powell 10–1 (40 ran)

1989 Little Polveir
  J. Frost 28–1 (40 ran)

1990 Mr Frisk
  Mr M. Armytage 16–1 (38 ran)

Mist (1953), Royal Tan (1954) and Quare Times (1955). Royal Tan's victory ruined one of professional punter Alex Bird's biggest bets. Bird had backed Tudor Line to win half a million pounds, only to see the horse fail by a neck to get to the winner after jumping to the right at the last, a habit which had previously been cured by fitting a 'pricker' to Tudor Line's bit: it was deemed unnecessary to use the pricker for the National, and another hard-luck story was born.

But the greatest hard-luck story ever told had to be that of the 1956 running, when the Queen Mother's Devon Loch leapt into the air and slithered to the ground fifty yards from home with the race totally at his mercy. The reason for his collapse remains a mystery. Did he catch sight of the water jump out of the corner of his eye and try to take it? Did he hit a patch of false going? Did he suffer a fleeting muscular spasm? He was quite sound afterwards, and the most likely explanation is that offered by his jockey Dick Francis: that the horse was scared by the wall of noise into which he was running. Whatever the cause, the name of Devon Loch is forever burnt into the fabric of Grand National history, a perpetual reminder that we should not count our winnings until the post is passed.

Seven years later that lesson might have been forgotten by backers of the seven-year-old Carrickbeg as he strode up the run-in under crack amateur jockey John Lawrence (now, of course, Lord Oaksey), but Carrickbeg's action went, and he was caught just before the post by 66–1 outsider Ayala (who failed to finish in the first four in ten subsequent appearances). The 1960s saw other oustanding finishes, with Team Spirit running down Purple Silk in the closing stages in 1964 and that wonderful battle between Jay Trump and Freddie in 1965. But the 1967 race had a perverse logic all its own, when Foinavon won only because he was so far in arrears after second Becher's that he was able to avoid the pandemonium at the twenty-third fence. Popham Down, after being brought down at the first, had continued riderless for another circuit and a half before deciding that the twenty-third was one fence too many to be negotiated without any human encouragement. Running up the inside at the head of affairs, he jinked to the right just before the fence and cannoned into the leaders, causing the other front-runners to come crashing to a halt. From the mêlée of birch and mud and stricken horses and men emerged the blinkered head of Foinavon to pop over the fence and maintain his gallop to the end.

If that was, in the words of the great trainer Peter Cazalet, 'an awful race', the 1973 running was awful in different ways. First it inspired awe, with the top weight Crisp and Richard Pitman skipping over the mighty jumps and putting up perhaps the finest display Liverpool had ever seen as they built up a huge lead. Then it became awful in another sense, as the realization dawned that Crisp's gallant effort might not be rewarded with the victory it so richly deserved. For throughout the final half-mile Red Rum, the only horse who had kept up a serious pursuit, was getting ever nearer, and on the run-in, with a weight advantage of twenty-three pounds, he bore down upon the leader as Crisp staggered from the effects of his monumental effort. Red Rum was full of running, Crisp was out on his feet, and at the post justice was denied by three quarters of a length. Red Rum won

'With a hundred yards to go and still no sound of pursuit, the prize seemed within our grasp. Eighty, seventy, sixty perhaps – and then it happened. In the space of a single stride I felt the last ounce of Carrickbeg's energy drain away and my own with it. One moment we were a living, working combination, the next a struggling, beaten pair. There was still hope – but not for long . . .

So abrupt and complete was Carrickbeg's collapse that in half a dozen strides the gap was closed and the race over.

To my dying day I shall never forget the sight of Ayala's head beside my knee. Two heartbeats later he was half a length in front, and although I dropped my hands before the post, I can honestly promise any aggrieved supporter that it made not one yard of difference.'

John Lawrence, *Horse and Hound*, 6 April 1963

Opposite: at the Chair fence in the 1990 Seagram Grand National, the winner Mr Frisk (Marcus Armytage) touches down just behind Uncle Merlin (Hywel Davies).

again (under top weight) in 1974 and then ran second in 1975 and 1976 before scooting clear of Churchtown Boy in 1977 to record an unequalled third victory.

Those halcyon days in the history of the race came at a time when its very existence was under threat, for changes in ownership of the racecourse at Aintree had cast a shadow over the Grand National for many years. The formidable Mrs Mirabel Topham, chairman of Messrs Topham Limited which had run the course since 1856, acquired the track in 1949. In the mid-1960s she tried unsuccessfully to sell the course, and during the long-drawn-out financial and legal wranglings that ensued the condition of the amenities deteriorated: the home of the National was in severe decline and the racing public was voting with its feet. The situation was not much improved when Mrs Topham finally sold out in 1973 to property developer Bill Davies. Two years on another new owner was lined up, but the deal fell through and again the days of the Grand National seemed to be numbered. Then at the end of 1975 Davies made an arrangement with Ladbrokes to run the course on a seven-year lease. At the end of that period – during which, under the inspired direction of Clerk of the Course John Hughes, not only the National but all racing at Aintree received a huge shot in the arm – the Jockey Club launched a public appeal for £7 million to purchase the course from Davies. The target was not reached; the deadline was extended; eventually Davies accepted less than half the originally agreed sum. The course passed into the control of the Jockey Club (coming under the umbrella of the holding company Racecourse Holdings Trust), and at last the National was safe.

If Red Rum's third victory brought the sort of rapture which made the threatened demise of the race unthinkable, emotion ran even higher in 1981 when Bob Champion, having conquered cancer, rode Aldaniti, who had three times broken down and had been nursed back to fitness by trainer Josh Gifford and owner Nick Embiricos, to a victory which transcended the confines of sport. This was truly a triumph of the spirit.

Since then we have witnessed many other wonderful occasions: 48-year-old Dick Saunders in 1982 becoming the oldest jockey ever to ride the winner when partnering Grittar; Corbiere, perhaps the best Liverpool horse since Red Rum, powering home in 1983; Last Suspect's whirlwind finish in 1985; Maori Venture at last bringing Jim Joel a National victory in 1987; Rhyme 'N' Reason getting up off the floor at Becher's to go on and win in 1988; and Mr Frisk demolishing the course record time when pushing away from the luckless Durham Edition in 1990. But none of these had the emotional charge of Aldaniti's victory. It epitomized the lure of the Grand National, the race apart that had inspired Bob Champion through the darkest hours of his illness, just as it has inspired so many others throughout the century and a half of its history.

Scottish National

Ayr: 4 miles 120 yards

Grade Three handicap steeplechase: five-year-olds and upwards

Now the highlight of the racing year in Scotland, the Scottish National began life as the West of Scotland Grand National at Bogside (not far from Ayr) in May 1867. Then run over three miles, it was won by The Elk, who started at 1000–15 for the 1870 Grand National at Liverpool but pulled up. The race first bore the name Scottish Grand National in 1881, when its distance was increased to three miles seven furlongs, thus providing a test of stamina not too dissimilar from the real thing at Liverpool, though the course itself – right-handed and undulating – was in no way comparable.

Between the wars several horses won both the Scottish race and the Grand National: Music Hall won at Bogside in 1920 and at Liverpool two years later; Sergeant Murphy (1922) won the Scottish as a twelve-year-old and the National itself in 1923 at a venerable thirteen; and Kellsboro' Jack won at Bogside in 1935, two years after his Aintree triumph (his owner had vowed that he would never have to face the Liverpool fences again after winning there in 1933). Kellsboro' Jack had run in that famous Cheltenham Gold Cup against Golden Miller and Thomond II (see page 149) shortly before his Scottish victory, and another of the runners in that legendary race was the greatest Scottish Grand National stalwart of the age. This was Southern Hero, who won the race three times – as a nine-year-old in 1934, an eleven-year-old in 1936, and a practically geriatric fourteen-year-old in 1939, when he carried twelve stone three pounds and gave six years, eleven pounds and an eight-length beating to the good chaser Glen Leven. Southern Hero was also second in 1937 and 1938. They don't make 'em like that any more.

Southern Hero's feat of winning three times was matched by Queen's Taste (1953, 1954 and 1956), and other noteworthy winners in the first decade after the war were Rowland Roy, who won in 1947 and landed the King George VI Chase later that year, and Wot No Sun (1949), second to Freebooter in the 1950 Grand National. The 1959 winner Merryman II came to Bogside having taken the Foxhunters' Chase at Liverpool, and within a year had won the Grand National. By the mid-1960s Bogside's days were numbered, but the penultimate running there of the Scottish Grand National produced one of the best finishes in its history and a heroic performance from a wildly popular Scottish horse destined to be best remembered for another narrow defeat. Freddie, trained on a sheep farm near Kelso, had graduated from point-to-pointing to become a hunter-chaser of

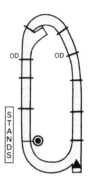

The runners in the Scottish National complete nearly three circuits of the course. There is a downhill run from the end of the back straight round the home turn and a gradual rise to the finish. The run-in from the last fence is 210 yards.

┌─WINNERS SINCE 1970─┐

1970 The Spaniard
  B. Brogan 8–1 (10 ran)

1971 Young Ash Leaf
  P. Ennis 12–1 (21 ran)

1972 Quick Reply
  M. Barnes 11–1 (17 ran)

1973 Esban
  J. Bourke 16–1 (21 ran)

1974 Red Rum
  B. Fletcher 11–8 (17 ran)

1975 Barona
  P. Kelleway 33–1 (17 ran)

1976 Barona
  P. Kelleway 12–1 (23 ran)

1977 Sebastian V
  R. Lamb 9–2 (18 ran)

1978 King Con
  Mr P. Craggs 33–1 (21 ran)

1979 Fighting Fit
  C. Hawkins 9–1 (19 ran)

1980 Salkeld
  D. Atkins 14–1 (23 ran)

1981 Astral Charmer
  J. L. Goulding 66–1 (21 ran)

1982 Cockle Strand
  D. Dutton 9–1 (15 ran)

1983 Canton
  K. Whyte 16–1 (22 ran)

1984 Androma
  M. Dwyer 7–1 (19 ran)

1985 Androma
  M. Dwyer 11–1 (18 ran)

1986 Hardy Lad
  M. Hammond 28–1 (24 ran)

1987 Little Polveir
  P. Scudamore 12–1 (11 ran)

1988 Mighty Mark
  B. Storey 9–1 (17 ran)

1989 Roll-A-Joint
  B. Powell 4–1 (11 ran)

1990 Four Trix
  D. Byrne 25–1 (28 ran)

such exceptional ability that he started at 3–1 on to win the 1964 Foxhunter Challenge Cup at Cheltenham, and did so by six lengths on the same day as the first Arkle–Mill House Gold Cup. After an unfortunate experience at Kelso when he unshipped his rider at the last, it was time for Freddie to take on top-class chasers, and he faced a strong field at Bogside, including Hoodwinked, winner of the 1963 Whitbread, Rainbow Battle, winner of the Welsh National earlier in 1964, Purple Silk, narrowly beaten by Team Spirit in that year's Grand National, and Peacetown, third in that race. It was Peacetown who made the pace after three fences, until Popham Down (who three years later would start the dominos falling in Foinavon's Grand National) took up the running on the second circuit. Freddie, ridden for the first time by Bill Rees, went with him, and for the best part of a mile they vied for the lead. At the last fence they were still locked together, but Freddie was conceding twenty-two pounds to his rival and on the run-in the difference began to tell: try as he might Freddie could not hold on, and Popham Down won by half a length as, according to *The Field*, 'the crowd erupted to an uninhibited roar audible in Arran'. A year later Freddie would go down in an even more rousing climax when just beaten in the 1965 Grand National.

Bogside closed in 1965, Brasher its last Scottish Grand National winner. The move to Ayr with the 1966 running strengthened the status of the race, for the Ayr circuit is one of the best in the country, and the distance of over four miles puts even more of a premium on stamina. In 1974 Red Rum came to Ayr just three weeks after his second Grand National triumph, and notched up the unique distinction of winning the Grand National and the Scottish Grand National in the same year: starting 11–8 favourite, he sprinted away from John Oaksey on Proud Tarquin. A statue of Red Rum now graces the paddock area at Ayr to mark his historic achievement.

In 1976 Barona won the Scottish Grand National for the second successive year just a week after coming fourth to Rag Trade at Liverpool, and in 1977 Sebastian V performed the rare feat of leading all the way. Toughness counts in this race. William Hill's sponsorship commenced in 1978 (when 'Grand' disappeared from the title), and the following year saw another advertisement of the class of the race when the novice Fighting Fit beat Aldaniti: the winner took the Hennessy Gold Cup that autumn, and we all know about Aldaniti.

In 1981 the 66–1 chance Astral Charmer went into a gargantuan lead in the early stages of the race. Despite trying to run out near the racecourse stables he was still nearly a fence in front of his rivals – whose jockeys seemed quite unconcerned – going out on to the final circuit. He tired rapidly in the home straight but kept going well enough to win by three lengths. Timeform delivered an acid comment on the riders caught out: 'We have seldom seen such an example of monumental stupidity on the part of experienced jockeys.'

Androma in 1984 and 1985 became the latest dual winner and Little Polveir won in 1987 before taking the Grand National in 1989 (thus joining Merryman II and Red Rum as the only post-war winners of both races), but the Scottish National also reminds us of the more sombre side of steeplechasing. Roll-A-Joint, winner of the Scottish race in 1989, was killed in the 1990 Grand National.

Whitbread Gold Cup

Sandown Park: 3 miles 5 furlongs 18 yards

Grade Three handicap steeplechase: five-year-olds and upwards

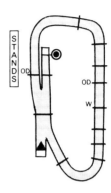

How's this for a line-up for a handicap chase in 1975? Top weight on twelve stone is Captain Christy, winner in 1974 of the Gold Cup (beating The Dikler) and the King George VI Chase (beating Pendil): for many experts the best since Arkle. The horse carrying a pound less runs in Arkle's colours, for like the now dead champion he is owned by Anne, Duchess of Westminster: this is Ten Up, fresh (if that is the word) from winning the Gold Cup from Soothsayer and Bula in such bottomless conditions that the rest of the Cheltenham meeting was abandoned as soon as the big race had been run. A stone further down the handicap is Crisp. Now twelve, he won a permanent place in the hearts of National Hunt racing enthusiasts by his performance in the Grand National two years earlier (see page 156), when just touched off by Red Rum after turning in an unforgettable front-running display. The public loves Crisp, and is hoping against hope that he may just be returning to his best after injury: he has not won in five outings this season, but was an eye-catching fourth to Summerville at Ascot on his last outing and could be on his way back. He concedes a pound to eleven-year-old Royal Relief, winner of the Two-Mile Champion Chase at Cheltenham in 1972 and 1974 and second in that race three times, most recently earlier in 1975, since when he has fallen when ridden by Lord Oaksey in the Grand National. Another victim of the Liverpool hurly-burly was the nine-year-old April Seventh, trained by Bob Turnell and ridden in the National by his son Andy, who in the Whitbread has plumped for the other Turnell runner Cuckolder, winner of the Yellow Pages Pattern Chase at Kempton. Then there's the mare Credo's Daughter, one of the most consistent staying chasers in recent years; there's Forest Rock, a brilliant hunter-chaser unbeaten in his last six races; Barona, who a week before won the Scottish Grand National; Noble Neptune, Highland Seal and Boom Docker. Twelve runners over three miles five furlongs around Sandown Park, from the spectator's point of view the best jumping circuit in the land; Ten Up is favourite at 11–4, with Captain Christy 5–1 and Crisp 11–2. Here's a race to savour.

As the runners stride up towards the enclosures and over the first they present one of the great sights of racing, a field of top-class chasers attacking Sandown fences in the spring sunshine. This is the essence of the Whitbread, and rarely has the race seen as good a field as the class of 1975. Forest Rock takes up the running, and leads throughout the first circuit. At the open ditch in front of the stands as

This is a testing course and distance for a chaser. The runners go uphill from the start, reach the highest point of the course beyond the winning post, then make a downhill run and take one fence (a tricky one) before turning into the back straight, which is practically flat. The three Railway Fences at the end of the straight come close together and demand accurate jumping, and are followed by the long sweep round to the Pond Fence (three out) before turning into the straight to face another haul up the hill. The runners make two complete circuits after they first pass the stands, with their final obstacle the plain fence which stands next to the open ditch by the enclosures.

Mr Frisk soaring clear in the 1990 Whitbread.

┌─ **WINNERS SINCE 1970** ─┐

1970 Royal Toss
  R. Pitman 20–1 (17 ran)

1971 Titus Oates
  R. Barry 11–1 (18 ran)

1972 Grey Sombrero
  W. Shoemark 16–1 (28 ran)

1973 Charlie Potheen
  R. Barry 11–4 (21 ran)

1974 The Dikler
  R. Barry 5–1 (16 ran)

1975 April Seventh
  S. C. Knight 16–1 (12 ran)

1976 Otter Way
  J. King 15–2 (14 ran)

1977 Andy Pandy
  J. Burke 4–1 (15 ran)

1978 Strombolus
  T. Stack 7–1 (15 ran)

1979 Diamond Edge
  W. Smith 7–1 (14 ran)

1980 Royal Mail
  P. Blacker 8–1 (12 ran)

1981 Diamond Edge
  W. Smith 5–1 (18 ran)

1982 Shady Deal
  R. Rowe 4–1 (9 ran)

1983 Drumlargan
  F. Codd 11–1 (15 ran)

1984 Special Cargo
  K. Mooney 8–1 (13 ran)

1985 By The Way
  R. Earnshaw 11–2 (20 ran)

1986 Plundering
  S. Sherwood 14–1 (16 ran)

1987 Lean Ar Aghaidh
  G. Landau 6–1 (9 ran)

1988 Desert Orchid
  S. Sherwood 6–1 (12 ran)

1989 Brown Windsor
  M. Bowlby 12–1 (18 ran)

1990 Mr Frisk
  Mr M. Armytage 9–2 (13 ran)

they come round again Cuckolder makes a dreadful mistake and Turnell has no chance of staying on board. The field swings to the right and hurtles downhill towards the back straight. Forest Rock still has the lead, followed by Noble Neptune, Crisp, April Seventh, Captain Christy and Credo's Daughter. Now they are really stretching, streaming over the succession of fences which makes the back straight at Sandown such a glorious vision. None is jumping more brilliantly than Crisp, measuring every obstacle with pinpoint accuracy and rapidly fuelling anticipation of the most popular result for years.

At the first of the Railway Fences, the jumps placed close together at the end of the far straight, Richard Pitman drives Crisp up to take the lead from Forest Rock, and as the course commentator announces Crisp's progress a huge roar goes up from the enclosures: he's going to do it! Whether or not they've backed him, everyone wants Crisp to win, and as he puts three lengths between himself and his rivals coming round the sweeping far turn the excitement becomes feverish. But those rivals are not going to let sentiment stand in their way, and though Crisp is still in front at the Pond Fence, three out, some of the others are closing, most ominously April Seventh. By the second last Steve Knight has brought April Seventh on terms with Crisp, and any lingering dream that the great Australian horse can erase the memory of that awful Grand National defeat with a famous victory here evaporates within a few seconds, for Crisp's back legs slither from under him on landing over the second last and his chance has gone. April Seventh is hammering up the hill, flies the last and makes for the winning post, now hotly pursued by Captain Christy. But the concession of twenty-nine pounds to the leader is too much for Captain Christy, who is one and a half lengths down at the line. Barona comes through late to deprive Crisp of third place.

April Seventh went on to win the Hennessy Gold Cup later in 1975, and Captain Christy put up one of the great performances of modern times when pulverizing Bula in the King George VI Chase. Crisp never ran again, but the shout that went up when he moved into the lead at the Railway Fences will go on echoing in the memory of those who were at Sandown that April afternoon.

The Whitbread is like that. So often it provides an emotional sub-plot to the race itself which raises the running above the level of simple sport – however high-class – to that of a great occasion.

For simple admiration, think of Arkle in 1965 beating Brasher with the greatest of ease.

For deep satisfaction at seeing a deserving cause rewarded, think of Mill House in 1967. Three years earlier, in his first race after the epic 1964 Gold Cup against Arkle, he had tried valiantly to concede forty-two pounds to Dormant in the mud and had lost the lead fifty yards out to go down by three lengths. By 1967 he was a shadow of his former self after all those unavailing attempts to dethrone Arkle, but even the shadow had its unshakeable place in the public's affection, and there was hardly a dry eye in the house when this mountain of a horse, dog tired, clung on to his lead up the run-in to hold off Kapeno.

For sheer joy in a wonderful performance, think of Desert Orchid skipping up the hill in 1988 to withstand Kildimo and confound those heretics who thought that he wouldn't stay. Or of Lean Ar Aghaidh's toughness when winning in 1987 so soon after his brave third in the Grand National. Even better, think of Mr Frisk's flamboyant display in 1990 when he became the first horse ever to win the National and the Whitbread.

For a hint of indignation and a lurking suspicion that perhaps justice may not have been done, think of Proud Tarquin and The Dikler in 1974. The Dikler had run second to Captain Christy in the Cheltenham Gold Cup. Proud Tarquin had, just a week before the Whitbread, been runner-up to Red Rum in the Scottish Grand National. John Oaksey rode Proud Tarquin and Ron Barry The Dikler, and Barry remembered the crucial moments in a controversial race:

> Going to the last I was challenging John, but Proud Tarquin was a neck in front on landing. Then on the flat he swerved to the left and The Dikler had to veer over, too, or we would have bumped. John immediately straightened his horse but mine had momentarily stopped in his gallop – he immediately went on and was gaining ground on Proud Tarquin when he passed the post, a head behind him.

After a lengthy enquiry the Stewards disqualified Proud Tarquin for interfering with The Dikler (though the two had not made contact) and reversed the placings. John Oaksey, disappointed that more account was not taken of Proud Tarquin's known habit of hanging to the left in finishes and his jockey's precaution of giving him a smack

JOHN OAKSEY'S DAY OF THE YEAR

The first Whitbread Gold Cup, won by Much Obliged in 1957, changed the face of British steeplechasing for ever. Followed quickly by the first Hennessy, it opened the era of commercial sponsorship and put paid to the Grand National's 200-year domination of the sport.

But the Whitbread has done much more than that. With the Hennessy, the King George and the Gold Cup itself, it means that any top staying chaser can nowadays earn fame as well as a fortune for his owner without ever going within miles of Becher's Brook. The race has also built its own distinguished roll of honour: Arkle, Desert Orchid, Pas Seul and Mill House all carried top weight to victory, while Larbawn and Diamond Edge each won twice.

As in so many of jumping's major prizes, Fulke Walwyn has been by far the most successful trainer. Of his seven winners, Mill House – with Arkle out of the way at last – got the warmest welcome ever heard at Sandown in 1967. It was only by inches that Special Cargo robbed Diamond Edge (trained, like him, by Walwyn) of a unique hat-trick in 1984. The four-horse battle Special Cargo won that day for the Queen Mother remains the most exciting finish I have ever seen.

Come right down to it, there isn't much doubt that if I were confined to just one more afternoon's racing my unhesitating choice would be Whitbread day at Sandown Park.

down the left-hand side to get him straight, has pointed out that 'two of the three stewards were beardless youths with negligible experience of steeplechasing'.

And for breathtaking wonderment at the spectacle which National Hunt racing can provide, think of the almost unbelievable race in 1984, when at the second last fence the one emotion you could safely rule out was a celebration of the Royalist cause. For of all the possibilities which this race still had up its sleeve in the closing stages, victory for the Queen Mother's Special Cargo was not one. He was too far behind to make any impact, and had not been in any hurry to respond to Kevin Mooney's urgings. Ahead of him Lettoch and Plundering were fighting out the result not only of this race but of that season's trainers' championship – for Lettoch would bring the title to Michael Dickinson, Plundering to Fred Winter. Diamond Edge, hanging on doggedly behind them at the last, was going for a unique third Whitbread at the age of thirteen, a win which would bring Fulke Walwyn his seventh triumph in the race; for good measure, Diamond Edge was jockey Bill Smith's final ride. Plundering and Lettoch set off up the run-in with very little between them, then Diamond Edge started to rally and just got his head in front. Then Lettoch fought back – and suddenly there was Special Cargo on the far side. The three flashed past the post together, but in a finish of two short heads Special Cargo had beaten Lettoch and Diamond Edge. It was for many people the greatest steeplechase ever.

Emotion apart, the Whitbread represents an important moment in the history of horse racing in Britain, for it was the first race to benefit from commercial sponsorship. It came into being at a time when increased television coverage of racing made sponsorship a highly attractive venture for the right sort of product, and the connection between racing and the output of Messrs Whitbread did not need much explaining. The race largely owes its existence to Colonel Bill Whitbread, chairman of the brewing company; himself a lifelong devotee of National Hunt racing, he had twice ridden his own Ben Cruchan in the Grand National (in 1925 and 1926), both times falling and remounting. On Colonel Whitbread's initiative the brewery proposed to the National Hunt Committee the founding of a valuable handicap chase to take place after the Grand National, a period when the jumping season was accustomed to a gradual and tedious winding down, with no significant races left to be run. 'Some of the Stewards thought sponsorship would "commercialise" the sport,' recalled Colonel Whitbread, but the traditionalists could not impede a move which was to alter the entire fabric of the jumping year, with the Hennessy Gold Cup (initiated later in 1957) providing a similar highlight for the early part of the season, and then a stream of sponsors moving in with a massive injection of prize money.

The first Whitbread Gold Cup was run on 27 April 1957, when Much Obliged beat 20–1 outsider Mandarin by a distance so short – though the official margin was a neck – that in the absence of the photo-finish some people who saw the race still believe that Mandarin won. A year later Mandarin was favourite at 9–2 but once more came second, this time to 100–6 shot Taxidermist, ridden by John

---

Fulke Walwyn's seven Whitbread winners were:

Taxidermist (1958)
Mill House (1967)
Charlie Potheen (1973)
The Dikler (1974)
Diamond Edge (1979, 1981)
Special Cargo (1984)

Lawrence. In 1959 Mandarin again found one too good, going under by a short head after a fierce tussle with Done Up, whose jockey Harry Sprague was a specialist hurdle-race rider and rarely tackled the bigger obstacles. Done Up was a notoriously lazy horse who needed pushing the entire distance, but Sprague never stopped shoving away and was duly rewarded. The effort took its toll, though, and on the way back to unsaddle Sprague, half-dead from exhaustion, threw up, losing his top set of teeth: report has it that winning trainer Ryan Price missed the celebrations in the unsaddling enclosure as he was scrabbling around in the dirt searching for Sprague's ejected dentures. His effort, like the jockey's, was rewarded.

In recognition of his gallant efforts in those first three Whitbreads, Mandarin in retirement at Lambourn enjoyed a pension of two bottles of Mackeson a day, courtesy of Bill Whitbread.

The innovation of the Whitbread clearly worked, and it was soon established not only as an important element in the structure of the jumping season, but as a contest which for excitement, quality and sheer spectacle had few rivals. In 1961 Pas Seul, winner of the Cheltenham Gold Cup in 1960, gave Grand National winner Nicolaus Silver twenty-one pounds and beat him four lengths. Then came the Neville Crump pair Hoodwinked (1963) and Dormant (1964), Arkle's victory in 1965 in the smallest Whitbread field yet (seven runners), What A Myth (ridden by Paul Kelleway) giving Ryan Price a second Whitbread in 1966, Mill House raising the roof in 1967 and Larbawn becoming the first dual winner in 1968 and 1969 (ridden on the latter occasion by Josh Gifford and the former by his late brother Macer). In 1973 the race was run at Newcastle while development work was under way at Sandown: Charlie Potheen won for Fulke Walwyn, but the day was clouded by the death of jockey Doug Barrott. In 1977 Andy Pandy gained handsome consolation for his fall in the Grand National when in the lead at second Becher's, and Diamond Edge in 1981 became the first horse since Larbawn to win the race twice when staging a remarkable rally up the run-in to typify the appeal of this great race: a top-class horse providing a wonderfully exciting denouement to a spectacular display of jumping and galloping.

The Whitbread – a celebration not only of the spectacle of Arkle in action but also of the emotion that wills on Crisp – is steeplechasing at its most magnificent. It's as simple as that.

> The most successful Whitbread jockey is Ron Barry, who won three times: Titus Oates (1971), Charlie Potheen (1973) and The Dikler (1974).

The last fence in the 1982 Whitbread: King Spruce (third) just leads from Whiggie Geo, Ottery News (second) and the winner Shady Deal.

INTERNATIONAL

Irish Grand National

Fairyhouse: 3½ miles

Handicap steeplechase: four-year-olds and upwards

The Irish Grand National takes up nearly two complete circuits of Fairyhouse, a galloping track with minor undulations.

WINNERS SINCE 1980

1980 Daletta
  J. P. Harty 11–1 (25 ran)
1981 Luska
  T. Finn 11–1 (20 ran)
1982 King Spruce
  G. Newman 20–1 (25 ran)
1983 Bit Of A Skite
  T. J. Ryan 7–1 (27 ran)
1984 Bentom Boy
  Mrs A. Ferris 33–1 (29 ran)
1985 Rhyme 'N' Reason
  G. Bradley 6–1 (23 ran)
1986 Insure
  M. Flynn 16–1 (15 ran)
1987 Brittany Boy
  T. J. Taaffe 14–1 (26 ran)
1988 Perris Valley
  B. Sheridan 12–1 (18 ran)
1989 Maid of Money
  A. Powell 10–1 (22 ran)
1990 Desert Orchid
  R. Dunwoody evens (14 ran)

Previous pages: the finish of the inaugural Arlington Million, August 1981: outsider The Bart (no. 4) is collared by John Henry as Lester Piggott rouses Madam Gay for a final effort.

Desert Orchid's foray to Ireland for the Jameson Irish Grand National on 16 April 1990 was the first time the grey horse had run in a steeplechase outside England, and he received a rousing reception from the crowd who had flocked to Fairyhouse – some twelve miles north-west of Dublin – for the most important race in the Irish jumping year. He rewarded his fans with a display outstanding even by his standards, galloping his rivals into the ground to such a degree that even a monumental blunder at the final fence could not interrupt him.

It was appropriate that Desert Orchid should produce a star turn in the Irish Grand National, for nowhere is the quality chaser more appreciated than in Ireland, and the race (first run in 1870) has gone to some of the very best. In 1904 it went to one of only two horses in its history who have won both the Irish National and the Liverpool equivalent. Ascetic's Silver – a half-brother to two other Grand National winners in Cloister and Drumcree – won at Fairyhouse in 1904 and Liverpool in 1906, a feat matched only by Rhyme 'N' Reason, who won the Irish for David Murray Smith in 1985 and the Liverpool race for David Elsworth in 1988. Between the wars one Irish Grand National which deserves to be remembered is that of 1929, when the mare Alike was ridden to victory by her owner, F. W. Wise, who had lost a leg in a flying accident in the First World War.

In 1942 Prince Regent carried twelve stone seven pounds and beat Golden Jack, to whom he was conceding twelve pounds, by a length. A measure of Prince Regent's phenomenal improvement that season is that late the previous year Golden Jack had given him fifteen pounds and beat him a short head. Prince Regent was second in the Irish National in 1943 and 1944.

Prince Regent was the first of trainer Tom Dreaper's ten Irish Grand National winners, which included seven in successive years from 1960 to 1966: Olympia (1960), Fortria (1961), Kerforo (1962), Last Link (1963), Arkle (1964: in the race immediately after his first Cheltenham Gold Cup victory he carried twelve stone and beat Height of Fashion, to whom he was conceding thirty-seven pounds), Splash (1965) and the superb but ill-tempered Flyingbolt (1966). Dreaper's son Jim trained the durable Brown Lad, winner of the race in 1975, 1976 and – at the age of twelve and carrying twelve stone two pounds – for a third time in 1978. And we should also mention Mrs Ann Ferris, the first lady jockey to win when partnering Bantom Boy in 1984: her sister Rosemary finished third.

THE IRISH CLASSICS

Irish Two Thousand Guineas
The Curragh: 1 mile
Group One: three-year-old colts and fillies

The Irish Two Thousand Guineas was first run in 1921, though like all the Irish Classics it was not run under strict weight-for-age terms until 1946: before that runners in the races had been subjected to penalties. It is now a crucial element in the early part of the season for three-year-olds, and it is common for horses who have run prominently in the equivalent race at Newmarket to go over to Ireland for a follow-up. Tirol, who in the 1990 Irish Two Thousand finally demolished any lingering suggestion that he may have been fortunate to beat Machiavellian on the Rowley Mile, was the third horse since the war to lift both races, following Right Tack (1969) and Don't Forget Me (1987), who like Tirol was trained by Richard Hannon. In the post-war period three horses have won the Irish Two Thousand en route to victory in the Derby at Epsom: Hard Ridden (1958), who had been bought as a yearling for just 270 guineas, Santa Claus (1964) and Grundy (1975). The Minstrel, short-headed by Pampapaul in 1977, went on to take the Derby, while Triptych in 1985 was the first filly ever to win the race.

Irish One Thousand Guineas
The Curragh: 1 mile
Group One: three-year-old fillies

The Irish One Thousand Guineas is a year younger than its sibling race, having first taken place in 1922. Like the Irish Two Thousand it is timed to encourage runners who have taken part in the equivalent Classic at Newmarket, though no filly since the war has won both races: the last One Thousand Guineas winner to attempt the double was On The House, third to Prince's Polly at The Curragh in 1982. In the 1980s the race has been won by two horses placed at Newmarket – Al Bahathri (1985), short-headed by Oh So Sharp in the One Thousand, and Sonic Lady (1986), third to Midway Lady in the English race – while in the same period two other winners, Ensconse (1989) and In The Groove (1990), had been beaten on the Rowley Mile, and L'Attrayante, heroine of the 1983 race, had won the French equivalent, the Poule d'Essai des Pouliches at Longchamp. The 1966 winner Valoris won the Oaks.

WINNERS SINCE 1980

1980 Nikoli
  C. Roche 5–1 (13 ran)

1981 King's Lake
  Pat Eddery 5–1 (13 ran)

1982 Dara Monarch
  M. J. Kinane 20–1 (14 ran)

1983 Wassl
  A. Murray 12–1 (10 ran)

1984 Sadler's Wells
  G. McGrath 10–1 (9 ran)

1985 Triptych
  C. Roche 7–1 (16 ran)

1986 Flash of Steel
  M. J. Kinane 9–2 (6 ran)

1987 Don't Forget Me
  W. Carson 6–4 (8 ran)

1988 Prince of Birds
  D. Gillespie 9–1 (14 ran)

1989 Shaadi
  W. R. Swinburn 7–2 (12 ran)

1990 Tirol
  Pat Eddery 5–4 (9 ran)

WINNERS SINCE 1980

1980 Cairn Rouge
  A. Murray 5–1 (18 ran)

1981 Arctique Royale
  G. Curran 7–1 (15 ran)

1982 Prince's Polly
  W. R. Swinburn 12–1 (24 ran)

1983 L'Attrayante
  A. Badel 4–1 (18 ran)

1984 Katies
  P. Robinson 20–1 (23 ran)

1985 Al Bahathri
  A. Murray 7–1 (15 ran)

1986 Sonic Lady
  W. R. Swinburn 4–1 (19 ran)

1987 Forest Flower
  T. Ives 4–1 (11 ran)

1988 Trusted Partner
  M. J. Kinane 10–1 (16 ran)

1989 Ensconse
  R. Cochrane 13–8 (13 ran)

1990 In The Groove
  S. Cauthen 5–1 (12 ran)

Irish Derby

The Curragh: 1½ miles

Group One: three-year-old colts and fillies

The Curragh is a wide and fair track with a long, sweeping right-hand bend into the straight, where the finish is uphill.

Although it was first run in 1866 (over an extended mile and three quarters, coming down to its present twelve furlongs in 1872), the history of the Irish Derby as a major international event begins with the 1962 running. The prime mover of the huge upgrading of the race's status was Joe McGrath, one of the most influential men in the history of Irish racing, both as owner and breeder (he won the 1951 Derby at Epsom with his home-bred Arctic Prince) and as Steward of the Turf Club. His vision was to arrange a substantial injection of prize money into the Irish Derby so that it would become an automatic target for the best three-year-olds in Europe, putting Ireland firmly on the map as a top-class Flat venue as well as a producer of top-class bloodstock; and the source of this extra prize money was the Irish Hospitals Sweepstakes, which McGrath had been instrumental in founding. At a stroke the whole status of Irish racing would be uplifted – if only the best horses would come to The Curragh.

They did, and the field for the inaugural running of the Irish Sweeps Derby on 30 June 1962 was appropriate to the occasion and to the purse – which at £50,027 to the winner compared highly favourably with the £34,786 won by Larkspur at Epsom three and a half weeks earlier. Larkspur (trained by Vincent O'Brien, greatest of Irish trainers) was in the line-up at The Curragh, the first of a succession of Derby winners to whom the Irish race would be the natural follow-up: ridden by Scobie Breasley, he started 9–4 favourite, but could only finish fourth behind the high-class French-trained colt Tambourine II, who beat the Irish Two Thousand Guineas winner Arctic Storm by a short head after a fierce battle through the final furlong. The Epsom winner may have been turned over, but the race was a huge success, and had heralded the beginning of a new age in Irish racing.

Sensation dogged the second running in 1963, when the Derby winner Relko went lame on the way to the start and was withdrawn. In his absence Ragusa, third at Epsom, won easily to announce the beginning of his development into one of the best Irish-trained horses of modern times: he went on to win the King George VI and Queen Elizabeth Stakes and the St Leger, and the following season took the Eclipse Stakes. In 1964 Santa Claus pulled off the Epsom–Curragh double at 7–4 on, becoming the first horse since Orby in 1907 to win both races. The following year the Epsom winner Sea Bird II did not run at the Curragh, and Meadow Court, second in the Derby, landed a handsome consolation prize. In 1966 Sodium, fourth at Epsom,

Vincent O'Brien trained the winner of the Irish Derby six times: Chamier (1953), Ballymoss (1957), Nijinsky (1970), The Minstrel (1977), El Gran Senor (1984) and Law Society (1985). Chamour, winner in 1960, had been trained by O'Brien but by the time of the race was in the charge of his brother Phonsie, as Vincent had been controversially suspended from training after Chamour had failed the dope test in a maiden race at The Curragh earlier that year. O'Brien's son David trained Assert, winner in 1982.

170

reversed Derby form with the winner Charlottown when taking the Irish race by a length: they ran against each other twice more, Charlottown thrashing Sodium at Newbury and then going down by a head to him in the St Leger. The first five runnings of the Irish Sweeps Derby had set a standard which has never slackened, and the race – now sponsored by Budweiser – is the third middle-distance peak of the early summer for three-year-olds (after the Prix du Jockey-Club and the Derby), and the springboard from which the best of the generation will take on older horses in races such as the King George: eight winners of the Irish Derby have gone on to take the Ascot showpiece – Ragusa, Meadow Court, Nijinsky, Grundy, The Minstrel, Troy and Shergar the same season, and Ballymoss (winner at The Curragh in 1957) as a four-year-old. The Curragh presents a very different proposition from Epsom (it is right-handed and mostly flat until a gradual uphill finish) and to win both Derbys demands a certain amount of versatility. Since Santa Claus in 1964 the feat has been managed by Nijinsky (1970), Grundy (1975), The Minstrel (1977), Shirley Heights (1978), Troy (1979), Shergar (1981), Shahrastani (1986) and Kahyasi (1988), while since Charlottown in 1966 six Epsom winners have failed at The Curragh: Sir Ivor (1968: 3–1 on), Blakeney (1969: 7–2), Roberto (1972: 15–8), Empery (1976: 5–4 on), Teenoso (1983: 2–1) and Quest For Fame (1990: 5–4). El Gran Senor, pipped by Secreto in that controversial Epsom finish in 1984, started at 7–2 on at The Curragh and stated his true worth when beating Rainbow Quest, while Old Vic in 1989 bypassed Epsom but added the Irish Derby to his victory in the Prix du Jockey-Club.

Yet none of these performances triggered off quite the excitement of Salsabil's achievement in 1990, following up her Oaks win with a smooth victory over Deploy at The Curragh to become the first filly to win the Irish Derby since Gallinaria in 1900. The way she swung out to cut down the leader in the straight, with Derby winner Quest For Fame already beaten and subsequent King George winner Belmez running on to be third, is not just the most recent of the many outstanding sights which this great race has provided; it will long linger as one of the very best.

In the 1990 Budweiser Irish Derby, Salsabil (Willie Carson) scores a famous victory by beating Deploy.

Irish Oaks
The Curragh: 1½ miles
Group One: three-year-old fillies

The Irish Oaks was first run in 1895, and took place over a mile until 1915, when it was extended to twelve furlongs. Commercial sponsorship began in 1963 with Guinness, who sponsored twenty-one runnings; in 1984 the race became the Gilltown Stud Irish Oaks, and since 1988 has been run as the Kildangan Stud Irish Oaks. Since sponsorship increased the value of the race six winners of the Oaks at Epsom have come over to score at The Curragh: Altesse Royale (1971), Juliette Marny (1975), Fair Salinia (1978), Blue Wind (1981), Unite (1987) and Diminuendo (who in 1988 dead-heated with Melodist at The Curragh). In the same period other Oaks winners were placed: Long Look (1965), Mysterious (1973), Circus Plume (1984) and Aliysa (1989) came second and Polygamy (1974) third. But perhaps the most remarkable Irish Oaks performance in recent memory was that of Dahlia, who started at 8–1 in 1973 and came right away from the Oaks winner Mysterious to make her dramatic entrance on to the international stage that she would grace until 1976.

Irish St Leger
The Curragh: 1¾ miles
Group One: three-year-olds and upwards

Here's one: which Classic winner of the last ten years made its racecourse debut when winning a maiden race at Catterick at 50–1? That the Classic in question is the Irish St Leger may be deemed further evidence of the decline of the event, first run in 1915, which completes the Irish Classic programme. The race comes so close to the Prix de l'Arc de Triomphe that it rarely attracts a top-class middle-distance horse, and it was in an attempt to improve the quality of the fields that the decision was made to open it to horses aged four and above: in October 1983 the four-year-old filly Mountain Lodge made history by becoming the first horse older than three legally to win an English or Irish Classic. In some ways the forgotten Group One race of the European Pattern, the Irish St Leger none the less has gone to some pretty good performers: Touching Wood added the race to his St Leger victory at Doncaster in 1982. And that Catterick newcomer? Opale, winner in 1984.

THE FRENCH CLASSICS

Poule d'Essai des Poulains
Longchamp: 1600 metres (1 mile)
Group One: three-year-old colts

Unlike its equivalent races the Two Thousand Guineas and the Irish Two Thousand Guineas, the Poule d'Essai des Poulains is not open to fillies. First run in 1883, it kept going through the Second World War, shifting to Auteuil in 1940 (when it was run in the autumn and won by the brilliant Djebel, who had won the Two Thousand at Newmarket earlier in 1940 and would take the Prix de l'Arc de Triomphe in 1942), to Le Tremblay in 1943 and to Maisons-Laffitte in 1944 and 1945. Since its return to Longchamp in 1946 it has been won by some notable horses, including Amour Drake (1949: beaten a head by Nimbus in the Derby), Tantieme (1950: winner of many big races including two Arcs), Right Royal V (1961: winner of the King George at Ascot), Relko (1963: winner of the Derby), Riverman (1972), Blushing Groom (1977) and Soviet Star (1987). Recitation, trained by Guy Harwood and ridden by Greville Starkey, took the prize across the Channel in 1981 (after Moorestyle had been runner-up in 1980). The race is generally less strongly contested than the English or Irish equivalents. (The literal meaning of 'poule d'essai des poulains' is: 'trial of the colts'.)

Poule d'Essai des Pouliches
Longchamp: 1600 metres (1 mile)
Group One: three-year-old fillies

The French equivalent of the One Thousand Guineas was (like its Classic *frère*) first run in 1883. The Second World War forced a cancellation in 1940, but it was run at Le Tremblay in 1943 and Maisons-Laffitte in 1944 and 1945. Since the war it has been won by many great fillies, and its timing allows a sufficiently forward filly to run both at Newmarket and at Longchamp. In 1947 Imprudence won the French race between victories in the One Thousand Guineas and the Oaks, and more recently the Poule d'Essai des Pouliches (the 'trial of the fillies') has gone to One Thousand Guineas heroines Miesque (1987) and Ravinella (1988). Allez France won the race in 1973 (with Dahlia third), and it fell to subsequent Arc winners Ivanjica in 1975 and Three Troikas in 1979.

WINNERS SINCE 1980

1980 In Fijar
G. Doleuze 52–10 (13 ran)

1981 Recitation
G. Starkey 24–10 (10 ran)

1982 Melyno
Y. Saint-Martin 17–10 (9 ran)

1983 L'Emigrant
C. Asmussen 28–10 (10 ran)

1984 Siberian Express
A. Gibert 34–10 (14 ran)

1985 No Pass No Sale
Y. Saint-Martin 9–10 (9 ran)

1986 Fast Topaze
C. Asmussen 4–5 (8 ran)

1987 Soviet Star
G. Starkey evens (14 ran)

1988 Blushing John
F. Head 6–10 (10 ran)

1989 Kendor
M. Philipperon evens (10 ran)

1990 Linamix
F. Head evens (7 ran)

WINNERS SINCE 1980

1980 Aryenne
M. Philipperon 13–10 (6 ran)

1981 Ukraine Girl
Pat Eddery 212–10 (10 ran)

1982 River Lady
L. Piggott 4–10 (9 ran)

1983 L'Attrayante
A. Badel 12–1 (10 ran)

1984 Masarika
Y. Saint-Martin 7–10 (11 ran)

1985 Silvermine
F. Head 38–10 (10 ran)

1986 Baiser Vole
G. Guignard 11–2 (18 ran)

1987 Miesque
F. Head 1–5 (8 ran)

1988 Ravinella
G. W. Moore 3–10 (8 ran)

1989 Pearl Bracelet
A. Gibert 503–10 (16 ran)

1990 Houseproud
Pat Eddery 9–10 (14 ran)

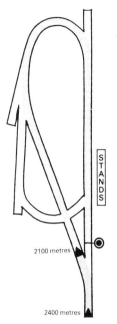

2100 metres

2400 metres

Chantilly is a fine galloping track with an easy right-handed turn and no major undulations.

WINNERS SINCE 1980

1980 Policeman
  W. Carson 538–10 (14 ran)

1981 Bikala
  S. Gorli 172–10 (12 ran)

1982 Assert
  C. Roche 22–10 (14 ran)

1983 Caerleon
  Pat Eddery 14–10 (12 ran)

1984 Darshaan
  Y. Saint-Martin 14–10 (17 ran)

1985 Mouktar
  Y. Saint-Martin 1–5 (11 ran)

1986 Bering
  G. W. Moore 1–2 (13 ran)

1987 Natroun
  Y. Saint-Martin 41–10 (17 ran)

1988 Hours After
  Pat Eddery 161–10 (16 ran)

1989 Old Vic
  S. Cauthen 47–10 (12 ran)

1990 Sanglamore
  Pat Eddery 95–10 (12 ran)

For the second successive year, the Prix du Jockey-Club Lancia goes to a British-trained horse, as Pat Eddery in 1990 drives the white face of Sanglamore past Epervier Bleu.

Prix du Jockey-Club
Chantilly: 2400 metres (1½ miles)
Group One: three-year-old colts and fillies

Any similarity which the Prix du Jockey-Club bears to its English equivalent, the Derby, stops well short of the surroundings in which the two races are run, for Epsom Downs cannot hold a candle to the elegance of Chantilly, where the Grandes Ecuries – the magnificent chateau stable block built by the Comte du Condé, who was convinced that he would be reincarnated as a horse – provides a breathtaking backdrop to the sport. Chantilly, twenty-seven miles north of Paris, is the Newmarket of France, with some 3,000 racehorses in training and a racing tradition stretching back to the early nineteenth century.

The Prix du Jockey-Club began life there in 1836, and its first two runnings went to Franck and Lydia, both owned by Lord Henry Seymour, who had been instrumental in founding the Société d'Encouragement pour l'Amelioration des Races de Chevaux en France – the French Jockey Club – and was one of the most influential figures in the establishment of French racing: many English expatriates trained at Chantilly in the nineteenth century, and the British influence is still strong there. Only very recently, however, has this influence stretched to the Prix du Jockey-Club itself. The race was closed to horses trained overseas until 1946, and it was not until Old Vic's storming victory by seven lengths from Dancehall in 1989 that an English-trained horse won; then Sanglamore followed up in 1990 for first-season trainer Roger Charlton. Ireland had scored twice in the 1980s with Assert (1982) and Caerleon (1983), both owned by Robert Sangster. Yves Saint-Martin, the greatest French jockey of the modern era, won the race on nine occasions (the same number as Lester Piggott in the Derby): his final victory was on the Aga Khan's Natroun in 1987. The legendary owner Marcel Boussac won twelve times, from Ramus in 1922 to Acamas in 1978.

Chantilly is a fine galloping track with an uphill finish which puts a premium on stamina, a far cry from the ups and downs and rights and lefts of Epsom. A field thundering past the Grands Ecuries is one of the finest sights of European racing – and so much finer when Old Vic or Sanglamore brings the top French Classic across the Channel!

Prix de Diane

Chantilly: 2100 metres (1 mile 2½ furlongs)
Group One: three-year-old fillies

The Prix de Diane – the French Oaks – is seven years younger than the Prix du Jockey-Club; first run in 1843, it remained (like the other Chantilly Classic) closed to foreign horses until 1946. Apart from the course over which it is run, its greatest variation from the Epsom equivalent Classic is its distance – one and a half furlongs shorter. This key difference makes it a reasonable target for a filly whose stamina may be open to question, such as Miesque, who in 1987 had won the One Thousand Guineas and the Poule d'Essai des Pouliches and in the Prix de Diane came up against Indian Skimmer, who had won the Musidora Stakes over an extended ten furlongs and then the Prix Saint-Alary over ten furlongs at Longchamp. It was Miesque's first attempt at beyond a mile, and once Indian Skimmer showed her outstanding turn of foot in the straight the result was never in doubt, Henry Cecil's grey filly striding home four lengths clear. Miesque ran on to be second, but was never again asked to race over so long a distance.

Indian Skimmer was just one of the great fillies of modern times to have won the race. There was Pistol Packer in 1971; Allez France, who beat Dahlia in 1972; and Pawneese, who took the 1976 running then went on to saunter home in the Oaks. Mrs Penny (1980), Madam Gay (1981) and Rafha (1990) brought the prize to England. But for English racing fans the finest occasion in the race's history came in 1974, when the Queen's Highclere stormed in from Comtesse De Loir to become the first filly to win the One Thousand Guineas and the Prix de Diane.

Prix Royal-Oak

Longchamp: 3100 metres (1 mile 7½ furlongs)
Group One: three-year-olds and upwards

First run in 1869, the Prix Royal-Oak is ostensibly the French version of the St Leger, though run over a furlong further than the Doncaster race and since 1979 open to horses over three. Sassafras won in 1970 (on the disqualification of Hallez) before beating Nijinsky in the Arc, and Exceller in 1976 was another winner from out of the top drawer. The next year the race was moved from mid-September to late October. Niniski added the Prix Royal-Oak to his victory in the Irish St Leger in 1979, and the following year ran sixth when the filly Gold River took the race: she won the Arc in 1981. Ardross, third in 1980, was a five-year-old when winning in 1981, and in 1982 just failed to add the Arc to his notable haul. The 1987 winner Royal Gait made his own mark on racing history when controversially disqualified in the 1988 Ascot Gold Cup. Opening the race to older horses may have removed the Prix Royal-Oak from the orthodox Classic programme, but it remains a lucrative prize for the cream of European stayers.

WINNERS SINCE 1980

1980 Mrs Penny
L. Piggott 82–10 (14 ran)

1981 Madam Gay
L. Piggott 9–1 (14 ran)

1982 Harbour
F. Head 12–10 (14 ran)

1983 Escaline
G. W. Moore 11–1 (17 ran)

1984 Northern Trick
C. Asmussen 46–10 (15 ran)

1985 Lypharita
L. Piggott 11–1 (10 ran)

1986 Lacovia
F. Head 2–5 (14 ran)

1987 Indian Skimmer
S. Cauthen 9–10 (11 ran)

1988 Resless Kara
G. Mossé 294–10 (16 ran)

1989 Lady In Silver
A. Cruz 138–10 (14 ran)

1990 Rafha
W. Carson 9–1 (14 ran)

WINNERS SINCE 1980

1980 Gold River
F. Head 7–1 (13 ran)

1981 Ardross
L. Piggott 23–10 (7 ran)

1982 Denel
Y. Saint-Martin 79–10 (13 ran)

1983 Old Country
Pat Eddery 27–1 (14 ran)

1984 Agent Double
F. Head 11–10 (11 ran)

1985 Mersey
J. L. Kessas 7–10 (12 ran)

1986 El Cuite
S. Cauthen 54–10 (10 ran)

1987 Royal Gait
A. Gibert 19–10 (11 ran)

1988 Star Lift
C. Asmussen 123–10 (16 ran)

1989 Top Sunrise
F. Head 28–10 (9 ran)

Prix de l'Abbaye de Longchamp

Longchamp: 1000 metres (5 furlongs)

Group One: two-year-olds and upwards

Somehow it sounds better in French: according to the official guide to the 1989 Ciga Weekend at Longchamp, the Prix de l'Abbaye '*couronne la saison de vitesse*' – the Abbaye (named after the abbey which once stood near where the Arc now starts) 'crowns the speed season'. Europe's top sprint, first run in 1957, has long been the curtain-raiser to the Arc (see opposite), a furious charge along Longchamp's remote five-furlong course and a regular cash-dispenser for the masses of visiting British punters needing a few extra francs for the Arc itself. In the twenty-two runnings between 1968 (when Be Friendly turned in a magnificent effort to win by two lengths) and 1989 (when John Matthias on Silver Fling beat the Canadian-trained Zadracarta and Nabeel Dancer by a short head and a head), the race has been won outright by a French-trained horse only three times. The Irish have won three, the British fifteen, and the French and British shared one.

The last French horse in that period to take the Prix de l'Abbaye was also the last two-year-old to win: Sigy, who led all the way to beat Solinus and Double Form – themselves both great sprinters – in 1978. The following year Double Form took his revenge, beating Kilijaro and Greenland Park with Sigy last. The hot favourite that day was Vincent O'Brien-trained Thatching, though those who backed him down to 6–4 on the Pari-Mutuel were obviously unaware of the notorious effect of the draw on Longchamp's five-furlong course, for Thatching was drawn twelve of the thirteen runners and had virtually no chance from that position: he finished ninth. But if the built-in unfairness of the draw has been the cause of some disaffection with the Abbaye as the sprint championship of Europe, the 1976 running produced a more specific controversy when British-trained 38–1 outsider Gentilhombre beat the home-trained Mendip Man – or so it appeared; then the judge announced a dead-heat, though many claimed that the photo clearly showed the British raider the winner. The next year Gentilhombre won by four lengths.

In the early 1980s the race was a benefit for top British sprinters as Moorestyle (1980) and Marwell (1981) both beat Sharpo into second place; then Sharpo gained a well-earned victory as a five-year-old in 1982, and the flying Habibti beat Soba and the two-year-old Sicyos (trying to emulate his dam Sigy, whose first foal he was). Committed in 1984 and 1985 and Polonia in 1987 took the prize to Ireland, and sensation dogged the 1988 running when Cadeaux Genereux beat Handsome Sailor by a head only to be disqualified for interfering with La Grande Epoque in the early stages.

Prix de l'Arc de Triomphe

Longchamp: 2400 metres (1½ miles)

Group One: three-year-olds and upwards

It has to be the greatest moment of the Flat racing year. The field for the Prix de l'Arc de Triomphe has set off from the shadow of the windmill way over to the left of the stands, raced behind the Petit Bois – the small wood which momentarily masks the runners from the sight of those in the stands – then climbed to the highest point of the course: helter-skeltering right-handed down the hill towards the enclosures, with less than two furlongs to go it straightens out for the final charge towards the winning post. At that moment the complexion of the whole of the European season on the Flat is in the melting pot, and what happens in the next few seconds determines not only the destination of the most valuable prize of the European calendar but so often also the way in which that season will go down in history. When Ribot or Sea Bird or Mill Reef came clear away from their fields, or Dancing Brave cut down the most valuable collection of bloodstock ever assembled for one race, the Arc was the stage on which true greatness was made manifest, and great seasons are made by great horses. And when Nijinsky failed to get to Sassafras, or Reference Point flopped behind Tony Bin – and worse, when Shergar and Nashwan failed to contest the race at all – the lack of a conclusive Arc result somehow left a question-mark hanging over that season. Or to put it more succinctly: the Prix de l'Arc de Triomphe is probably the finest horse race in the world.

The essence of the Arc – that it should be a truly international quest for the best middle-distance horse around – was established with its

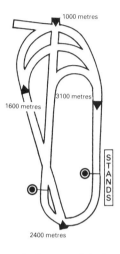

With its gradual turns and climb to the highest part of the course at the farthest point from the stands, Longchamp places an emphasis on seeing the trip out, with a fair degree of balance required for the downhill run towards the straight. The five-furlong course is straight and flat.

The 1989 Ciga Prix de L'Arc de Triomphe: Carroll House powers home from Behera.

177

first running in 1920. (The selling race which had been run under the same name some years earlier was in no way the precursor of the present-day Arc.) The Grand Prix de Paris had long been the most important race run at Longchamp, and the Société d'Encouragement hatched a plan to found a race of similar status run in the autumn and designed to bring to Paris the *crème de la crème*, a field of Classic winners and other top horses from around the world, to compete for a huge prize in what would be acknowledged as the middle-distance championship of Europe. The first winner admirably fulfilled the international requirement: Comrade was owned by Frenchman Evremond de Saint-Alary (who had bought him as a yearling for twenty-five guineas – not a bad price for an Arc winner, even in those days), trained at Newmarket by Peter Purcell Gilpin (who had trained Pretty Polly) and ridden by the Australian jockey Frank Bullock.

In 1922 Bullock won again on Ksar (who had also won the 1921 running) and victories for Italy with Ortello in 1929 and Crapom in 1933 crystallized the international character of the race; Corrida in 1936 and 1937 remains the only mare to have won twice. Nevertheless, by the time the Second World War caused the cancellation of the race in 1939 and 1940 the Arc was still well short of the prestige it has today. It returned to Longchamp for the 1941 and 1942 runnings and was then transferred to Le Tremblay, finally settling back at Longchamp in 1945.

After the war the Arc rapidly increased in stature, with the Aga Khan's Migoli winning for English trainer Frank Butters in 1947 and Tantieme scoring in 1950 and 1951. But it was the next dual winner who really left his mark on the 1950s: Ribot, the greatest horse ever to come out of Italy. Though bred by Federico Tesio at his stud on the shores of Lake Maggiore, Ribot actually drew his first breath in 1952 in the less exotic environs of West Grinstead in Sussex, at that time home of the National Stud where Ribot's sire Tenerani was standing and awaiting another visit from his dam Romanella. Nicknamed *il piccolo* on account of his diminutive stature as a foal, Ribot grew into a magnificent looking horse whose racing ability fully matched his appearance. He had won several races in Italy before taking the 1955 Arc at 9–1, and by the time he returned a year later was unbeaten in fifteen races, including the 1956 King George VI and Queen Elizabeth Stakes. At Longchamp he faced a field so strong that Fisherman, who had won the Washington International in 1954, was in the line-up as a pacemaker to another American raider Carcer Boy, second in the Belmont Stakes. There were two Irish Derby winners in Zarathustra and Talgo and the Oaks winner Sicarelle as well as a strong French team, but Ribot strode away from them as if they had mistaken the Prix de l'Arc de Triomphe for its old guise of a selling race, putting up as brilliant an individual performance as any since the war.

Nine years later – during which time the status of the Arc had been upheld by such winners as Ballymoss (1958) and Exbury (1963) – there took place a finish as astonishing as that of Ribot's in 1956. Unlike the Italian horse, Sea Bird II did not come to the Arc with an unblemished record. He had been beaten once as a two-year-old, but as a three-year-old had proved himself one of the all-time greats, most tellingly with a performance in the Derby which was so easy that jockey Pat Glennon's only worry was whether he would be able to slow Sea Bird down before they reached the road which crossed the Epsom course after the finish. At Longchamp he faced another unbeaten French three-year-old – Reliance, winner of the Prix du Jockey-Club – and eighteen other opponents, including Meadow Court, Tom Rolfe from the USA and Anilin from Russia. Sea Bird slaughtered them, sweeping past Anilin at the entrance to the straight and going further and further clear as Reliance mounted a vain pursuit. In the closing stages Sea Bird veered diagonally across the course – still going so easily that he could have signed autographs for his fans in the enclosures – but none the less had a six-length advantage at the winning post. Like the Irish steeplechaser who was illuminating the jumping scene that year, Sea Bird was a freak.

In 1968 the Arc produced another dazzling display when Vaguely Noble, who had been trained in England as a two-year-old before being sold for 136,000 guineas in December 1967 and moving to the Chantilly stable of Etienne Pollet, showed a breathtaking turn of foot to beat Sir Ivor by three lengths. Lester Piggott, Sir Ivor's jockey, partnered the runner-up again in 1969 when the mare Park Top went down by three quarters of a length to the Irish-trained Levmoss (who started at 52–1), but was widely expected to land his first Arc in 1970. His mount Nijinsky, the unbeaten winner of the Triple Crown, was clearly a cut above the fourteen other runners, and he started at 5–2 on to wind up his career with Longchamp glory. Fate decreed otherwise. At the top of the hill Nijinsky was well behind, but as the runners made the descent towards the straight he started to make up

JOHN FRANCOME'S DAY OF THE YEAR

For the high point of my racing year it's a close call between two very different occasions – Stratford on the last day of the jumping season, and Arc day in Paris early in October. Longchamp just gets the verdict.

Arc day has everything. Europe's top middle-distance horses in the main race and the very best of the sprinters in the Prix de l'Abbaye, the Prix du Rond-Point, the Prix Marcel Boussac – won in 1989 by Salsabil in brilliant style – and the Prix de l'Opera.

But it's not just the unrivalled standard of the racing (after all, no other day in Europe has three Group One races) that raises this day above all others: Arc day has an unparalleled atmosphere. A huge contingent of English racing fans make the trip every year and bring to the occasion that extra spice of seeking the spoils in foreign lands. Whether we've backed it or not, we greet every English-trained winner with rabid enthusiasm. An English victory on Arc day is racing's equivalent of an away win, and it gives a special buzz to follow our challengers over to France and see them beat the home opposition – which we do with great regularity in the Abbaye and often enough in the other big races.

Win or lose, it's the best day's sport in European racing, a great day out, and a fixture which never fails to quicken my pulse. Along with Stratford in June, of course.

ground, with Piggott looking for a run through on the inside. Less than two furlongs out Sassafras, ridden by Yves Saint-Martin, took the lead and made for home as Nijinksy, unable to find a passage through on the inside, was switched to the outer. Though several lengths down on Sassafras, Nijinksy was now in full flight and with Piggott driving for all he was worth got to the leader with two hundred yards to go. Nijinsky's surge would surely carry him to victory: he went a neck up, but then moved left under pressure, giving Saint-Martin the signal that all was not lost. Sassafras clawed his way back gamely and as the post loomed up forced his nose in front to win by a head. It was the first of Yves Saint-Martin's four Arc victories and had been won in never-say-die style by both horse and jockey, but the post-race attention unsurprisingly centred on the beaten Nijinsky. Had Piggott given his partner too much to do and expected him to make up an impossible amount of ground in the short Longchamp straight? Had the horse properly recovered from the attack of ringworm which had affected his preparation for the St Leger, his last run before the Arc? Had he failed to stay the trip in such company and over such a stiff course? Or was he simply not the wonder horse that he had been billed? Whatever the reasons for Nijinsky's defeat, his failure in the Arc was one of the saddest moments in the race's history – a sadness compounded by his failure to get to Lorenzaccio in the Champion Stakes less than two weeks later. Sassafras did not run again.

If Nijinsky's downfall caused regret and soul-searching, the rest of the 1970s brought all sorts of wonderful moments. Mill Reef blazed away from Pistol Packer in 1971, Rheingold gave England another victory in 1973 when beating Allez France (and giving Lester Piggott his first Arc), and Allez France herself threw all Paris into rapture when holding Comtesse De Loir by a head in 1974. In her third Arc in 1975 Allez France started favourite for the third time, but could finish only fifth as Greville Starkey steered Star Appeal – who had won the Eclipse Stakes earlier in the season – through to win at odds of 119–1. That starting price is what lingers most in the memory from the 1975 Arc, but the finishing burst which made Star Appeal the first German-trained winner of the race was truly astounding.

Less spectacular, perhaps, but no less telling, were the tactics applied by Lester Piggott to win on Alleged in 1977. The opening pace had been slow, and Piggott took the Vincent O'Brien three-year-old into the lead at the Petit Bois; thereafter he dictated the running, taking the field along at a leisurely clip then suddenly speeding up at the entrance to the straight. Alleged had a formidable burst of acceleration, and by producing it here rather than waiting until closer to home Piggott left his rivals flat-footed. At the line he had one and a half lengths to spare over the fast-finishing Balmerino, a much-travelled New Zealand horse whose presence in the Arc field further underlined the international stature of the race. A year later Piggott was happy to wait with Alleged until the final three hundred yards before unleashing that burst of speed, but again the effect was devastating, Alleged coasting home two lengths ahead of Trillion (the dam of Triptych).

In 1979 Derby winner Troy was an odds-on favourite but could only finish third behind Three Troikas, who started a run of victories in the race for fillies. She was followed by Detroit, in 1980 giving Pat Eddery his first Arc triumph; the four-year-old outsider Gold River in 1981; Akiyda in 1982, who withstood the furious finish of Lester Piggott on Ardross by a head in the first sponsored Arc (Trusthouse Forte being the benefactor); and All Along, who was ridden by Walter Swinburn to a one-length victory over the Oaks winner Sun Princess in 1983. Daniel Wildenstein, owner of All Along, took the race again with Sagace in 1984 and in 1985 must have thought that a third successive Arc was in the bag when the same colt got the better of Rainbow Quest by a neck after a prolonged battle in the closing stages. But Sagace had twice bumped Rainbow Quest in the straight, and Pat Eddery on the runner-up lodged an objection against Eric Legrix on the winner: at the subsequent enquiry the placings were reversed, making Rainbow Quest the first English-trained winner since Rheingold and the fourth since the war.

If that English victory was gained only in the Stewards' room, no such controversy attached to Pat Eddery's triumph in the same colours of Khalid Abdullah the following year. For Dancing Brave's powerhouse finish up the outside to sweep past Bering, Triptych, Shahrastani, Shardari and Darara in 1986 was a performance which put the Guy Harwood colt in the very first rank of post-war Arc winners. Trained in Sussex, bred in the USA, owned by a Saudi prince, ridden by an Irish jockey based in England, Dancing Brave epitomized the international nature of modern racing.

Eddery won for the third successive year when conjuring a phenomenal finishing run from Trempolino to beat Tony Bin and Triptych (third for the second time) in 1987, and Tony Bin returned as a five-year-old in 1988 to repel the late flourish of Mtoto and advertise yet again the international context of the Arc: Tony Bin was English-bred, Italian-owned and trained (highly fitting for the first occasion on which the race was sponsored by the Italian-based hotel company Ciga), and ridden by John Reid, born in Ulster. The theme continued with 1989 winner Carroll House: owned by the Italian Antonio Balzarini, trained in England by Michael Jarvis and ridden by the leading Irish jockey Michael Kinane, by the end of the season Carroll House had been campaigned in England, France, Ireland, Germany, Italy and Japan.

But for all the international aspects of each running, the essence of the Prix de l'Arc de Triomphe is in that moment, on the first Sunday in October in the Bois de Boulogne in Paris, when the field turns to face the winning post. Wherever they have come from, that is the moment of truth.

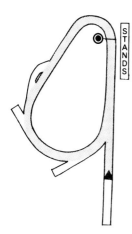

The Flemington circuit is like a compact version of Doncaster: the Melbourne Cup runners start towards the end of the straight course and make a fairly tight left-hand turn after the stands, then a gradual turn into the short home straight.

WINNERS SINCE 1980

1980 Beldale Ball
  J. Letts 11–1 (22 ran)

1981 Just A Dash
  P. Cook 15–1 (22 ran)

1982 Gurner's Lane
  L. Dittman 8–1 (23 ran)

1983 Kiwi
  J. Cassidy 9–1 (24 ran)

1984 Black Knight
  P. Cook 10–1 (19 ran)

1985 What A Nuisance
  P. Hyland 15–1 (23 ran)

1986 At Talaq
  M. Clarke 10–1 (22 ran)

1987 Kensei
  L. Olsen 12–1 (21 ran)

1988 Empire Rose
  T. Allan 5–1 (22 ran)

1989 Tawrrific
  R. S. Dye 30–1 (23 ran)

Melbourne Cup

Flemington: 3200 metres (2 miles)

Handicap: three-year-olds and upwards

Melbourne Cup day is one of the great occasions of world racing. A crowd of over 100,000 packs into the enclosures at Flemington to indulge in a carnival which is like Royal Ascot in its appeal to the socially aware and fashion-conscious, and like Derby Day in being essentially a popular celebration. On the racecourse the cream of society in morning-suits rubs shoulders with – and, as the day progresses, dances boozily with – the lower orders in wild fancy dress. And off-course Cup fever runs high. The first Tuesday of November is a public holiday in the state of Victoria, and the city of Melbourne pays due regard to its showpiece event, with a parade to sustain the excitement, and even a Racing Fraternity Mass at which the help of the Almighty is invoked to ensure the well-being of the racing community over the coming year. The rest of the nation contrives to find a way of being in front of the television at 2.40 that afternoon, and Australia effectively suspends operations while the race is run.

That the contest which is the excuse for all this celebration is not some weight-for-age Classic but a two-mile handicap is irrelevant to the appeal of the Cup, which seized the national attention with its very first running in 1861. It emerged after the race that the winner, Archer, who beat the top-weight Mormon, had walked the 550 miles from the New South Wales stable of trainer Etienne Livingstone de Mestre – clearly steady road work brought the horse to peak fitness – and he became a popular hero, winning the race again from Mormon in 1862 under ten stone two pounds.

Most of the great Australasian horses have won the Melbourne Cup. Carbine carried ten stone five to victory in 1890. Phar Lap (bought as a yearling for 160 guineas) was third in 1929, defied nine stone twelve to win in 1930 at 11–8 on (the shortest-priced favourite in the history of the race) and was lumbered with ten stone ten in 1931, finishing eighth in his last race in Australia. Rain Lover in 1969 became the first horse since Archer to win the race in successive years, but Tulloch – for many experts the best Australian horse since the war – was anchored by ten stone one in 1960 and made no impression. Recently the Cup has reflected the growing internationalization of racing, with Robert Sangster's Beldale Ball winning in 1980 and the 1986 race going to Sheikh Hamdan Al-Maktoum with At Talaq, who had finished fourth to Secreto in the Derby at Epsom in 1984.

Japan Cup

Tokyo: 1½ miles

Group One: three-year-olds and upwards

Some of the figures about racing in Japan make interesting reading. In 1989 the average prize money per race was the equivalent of £105,719. The average amount wagered on the totalisator each day was £39,074,281. The attendance over the 288 days' racing that year exceeded nine million, at an average daily attendance of 31,733. But the picture of Japanese racing is not painted simply by mind-boggling numbers, and careful buying of stallions from the West is steadily improving the quality of the country's bloodstock.

The founding in 1981 of the Japan Cup, to which the Japan Racing Association invites the best horses from around the world, was a significant step forward in the Japanese breeding and racing industry's move to establish itself in the world arena. The prize money is vast (Horlicks in 1989 won £589,162 at the prevailing exchange rate), and the comparative ease of international horse transport makes it a realistic target well worth going for, even if it comes – for European and American horses – very late in the year.

The inaugural running went to the US-trained Mairzy Doates, ridden by Cash Asmussen, and the second to another American challenger, Half Iced, who beat All Along, April Run and Stanerra, with the legendary John Henry in arrears. Stanerra, a wonderfully tough mare owned and trained in Ireland by Frank Dunne, had won twice at Royal Ascot in 1983 and run a close-up sixth to All Along in the Arc. Starting at a shade over 3–1 in the Japan Cup she swooped through in the final few yards to head Kyoei Promise. Two home victories followed, from Katsuragi Ace in 1984 and Symboli Rudolf in 1985, but the climax of the 1986 running was strictly a British affair. To win the Japan Cup the horse has to be tough and the connections adventurous, and both criteria were amply met by Jupiter Island, whose trainer Clive Brittain had long since established a reputation for having a go. At the age of seven Jupiter Island, ridden by Pat Eddery, experienced his finest hour when pipping another English raider Allez Milord (Greville Starkey) by a head.

By the time of the 1989 race the Japan Cup had gone twice to the home side, three times to the USA and once apiece to Ireland, France and Britain. A new continent joined the roll of honour that year with the six-year-old New Zealand mare Horlicks, who beat Oguri Cap by a neck with the previous year's winner Pay The Butler third and the Arc winner Carroll House well behind. More figures: a crowd of 144,295 crammed into the stands at the Fuchu racecourse and bet one fifth of the £89,400,000 placed on the race across the nation.

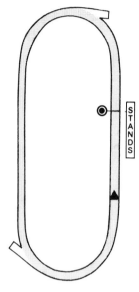

Similar in configuration to an American track, the Tokyo course at Fuchu features a gradual climb into and round the final turn.

WINNERS SINCE 1981

1981 Mairzy Doates
   C. Asmussen 11–1 (15 ran)

1982 Half Iced
   D. MacBeth 31–1 (15 ran)

1983 Stanerra
   B. Rouse 32–10 (16 ran)

1984 Katsuragi Ace
   K. Nishiura 396–10 (14 ran)

1985 Symboli Rudolf
   Y. Okabe evens (15 ran)

1986 Jupiter Island
   Pat Eddery 139–10 (14 ran)

1987 Le Glorieux
   A. Lequeux 76–10 (14 ran)

1988 Pay The Butler
   C. McCarron 139–10 (14 ran)

1989 Horlicks
   L. O'Sullivan 19–1 (15 ran)

THE US TRIPLE CROWN

Kentucky Derby
Churchill Downs (Louisville, Kentucky): $1\frac{1}{4}$ miles on dirt
Grade 1: three-year-olds

'Until you go to Kentucky, and with your own eyes behold the Derby, you ain't never been nowheres and you ain't never seen nothing.' Such was the opinion of local sage Irving S. Cobb, and few American racing fans would disagree. For however much excitement is engendered by the Breeders' Cup, the Kentucky Derby is still the focal point of the American racing year. And that point comes early in the season, for the Kentucky Derby is traditionally run on the first Saturday in May, at Churchill Downs, the course with the distinctive twin spires on top of the grandstand. Other traditions accompany the race: the consumption of mint juleps, that famous local tipple with the unassuming taste and the after-effect which ambushes your head; the communal singing of 'My Old Kentucky Home' before the big race; and the garland of roses which since 1896 has greeted the winner – a custom which in 1925 led the New York journalist Bill Corum to dub the Kentucky Derby 'the Run for the Roses', a nickname it still bears.

The race was first run in 1875 over one and a half miles, and was instigated by Colonel M. William Clark, who after two years studying the racing business in Europe returned to the USA determined to draw attention to the local bloodstock industry by founding the richly endowed stakes race which he named after the most famous English event. Although its early years were financially shaky for Colonel Clark, the Kentucky Derby was hugely popular with racegoers, and by the early part of the twentieth century the race (which had been reduced to its current distance of ten furlongs in 1896) was attracting fans from all over the country. As the race became linked with the Preakness and the Belmont to form the Triple Crown its appeal increased further, and after the infield was opened up in 1938 a six-figure crowd became possible. The attendance for the 1974 running was 163,628, the largest ever at an American racecourse.

But what of the horses? The eleven Triple Crown winners are listed in the panel, and though every Kentucky Derby is a memorable race run in a frenetic atmosphere, some performances stand out, including Northern Dancer's brave struggle with Hill Rise in 1964, Spectacular Bid's relentless finish at 5–3 on in 1979, and the game effort of Clive Brittain's Bold Arrangement – the first British challenger in the history of the Kentucky Derby – when second to Ferdinand in 1986.

Preakness Stakes

Pimlico (Baltimore, Maryland): 1 mile 1½ furlongs on dirt
Grade One: three-year-olds

First run in 1873 (two years before the first Kentucky Derby), the race which now forms the middle leg of the Triple Crown was named after a local equine hero who had won twice at the inaugural Pimlico meeting in 1870. Until 1889 the race took place over a mile and a half, and did not take place at all between 1890 and 1893 while racing at the track was suspended: it resumed in 1894 at Gravesend and returned to Pimlico in 1908. Triple Crown winners apart, the most famous winner of the Preakness is probably Man O' War, who in 1920 was not in the line-up for the Kentucky Derby as his owner Samuel Doyle Riddle thought that race too stern a test too early in the season: the Pimlico race was his first of the season, but he had no trouble in disposing of Upset (who as a two-year-old was the only horse ever to beat him) before going on to win the Belmont. Man O' War would surely have won the Triple Crown had he run in the Derby.

Belmont Stakes

Belmont Park (Jamaica, New York): 1½ miles on dirt
Grade One: three-year-olds

The final leg of the Triple Crown is the oldest (founded in 1867 at the now defunct Jerome Park in the Bronx) and the longest, and sometimes that extra distance thwarts Triple Crown ambitions: Northern Dancer, for instance, won the first two legs in 1964 but failed to stay at Belmont and went down to Quadrangle and Roman Brother. Spectacular Bid in 1979, Alysheba in 1987 and Sunday Silence in 1989 are more recent examples of horses who have won the first two and failed in the third. But to the Belmont Stakes goes the honour of staging perhaps the single most breathtaking individual performance seen in a Flat race in modern times, when in 1973 Secretariat fought a head-to-head duel with Sham along the back stretch and then began to pull away. He went further clear . . . and further . . . and further: as he came into the home stretch he was twenty-eight lengths ahead, and at the post the winning margin was thirty-one. This stupendous display of power galloping was aptly evoked by the writer Charlie Hatton: 'He could not have moved faster if he had fallen off the grandstand roof.' In the 1990 running Go And Go, trained in Ireland by Dermot Weld, made history when becoming the first European-based winner of one of the US Triple Crown races – and he did it in some style, barrelling home by eight and a quarter lengths from Thirty Six Red, with Kentucky Derby winner Unbridled unplaced.

Arlington Million

Arlington International (Chicago, Illinois): 1¼ miles on turf

Grade One: three-year-olds and upwards

Both on and off the track, the short life of the Arlington Million has been one of excitement and drama. Take the inaugural running of the world's first million-dollar horse race on 30 August 1981. The committee responsible for issuing invitations to the best middle-distance horses around the globe had done its job well, and runners from the USA, Canada, England, Ireland and France were there – including English-trained Madam Gay, winner of the Prix de Diane and second to Shergar in the King George, and Fingal's Cave, third in that race, and Argument from France. But the star attraction was the six-year-old gelding John Henry, one of the most popular horses ever to race in America and ridden by the ageless Bill Shoemaker, the most successful jockey in history. John Henry disliked the soft going and seemed well held with half a mile to go, but he started to make up ground as the 41–1 outsider The Bart went for home in the straight. John Henry got to The Bart right at the wire and the two flashed over the line together. John Henry had made it by a nose.

The 1982 race went to Perrault, who had previously been trained in France and was then with Charlie Whittingham in California. British raiders Be My Native and Motavato were second and third, but 1983 saw the first British victory when Pat Eddery conjured a whirlwind finish out of Tolomeo (who started at 38–1) to beat John Henry by a neck. John Henry ran in the race for the third time at the age of nine in 1984 and raised the roof of Arlington when beating Royal Heroine, but a year later that roof had become part of the smouldering ruins of the Arlington Park grandstand, which had burnt down less than a month before the 1985 race was due to be run. The Million – in the circumstances deserving its epithet 'The Miracle Million' – went ahead with a crowd of 35,000 accommodated in temporary stands, and they were rewarded for their discomfort with an outstanding race as Teleprompter took a little over two minutes to quintuple what he had previously earned in four seasons: the manner in which Lord Derby's gelding held off the challenge of Greinton remains one of the greatest memories of modern English racing.

The 1988 running was transferred to Woodbine in Toronto so that the rebuilding work at Arlington could be completed, and the race returned to Chicago in 1989. That the course rose from the ashes without compromising the high international standing of its flagship race is a tribute to Richard Duchossois, the owner of the track and an inspirational force behind getting the Million to the very forefront of the international racing year, and keeping it there.

THE BREEDERS' CUP

The inauguration of Breeders' Cup Event Day in 1984 significantly altered the complexion of the racing year, bringing on to the international calendar a day of racing so richly endowed as to make its races a natural target not only for American horses but for the best performers from Europe, where the season at the highest level had customarily started to wind down after the Prix de l'Arc de Triomphe in early October. For middle-distance horses the Arc had been the climax of the season. Now the Breeders' Cup beckoned, offering glittering prizes at a time when the European horses would normally be tucked up for the winter. The increased ease of international travel removed many of the practical difficulties associated with challenging for American races, so that the top US and Canadian events were more and more attractive to transatlantic raiders. The age of truly international racing had arrived.

The Breeders' Cup programme was the idea of John R. Gaines, owner of the Gainesway Farm near Lexington, Kentucky (where Dancing Brave was bred) and where stand such stallions as Blushing Groom, Lyphard and Trempolino). Gaines's notion was to give American racing – which he thought to be in some decline – a huge shot in the arm by staging on a day late in the season a programme of races over different distances and for different sorts of horse which would be in effect the world championship of horse racing, an event to

<table>
<tr><td colspan="2">THE VENUES</td></tr>
<tr><td>1984</td><td>Hollywood Park, California</td></tr>
<tr><td>1985</td><td>Aqueduct, New York</td></tr>
<tr><td>1986</td><td>Santa Anita, California</td></tr>
<tr><td>1987</td><td>Hollywood Park, California</td></tr>
<tr><td>1988</td><td>Churchill Downs, Kentucky</td></tr>
<tr><td>1989</td><td>Gulfstream Park, Florida</td></tr>
<tr><td>1990</td><td>Belmont Park, New York</td></tr>
<tr><td>1991</td><td>Churchill Downs, Kentucky</td></tr>
</table>

BROUGH SCOTT'S DAY OF THE YEAR

Live television in the open air is always exciting, but there's nothing like a new field we have yet to conquer. That's why Breeders' Cup Day is at present the greatest challenge for me on Channel Four.

For this is a racing day into which America's NBC network has committed the sort of money and hardware normally associated with a space shot. Having worked with them (as a tame European) from the blazing heat of California's Santa Anita racetrack to the misty chill of New York's Aqueduct and the squelching mud of Kentucky's Churchill Downs, I know how outrageously outsize an event this is, and I want Channel Four to be part of it.

Whether we agree with all its conditions or not, the Breeders' Cup is the nearest thing to equine Olympics. It gives enormous home advantage to the Americans, who are racing to their own rhythm over their own tracks, but if you have any wish to prove British horses are the best in the world we've got to go there and play with them. Pebbles did it unforgettably in 1985, but we were not there, and all the other attempts have been disasters. The big day is going to come, and if we are there to bring it to you, there will be dancing across the kingdom.

THE WINNERS

Sprint

1984 Eillo
  C. Perret 13–10 (11 ran)

1985 Precisionist
  C. McCarron 34–10 (14 ran)

1986 Smile
  J. Vasquez 11–1 (9 ran)

1987 Very Subtle
  P. Valenzuela 164–10 (13 ran)

1988 Gulch
  A. Cordero 58–10 (13 ran)

1989 Dancing Spree
  A. Cordero 166–10 (13 ran)

Juvenile Fillies

1984 Outstandingly
  W. Guerra 228–10 (11 ran)

1985 Twilight Ridge
  J. Velasquez 6–10 (12 ran)

1986 Brave Raj
  P. Valenzuela 4–1 (12 ran)

1987 Epitome
  P. Day 304–10 (12 ran)

1988 Open Mind
  A. Cordero 7–10 (12 ran)

1989 Go For Wand
  R. Romero 5–2 (12 ran)

Distaff

1984 Princess Rooney
  E. Delahoussaye 7–10 (7 ran)

1985 Life's Magic
  A. Cordero 2–5 (7 ran)

1986 Lady's Secret
  P. Day 1–2 (8 ran)

1987 Sacahuista
  R. Romero 29–10 (6 ran)

1988 Personal Ensign
  R. Romero 1–2 (9 ran)

1989 Bayakoa
  L. Pincay 7–10 (10 ran)

Mile

1984 Royal Heroine
  F. Toro 17–10 (10 ran)

1985 Cozzene
  W. Guerra 36–10 (14 ran)

1986 Last Tycoon
  Y. Saint-Martin 359–10
  (14 ran)

grab the attention of the whole sporting world. The programme would be funded primarily from two sources: the payment by breeders of an annual sum equivalent to the stud fee of each stallion they wished to nominate (which effectively means every leading stallion in the world), and an additional fee to nominate to the programme each foal. The support of other major breeders was enlisted and a connection effected with the European Breeders' Fund to involve European horses, and the scheme was off the ground.

The money raised for each year's programme is divided among the Event Day (worth $10 million in 1989), sponsorship of existing stakes races throughout North America, and a Special Stakes Fund to establish new sponsored races. But it is the big day which commands most attention, and Gaines's vision of the race competing with the biggest sporting events in the world is being fulfilled. The venue moves from year to year (see panel). Wherever the day is staged, the programme remains the same:

Breeders' Cup Sprint
6 furlongs on dirt
Grade One: three-year-olds and upwards

Breeders' Cup Juvenile Fillies
1 mile 110 yards on dirt
Grade One: two-year-old fillies

Breeders' Cup Distaff
1 mile 1 furlong on dirt
Grade One: three-year-olds and upwards, fillies and mares

Breeders' Cup Mile
1 mile on turf
Grade One: three-year-olds and upwards

The Mile is the race in which European raiders have been most successful, France winning with Last Tycoon in 1986 and the following two years with Miesque, who brilliantly beat Show Dancer and Sonic Lady at Hollywood Park and then came right away from Steinlen and Simply Majestic at Churchill Downs, with the favourite Warning second last. Warning had come to the Breeders' Cup after a brilliant victory in the Queen Elizabeth II Stakes at Ascot, and in 1989 Zilzal did likewise, only to provide one of the biggest British disappointments: he completely failed to fire and came in seventh behind Steinlen, having got stirred up in the preliminaries and being caught flat-footed when the stalls opened: 'As soon as the gates opened', reflected trainer Michael Stoute, 'I thought to myself: "We might as well be in Newmarket".' Zilzal's sad flop – his first defeat – emphasized again how difficult winning a Breeders' Cup race can be for a European horse, for not only did the race come very late in the season for him, not only were the surroundings highly unusual and thus an additional problem to a notoriously edgy character, but the nature of the race itself demanded a different style of running than he was used to. The tight turns of Gulfstream Park are a far cry from

Newmarket or Ascot, and to miss the break in the Mile was disastrous. Immediately after the race Zilzal was whisked off to stand at stud in Kentucky.

Breeders' Cup Juvenile
1 mile 110 yards on dirt
Grade One: two-year-old colts and geldings

Breeders' Cup Turf
1½ miles on turf
Grade One: three-year-olds and upwards

The Turf has provided the agony and the ecstasy for the British raid on the Breeders' Cup. The ecstasy came first, when Pebbles repaid Sheikh Mohammed's confidence in supplementing her for the race at a cost of $240,000 by shooting up the inside under Pat Eddery to hold off Strawberry Road by a neck at Aqueduct in 1985. It was the first British victory in the Breeders' Cup, and a year later at Santa Anita a second looked a formality, for the Arc winner Dancing Brave could surely not be beaten in the Turf. But he was: prominent enough along the backstretch, he failed to improve his position off the final bend and finished fourth behind Manila, beaten nearly seven lengths. Less agonizing because preceded by less expectation was Indian Skimmer's brave third in the Turf behind Great Communicator at Churchill Downs in 1988.

Breeders' Cup Classic
1¼ miles on dirt
Grade One: three-year-olds and upwards

The Classic is the richest race of the day, and has produced not only some of the finest Breeders' Cup finishes but two of the greatest races ever seen: the battle between Ferdinand and Alysheba, both winners of the Kentucky Derby, at Hollywood Park in 1987, and – after Alysheba had found consolation by winning the race in 1988 – the heart-stopping finish between Easy Goer (winner of the Belmont Stakes) and Sunday Silence (winner of the Kentucky Derby and the Preakness) up the stretch as night came down in 1989.

The Breeders' Cup is not without its problems. The bitter disappointments of Dancing Brave and Zilzal have made some wonder whether it is fair to expect horses to produce their best form so late in the year and over terrain so alien (though plenty of other European horses have managed it), and the permitted use in some US states of race-day medication which is prohibited in Europe brings in the issue of how much the horses are competing on equal terms. But the true worth of the enterprise lies in the number of famous performances and great races which it has given us in its short life, and the names of Pebbles, Miesque, Steinlen, Ferdinand and Alysheba, Easy Goer and Sunday Silence are eloquent testimony to its pre-eminent place in the racing year.

Winners, Mile, *cont.*

1987 Miesque
F. Head 36–10 (14 ran)

1988 Miesque
F. Head 2–1 (12 ran)

1989 Steinlen
J. A. Santos 18–10 (11 ran)

Juvenile

1984 Chief's Crown
D. MacBeth 7–10 (10 ran)

1985 Tasso
L. Pincay 56–10 (13 ran)

1986 Capote
L. Pincay 12–5 (13 ran)

1987 Success Express
J. A. Santos 41–10 (13 ran)

1988 Is it True
L. Pincay 92–10 (10 ran)

1989 Rhythm
C. Perret 26–10 (12 ran)

Turf

1984 Lashkari
Y. Saint-Martin 534–10 (11 ran)

1985 Pebbles
Pat Eddery 22–10 (14 ran)

1986 Manila
J. Santos 88–10 (9 ran)

1987 Theatrical
P. Day 9–5 (14 ran)

1988 Great Communicator
R. Sibille 124–10 (10 ran)

1989 Prized
E. Delahoussaye 88–10 (14 ran)

Classic

1984 Wild Again
P. Day 313–10 (8 ran)

1985 Proud Truth
J. Velasquez 74–10 (8 ran)

1986 Skywalker
L. Pincay 101–10 (11 ran)

1987 Ferdinand
W. Shoemaker evens (12 ran)

1988 Alysheba
C. McCarron 6–4 (9 ran)

1989 Sunday Silence
C. McCarron 2–1 (8 ran)

INDEX

Each horse's entry in this index refers to the mention in the main text of victories in races featured in the book.